A GLOBAL COUP

ANNEXES (PART IV)

GUILLAUME FAYE

A GLOBAL COUP

ARKTOS
LONDON 2017

Printed in the United Kingdom.

ISBN	978-1-912079-82-7 (Paperback)
	978-1-912079-81-0 (Hardback)
	978-1-912079-80-3 (Ebook)
TRANSLATION	Roger Adwan
EDITING	Martin Locker
	Roger Adwan
COVER DESIGN	Andreas Nilsson
LAYOUT	Tor Westman

www.arktos.com

CONTENTS

CHAPTER V

CHAPTER VI

CHAPTER VII

CHAPTER VIII

ANNEXES (PART IV)

Introduction

What follows is a summary of the views and arguments that I intend to develop in this book.

Since the disappearance of the USSR, the classic form of American imperialism has been replaced by a New American Imperialism (NAI). The latter is of a far more brutal, straightforward yet clumsier kind, because it overestimates its own power.

The campaigns that have taken place in Serbia, Afghanistan and ultimately Iraq have established the ever-increasing power of the NAI, whose initial formulation actually predates the 9/11 attacks. Ideologically, it is supported by the *neoconservatives*, who currently hold the reins of power and have formed an unprecedented and novel alliance that brings together rigourist Protestant milieus and Zionistic Jewish circles supportive of the Likud. Having said this, in no way do I consider myself to be an 'anti-Zionist', nor even a Zionist for that matter, since I do not take sides in causes that have no impact whatsoever on me.

What the NAI does is reinforce the USA's self-proclaimed messianic legitimacy, which aims to impose Goodness upon the earth — i.e. its own political and social model — and combat Evil. Founded upon a bizarre ideology that merges Machiavellianism and Bismarckism with a theory advocating the USA's moral predestination, the NAI's strange patchwork associates a Schmittian doctrine of power (which serves as its law source) with an anti-Schmittian one that preaches the existence of a single, intrinsically authorised source of power (meaning the USA itself, in what has been labelled 'unilateralism'). All this while simultaneously combining certain Kantian and Hegelian philosophical elements (which had hitherto been incompatible) with a few snippets of isolationism, unbridled interventionism and a neo-Keynesian, perhaps even neo-autarchic economic dirigisme, paired with the pursuit of an ultra-liberal and highly hypocritical global policy.

The NAI's global, novel and original doctrine follows three central geostrategic axes: the principle of *unequal bilateralism*, the *deficient sovereignty* theory, and the concept of *legal recession* and declining international institutions.

First of all, according to the principle of unequal bilateralism, in no way does the USA strive to establish a 'global government'. Instead, it takes heed of the fact that the world is now divided into two parts: on the one hand, there's the USA, with its sphere of 'new European' vassals, meaning Great Britain, Poland, Italy, Spain and so on, while on the other, we have the so-called 'Rest of the World' (ROW). The USA is thus no longer the *leader* (or 'conductor') of the free world, but its actual *ruler*, i.e. the 'police force' that governs all other peoples and nations. It does not consider itself at all to be the principal Crusader of western civilisation, nor the first rock upon which a democratic, global and liberal state can be founded (in harmony with Carter's doctrine). Instead, it thinks of itself as the sole superpower with the right to arrogate to itself the maintenance of planetary order in a manner that, above all else, serves its own interests, but automatically also those of the other nations which, to some extent, wallow in obscure ignorance. Europe is envisioned to be the empire's 'first realm', in the same fashion that Rome looked upon its closest allies, the *foederati*.

The NAI thus rejects and dismisses Samuel Huntington's views regarding a 'clash of civilisations', as well as the ideas defended by Francis Fukuyama with regard to the 'end of history' and the UN 's global government.

As a result of this, the doctrine of 'deficient sovereignty' postulates that the moment a certain state succumbs to 'deficiency' (meaning that it becomes part of the 'axis of evil'), it is considered a *rogue state*, a

'heinous state' against which none but the USA has the duty to intervene and thus guarantee its own security and, on a secondary level, that
of the surrounding world. The criteria that this 'deficient sovereignty'
resorts to are of three kinds:

1) The presence of evidence or, in some cases, mere suspicion that one
   foments or supports 'terrorist activity'.

2) The possession of weapons of mass destruction.

3) The presence of a political regime considered tyrannical, dangerous, etc.

No country is thus, theoretically speaking, immune from inclusion in
this black list.

The third doctrine is that of legal recession and the decline of
international institutions, meaning the UN, of course, but lately also
NATO. The NAI's ideologists have now taken heed of the fact that the
United Nations is a rather useless organisation (a previously Gaullist
acknowledgement) which cannot maintain peace and that international legality itself lacks the necessary efficiency. This deficient legality
must therefore be superseded by a more efficient one — that of the
United States.

The NAI thus draws its conceptual inspiration from every conceivable source: a bit of Metternich here (in memory of Kissinger,
perhaps?), a little 'restricted sovereignty' inspired by 'Brezhnev's communist doctrine' there, etc. Most of all, however, one notices a transi-
tion from an implicit and indirect form of imperialism to a different
kind, one that is marked by explicitness and directness. What the NAI
actually offers is an uninhibited kind of imperialism. The pangs of the
Vietnam war have long been forgotten.

In terms of ambition, the NAI far surpasses traditional American
imperialism, i.e. the same overly cautious imperialism which Nixon,
for example, adhered to. Both its aims and its means are thus compara-
tively higher in number.

With regard to the NAI's ambitions, the military campaign in Iraq has demonstrated that it is not merely a question of securing oil reserves, but also a matter of transforming Middle-Eastern Muslim countries into 'democratic vassals' and, above all, establishing a security belt around the Jewish state, a state that now finds itself in a desperate situation, even if it has not necessarily lost the fight yet thanks to the immemorial tenacity of the Jewish people. The NAI's main objective, however, is to neutralise the potential birth of a European power stretching along a Paris-Berlin-Moscow axis, a power that I have christened 'Euro-Siberia' and whose existence embodies a genuine nightmare for the American thalassocracy. There is, of course, a further objective — that of neutralising the increasing power of India and China. The NAI thus wages war on all fronts.

The NAI's methods are global in character, and it resorts to all available means, including the strengthening of the Pentagon's powers; the reinforcement of military-industrial facilities; a global control policy over all information networks; a strategy to weaken and dismantle the European Union that relies particularly on encouraging the massive Islamic presence on the latter's soil (by advocating Turkish E.U membership, supporting the Muslims in the Balkans, calling for the establishment of a multiracial Europe, and so on); and the seduction of Central European states (which were previously under Soviet influence) in an attempt to turn the area into a protectorate. What should be noted is that the NAI has no intention whatsoever to combat Islam and the Third World. Its ambition is rather to exploit them both in its struggle against Europe and rob the latter of its identity.

The NAI also draws upon a hitherto unused method: that of direct interference in the domestic affairs of other countries without taking any diplomatic precautions, especially if these countries happen to be European ones. This is achieved through the issuing of 'directives', the official expression of wishes, and the use of explicit injunctions and threats, as witnessed recently in the case of the crude pressure exerted upon those enlarged future European institutions. Any protests are voiced so timidly that Washington only feels encouraged in this regard, for its vassals overestimate its power as much as it itself does.

Despite the enormous rhetorical intelligence that characterises its aims and means, the NAI has bitten off more than it can chew. Thanks to this novel imperialism, the USA has reached the *apparent peak* of its own power and is actually commencing its decline, having succumbed to both *hubris* and power intoxication. For the NAI is counterproductive: in the medium term, it will only bring about an increase in terrorism and exacerbate anti-American sentiments on a worldwide scale. The sheriff has gone insane and, unlike John Wayne in *High Noon*, will find himself unable to restore the *Pax Americana*. The Iraqi campaign has proven that in order to defeat a small and already bled-dry country, the world's foremost superpower was forced to mobilise more than 50 % of its military means and ask its British auxiliaries for assistance, and yet was still unable to evade the quagmire of the post-war period. This constitutes a powerful signal: Iran, Pakistan and other middle powers have little to fear when faced with this toothless American tiger.

On the other hand, it is obvious that this American warmongering will incite many countries to acquire nuclear weapons as a precaution. Furthermore, the NAI pays neither heed to the frailty of the American economy, nor to the abysmal deficit of its commercial balance. In spite of its remarkable technological strength and labour power, the USA inhabits the sandcastle of a speculative economy, a 'casino-like economy' whose deficit was more than 500 billion dollars in 2003. This miracle will last as long as a rose in bloom: a mere morning.

Let us also bear in mind the ever-growing weakness of the American ground troops, increasingly forced to turn to Latin American foreign mercenaries; the numerical and demographic decline of the WASPs in the United States; the highly temporary aspect of the NAI that relies on the future electoral victories of the neoconservatives; the peacefully increasing power of the Chinese and Indian blocs, whether on the military level or from the industrial, technological, commercial and demographic perspective; the ancestral power of Islamic *jihad*, which now targets the USA (having initially burdened Europe); and so on.

In short, the *new American dream* of becoming the third thalassocratic Rome in the course of the 21st century has hardly any hope of coming true.

***

What is more, the 'resistance' to the NAI displayed by the Paris-Berlin-Moscow axis lacks any sort of credibility at this time, regardless of how much of a 'divine surprise' it is to some people. The French and the Belgians partake in the preaching of the humanitarian, Kantian and legalistic ideology. In their opposition to the campaign in Iraq, the governments of both countries were far more motivated by their desire not to offend the enormous Muslim-Arab communities that they shelter than by any genuine European policy to resist the NAI. Inspired by the SPD's favourite electoral topic, the Germans play the pacifist card. As for Russia, it is but a ruined castle compared to the USSR, and its real power (namely its military and economic potential) is not even a patch on China's, a fact that the Americans are very well aware of.

Despite its immense weaknesses, the NAI could never be threatened by 'a Europe of verbal policies and conference debates', nor by a Europe that relies on the lyrical sermons given by the likes of Mr. Michel and Mr. Villepin. A genuine European superpower, including its Russian sibling of course, could only be founded upon actions, never sentiment, and be rooted in both practice and effort, not mere theory and criticism.

For it is absolutely useless for one to 'criticise' the NAI or 'theorise' about its wrongdoings if one does not endow themselves with specific technological, economic, cultural, demographic and other means to counteract its actions. In this respect, the above-mentioned European axis is something to pray for, a headline-grabbing global event that begs to be committed to action. History is, after all, comprised of a 99 % action rate, with words making up the remaining 1 %.

In parallel with this New American Imperialism, we have witnessed the development of what I, for reasons of convenience, have christened *'Obsessive and Hysterical Anti-Americanism'* (OHAA), a development that has afflicted Europe, particularly France, and that I shall now criticise. OHAA concerns numerous milieus: it is found among Communists, Trotskyites, neo-Gaullists (who bear no connection to genuine Gaullism), progressive Christians, and, of course, Muslims, Islamophiles, those favourable to immigration and supportive of the Third World, pro-Palestinian individuals, etc.

OHAA reinforces the NAI: as a result of its own extremism and delirium, obsessive anti-Americanism provides American imperialism with the necessary justifications. The former is, in fact, probably financed or, at the very least, manipulated by American intelligence agencies, in whose interest it is to give anti-Americanism the image of an ideology embraced by dangerous madmen. In no way is the purpose of OHAA, even in its Right-wing elements, to defend our European identity. What it strives for, in truth, is the actual Islamisation and 'Third-Worldisation' of Europe, all in the name of a perverse sort of sophism that claims to detect a solidarity uniting Islam, the Third World and Europe against the Great American Satan and the Little Zionist Satan. In its dualistic and binary vision of the world, OHAA is incapable of thinking in ternary terms and of understanding that Europe has *neither* the duty to be reduced to an American protectorate *nor* the obligation to become another land of conquest claimed by the Muslim-Arab world. OHAA generates the impression that being anti-American means espousing Islamophilia, especially since the military campaign in Iraq.

Just like Islam and messianic American imperialism, OHAA resorts to demonisation, anathema, excommunication and invectives. Its attitudes belong to the sphere of passions, and its followers are highly reminiscent of the 'anti-fascist' European battalions that fell prey to Soviet manipulation during the 1930s and 1960s.

It is not merely certain American intelligence agencies that lie at the source of the manipulation that these impassioned minds and derealised, excited intellectuals have fallen victim to, but, in all likelihood, also some immigrationist and Islamophilic milieus. Indeed, by labelling the USA 'the Great Satan' and presenting the latter as a mortal threat, OHAA fulfils one of its main functions, namely that of lulling the masses into forgetting and/or accepting the ongoing immigrational colonisation and Islamisation of Europe. Yet again, the NAI and OHAA pursue the same goal in this respect, even if their schemes are different. They are thus to be objectively regarded as historic allies against Europe.

In harmony with my previous essays, I reaffirm my contention that the USA is Europe's *principal adversary*, not its *chief enemy*. In doing so, I base my opinion on facts and not on intellectual reveries and speculation. Our chief enemy is embodied by the colonising masses whose identity the laws of our gradually occupied country ban me from specifying, as well as by our zealous indigenous collaborators.

The NAI has an irreducible number of adversaries within 'White' American nationalistic milieus, in whose view Washington had better concern itself with protecting the US-Mexican border against ethnic invasion and safeguarding the USA from the ravages of immigration rather than with playing cowboy in Mesopotamia. Pro-European in essence, they are far from being 'Zionists' or 'anti-Zionists' and believe the NAI to be defending a multiracial and policing (i.e. Orwellian) vision of the world. Last but not least, what they propose is a notion that I shall develop in the conclusion, at the end of this essay: that of a global and intercontinental union banding all peoples of European descent together.

CHAPTER I

The Ideology Behind the New American Imperialism

A. American Imperialism's New, Hazardous Strategy

The word 'imperialism' is not to be taken pejoratively here, but rather understood from a descriptive angle.

The new American conception of war is that of an international police force governed by the USA and targeting all states characterised by a '*deficient sovereignty*'. The actual use of the term 'war' is completely banned. The new, *neoconservative* American administration thus attempts to unbalance the notion of national sovereignty as defined globally during the past two centuries.

Richard Haas, Director[1] of Policy Planning for the United States Department of State, is the man who first proposed the notion of '*deficient sovereignty*' (in connection with international responsibility) to describe any regimes that:

1) support terrorist movements;

2) possess or attempt to produce nuclear, bacteriological or chemical weapons of mass destruction;

3) violate 'human rights'.

---

1   TN: Now former Director.

If all three facts are confirmed, the states in question are thus stripped of the right to enjoy their sovereignty and become the potential targets of a legitimate attack at the hands of a 'coalition' headed by (none other than) the USA. These states are thus viewed as zones of lawlessness. The whole UN charter and its stipulations regarding both national sovereignty and the authorisation of military action solely in matters of legitimate defence is thus denied. From this perspective, every state is subject to preventive attacks the moment it is suspected (by the US, of course) of meeting the three sinful conditions listed above, as witnessed recently in Iraq.

Haas' theory was inspired by the document entitled *Strategy on National Security*, published by the White House in October 2002. It is no longer a matter of entrenching, encircling and smothering dangerous countries (in accordance with McNamara's containment theory), as was the case during the Cold War, but of attacking them pre-emptively in order to neutralise them. As might be expected, any threat to American interests is seen as the decisive criterion, since American interests are equated with those of the entire world...

Rogue states are placed on the same level as terrorist networks and criminal organisations. This revolutionary American doctrine is convinced of the fact that, as a result of globalisation, the immediacy of human communications and the new techniques of mass terrorism, the urgency of pre-emptive strikes abolishes the laws of war, as well as any respect for another country's sovereignty. Two new countries have been added to the black list of the Axis of Evil: the Yemen, the breeding ground of Al-Qaida, and Nigeria, where the Islamists may well end up appropriating the immense oil reserves. In an interview with *Minotaure* magazine (spring 2002), geopolitician Guillaume Dasqué made the following comment:

> Coming from a country endowed with a powerful sovereignty (the USA), these sudden changes denature the essence of both international law and the relations between different states by introducing a new imbalance between those capable of conducting global policing operations and the others.

In fact, this 'new' strategy of American imperialism is utterly *archeo-futuristic*, since there is nothing really new about it. It embodies a revolutionary return to the conceptions that prevailed from Antiquity to the end of World War I. In the eyes of the neoconservatives, the American territory represents a sort of 'sanctuarised police station' or neo-medieval fortress, from which the Lord conducts his campaigns to maintain order on his vassals' lands. The USA is thus abolishing the very same rules that it itself established after 1919 through the founding of the UN and embracing European notions instead, whereas Europeans, especially the French and the Germans, are adopting the legalistic ideology of a 'legitimised self-defensive war'.

The Americans are returning to the good old principle of pre-emptive attack used by the Romans for more than five centuries against the troublesome barbarians who they fought beyond their own *limes*; by Louis XIV against a small, subversive and free Holland; by Napoleon in his ambition to 'liberate' the peoples of Germany and Italy from the clutches of dangerous tyrants; by the Austro-Hungarian empire in its desire to neutralise Serbia; etc. The examples are beyond count. Through the notion of 'humanitarian intervention' ever so dear to Bernard Kouchner, this doctrine has, to some extent, rubbed off on France as well, the difference being that, in the French mentality, the campaign in question must first be sanctioned by the UN.

The problem is that, despite their apparent power, the Americans can rival neither the Roman empire nor Napoleonian France in terms of their power relations with the surrounding peoples. Currently governed by a group of neoconservatives whose capacity for strategic programming is as limited as President Bush's intelligence and political culture, the USA is high on its factitious power. The latter's technological sophistication, which they so stupidly idolise, is not a miracle potion that could enable it to dominate the world in the face of the archaic and eternal forms of war. The difficulties that the Americans have encountered in Iraq, their geopolitical failure in Afghanistan, their setback in Somalia and their defeat at the hands of general Giáp in the open Vietnamese terrain (which has not been forgotten in any way) have proven to the whole world that they lack the necessary human means to successfully implement their new imperialistic military doctrine. The reason for this is that they are either not or no longer able to use their ground troops with the necessary degree of effectiveness to pacify the territories that they control. Their capacity to conduct strikes and their technological supremacy are both compelling, yet still remain highly insufficient.

Disguised as a 'preventive international police', in no way does this doctrine strive to establish a secure and humanistic super-state of global law under American control. Prosaically, its ambition is rather rooted in the cynical construction of an empire in the traditional and Roman sense of the word, comprising various federated and obedient peoples that act as its auxiliaries (all thanks to its 'coalition' concept).

Two difficulties surface at this stage:

1) Apart from Great Britain, the above-mentioned auxiliaries are microscopic on a military level, especially Poland and Spain, whose armies lack any achievements worth mentioning;

2) Militarily speaking, the USA would not even be able to bring a middle power into line. Taking on a country that has a *'deficient sovereignty'* and that belongs to the Axis of Evil would only be a successful endeavour if the USA targeted a tiny and defenceless state. The Americans would never, for instance, dare attack Pakistan, Iran or even Syria. By contrast, a military intervention against Cuba cannot be excluded. The extravagant claims expressed by the neoconservatives (and vehemently denounced by genuine and serious American nationalists) cast the darkest shadows upon American diplomacy.

***

In other words, the new American imperialist doctrine is intellectually seductive, skilful and suited to our current world, but this applies solely to its intellectual and theoretical aspect, not the practical one. The new American executives are rediscovering the old imperial doctrines that mirrored ancient Europe's realistic approach to power. They do so in a most naïve fashion, as if they were big children, and fail to comprehend the latter's essence. Stemming from Protestant biblical sects, these neoconservatives lack the historical intelligence and strategic perspicacity that typify the Jewish people, the very people that they admire so much and long to protect at any cost, believing themselves to be the Jews' rightful messianic successors.

Current American leaders (who should not be confused with any other US elites) make the severe mistake of overestimating themselves, while simultaneously underestimating the extraordinary anti-American enmity that they have awakened on a global scale, even outside the borders of Muslim countries. The new American will is but a fancy — the fancy of a declining world power.

***

The USA will find itself unable to realise its dream of superseding the Roman Empire in its role of global police force under the guise of international morality and 'antiterrorism'. For China is present, watching the Americans just as it watches us Europeans. The war that the USA wages against Iraq is a kind of fallacious theatre: the latest manifestation of the American pseudo-power, which mobilises more than half of its armed forces without actually succeeding in resolving the problem it faces (exacerbating it even) is certainly a good reason for certain strategists to wonder whether the great nuclear power embodied by the USA will not end up collapsing instantly in the event of an outbreak of genuine war.

The mistake made by the Europeans is that they consider the USA to be a 'superpower', a notion invented by our stupidly anti-American French diplomacy. In actual fact, America is weak, especially on the military level, and only comes across as being powerful, thus resembling the Roman Empire of the 4th century.

B. 'Unilateralism' or 'Unequal Bilateralism'?

Robert Kagan, who is both a Machiavellianist and a theoretician of the NAI, justifies this new form of imperialism through the UN's impotence and utopian 'international agreement', since the UN is incapable of maintaining order. Bush followed in his footsteps when expecting post-war Iraq to be temporarily overseen by the USA, not the UN. In his essay entitled *Power and Weakness*, Kagan castigates those naïve enough to believe that law and order should not be maintained through the justice of the strong but the legalism of the weak, insisting that the latter could, on the contrary, only lead to anarchy and anomie. As an example, he mentions the film *High Noon*, in which the cowardly locals attempt to drive the courageous avenger away so as to avoid enraging the bandits.

From the traditional American perspective, the new form of imperialism is both highly pragmatic and moralising: only the USA has the power to actually force the world to respect what is Good (democracy and freedom), for it embodies the very essence of all the Forces of Good on Earth (the so-called *Manifest Destiny*, which the Americans, as God's protégés, allegedly enjoy). Gary Schmidt, the executive director of the Project for the New American Century (an institute focused on strategic research), gave the following explanation in *The Los Angeles Times* (08/04/2003):

> If the USA lacked the courage to take action, no other country would have the necessary political will and military means to take on the world's villains.

Thomas Donnelly, an expert at the American Enterprise Institute, points out:

> It is necessary to introduce fundamental changes to international institutions, which applies to both the UN and NATO, so as to re-establish the connection between the passing of international law and its effective implementation.

In other words, to be entirely clear about things, the USA is to be-come the sword arm of a UN organisation governed by the Americans themselves. Furthermore, in order to be implemented, international law must always be validated by the USA, which, as the world's sole superpower, should be alone to enjoy the right of veto at the Security Council and thus be able to sway any decision, even when a majority opposes it.

This maximalism is taken even further by Richard Perle, a man who contributed to the onset of the war in Iraq (Perle also happens to be the former advisor of Donald Rumsfeld, the former American Secretary of Defence who was forced to resign in early April 2003 because of his involvement in financial corruption affairs relating to the armament industry). In his view, the UN's achievements in matters of security are *'quite simply abject'*. He gives the following examples: it was the USA and not the UN that liberated Eastern Europe and enabled the collapse of the USSR, just like in South Korea in 1951, where Communism was made to retreat; it was also Israel, not the Blue Berets, that managed to beat back the Arab attacks in 1967 and 1973; as for Great Britain, it reclaimed the Malvinas[2] on its own, without any UN involvement. These arguments are, however, absolutely specious since, in accordance with its own charter, the UN is not required to intervene whenever a direct attack targets a given country on its own soil, which was the case with South Korea, Israel and Great Britain. For the 'falcons', Chirac's *'multipolar system'* is fallacious, utopian, impotent and protective of tyrants, and is but a sign of arrogance on the part of the French, who long to maintain their position in the Security Council and throw a spanner in the works of the American avenger. They question the following fact: when it comes down to it, do France, Russia, Germany and China actually have the means and will to overthrow despotism? In this regard, one must admit that their argument is a rather valid one. Since 1945, have the Blue Berets and the

---

2   TN: The Falkland Islands occupied by Argentina.

various UN peacekeeping forces representing the famed 'international community' ever achieved anything?

William Wohlforth, another 'falcon' ideologist, argues against the multipolar Franco-Russian view of the world:

> On the contrary, it is unipolarity that offers the best guarantee of peace and security. The greatest danger lies in American retreat. [...] Thanks to its power, the USA is more at liberty to ignore the international system than any other country. But since this very system has been erected around the USA itself, the demand for US involvement is constant. The more efficiently Washington responds to such demands, the more durable and pacifistic this international system will prove to be. (*Le Figaro*, 10/04/2003)

The ideological views advocated by the *neocons* are thus confirmed: the collective security system is to become one with the American will, since the USA alone holds the necessary power and is the sole guarantor of the prevalence of Good over Evil. What we are faced with here is thus a bizarre hybrid not only between universalistic biblical messianism and power politics, but also between naivety and brutal realism.

This messianism has been theorised by James Woolsey, the former head of the CIA under Clinton who has since joined ranks with the Bush administration. Woolsey is the perfect embodiment of the Uncle Sam figure, the Bible in one hand, a colt in the other. He gives a confounding answer to all those who would object and say that this unilateralist vigilantism might not end well, that the Americans are not always necessarily driven by righteous and saint-like sentiments, that American military strikes tend to result in considerable damage, that the most sordid economic interests often come into play and that, last but not least, the NAI may well end up drifting into some form of archeo-imperialism akin to the one embraced by Caesar, Genghis Khan and Tamerlane. For Woolsey's response is identical to the Muslim justification of Islamic *jihad*.

Keeping an absolutely straight face, Woolsey explains that '*God watches over America*', a land that has been '*blessed by God*' since, metaphysically speaking, *'America always has the best possible inten-tions'*. (The CIA's!) American puritans have simply adopted the *Gott Mitt Uns* slogan. Thinking of their country as a *genuine Israel*, they subordinate their entire foreign policy to a theocratic legitimisation, just as the Muslims do. It therefore comes as no surprise that the American policy in the Middle-East is seen by Muslims as a war of religion (yet those naïve neoconservatives are still taken aback).

This theological providentialism, however, which presents America as the very instrument of God, has an answer to every objection, in-cluding questions such as: 'How does one account for the fact that the USA, while overthrowing certain despots, often supports and estab-lishes other tyrannical rulers through its foreign policy?'; 'Is American moralism not merely the comely mask that conceals the America's imperialistic ambitions'? Not at all, according to Michael Leeden, a neoconservative essayist, who had this to say when interviewed by *The New York Times* (07/04/2003): *'America has always been to dictators the most disloyal of allies'*. In his eyes, it is for temporary tactical rea-sons that the US has associated with, established and not taken action against dictators such as Saddam Hussein, Stalin, Franco, Pinochet, nor against any of the current rulers in Muslim countries and the vari-ous Asian or South American military dictatorships (all of which are more or less despotic); he asserts that it has never been a matter of protecting American interests. As soon as the opportunity arises, the valiant Americans always reinstate Good, freedom and democracy. Leeden concludes his statement with the following words: *'We always return to the warpath in our defence of freedom. The war in Iraq is the most recent proof of this'*. How moving. One is left wondering whether such statements are actually hypocritical or sincere. The appalling truth is that such claims are, surprisingly, often honest.

***

Indeed, as a result of the *divine benediction* that has always presided over American foreign policy, all instances in which the US Air

Force bombards and kills civilians, including the horrific massacres committed during World War II, are described as being 'mistakes' or 'necessary evils'. The end justifies the means, just like in Lenin's case: the definitive triumph of Good over Evil justifies temporary suffering. Evil cannot, therefore, be encountered on the American side. When wreaking death, the American sword of God kills to ensure mankind's salvation. In this respect, the American foreign policy is driven by similar legitimising principles to those of Islam, Communism and the French revolutionaries of the Vendean wars.

On the other hand, this new unilateralist doctrine seems to contradict the 'multipolar' discourse embraced by France and Russia, as well as the UN's desire to introduce a global rule of law in harmony with Kantian utopias. And yet the USA does not renounce the prospect of a global state at all. It is simply not the kind that one might be inclined to expect. America does strive for a global state, but one that submits to its own will. The Americans long to achieve the following objective: being the sole entirely independent and omnipotent power on earth (just like God), the USA is to stand above all countries, governing an obedient *Rest of the World*, i.e. an agglomeration of countries that adhere to the UN. Instead of being labelled 'unilateralist', this position should rather be described as 'unequal bilateralism'.

The latter is a genuine reformulation of the Roman imperial doctrine, expanded to apply on a global scale. This worldwide empire is meant to be governed by the New Rome (the USA), which acts as both the protector and the suzerain of the *foederati*, a global ensemble of vassal nations that could never acquire the power of the Centre and thus contest its legitimate position of *gobernator universalis*, i.e. 'the world's helmsman'.

***

The problem with this new world order is that it is inapplicable. The NAI misestimates its own capacities in a most woeful fashion, particularly when ignoring the relevant economic and demographic data.

Indeed, the latter have led to the fact that, globally speaking, the power of the United States has been decreasing incessantly, slowly but surely, for a period of thirty years. There is yet another factor that has been neglected: the presence of China, a country which, by 2020, will most probably have managed to become a superpower rivalling, if not surpassing, the USA, thus taking us back to a state akin to the Cold War (1945–1991).

In fact, American unilateralism (or rather 'unequal bilateralism') is as utopian in character as the French notion of a legalistic and multipolar world governed by the UN. Wisdom would have us seek a third path. The latter could only be found in the Metternichian theory of a Concert of Great Powers (1815), which is founded upon three paradigms:

1) The world was, is and ever will be a jungle in which power will always shape legality. However, this jungle must be disciplined;

2) No world power could ever achieve a status of absolute dominance, as demonstrated by the tragic end that befell the Napoleonic saga;

3) International security policies can only be rooted in temporary alliances characterised by a balance of power.

If we are to succeed in countering the disastrous American foreign policy, therefore, we cannot resort to mere moral arguments, neo-Kantian legalism of the Franco-Belgian or German kind, hymns to the glory of the UN (which will always be the 'thingy' denounced by de Gaulle, a sound opinion that Washington has now adopted) and anti-American demonstrations in the street. The real solution lies in the actual establishment of counter-powers to American hegemony, both on an economic and military level. Silently, China and India are working to achieve this very purpose. Beyond the endless musings regarding the birth of a Paris-Berlin-Moscow axis, everyone anticipates its actual creation. What is noteworthy is that every single UN Secretary General has come from a small country lacking international influence, and not a single one has ever had a strong personality. One must wonder why this is always the case. Kofi Annan, the UN Secretary General who valiantly attempted to resist the American power grab, lacked the necessary means to assert his authority.

It is neither in hateful anti-American imprecations, nor in idealistic and pacifistic reveries that the counterweight to American unilateralism can be found, but in European military budgets and sustained efforts towards techno-economic efficacy and, more generally, the acquisition of palpable power. The first stage of this process is epitomised by our continent's liberation from the ongoing invasion at the hands of Islam and the Third World, an invasion which, in my view, is more of a threat that American political posturing.

C. As the USA Adopts the Soviet Doctrine of 'Limited Sovereignty'

The anger expressed by the Americans at the French objection to the war in Iraq has brought to light a now explicit fact which had, until recently, only been implicit, going beyond what is termed 'unilateralism': the USA (or rather its *neocon* administration) now espouses the view that the rest of the world is only entitled to a limited independence in relation to its own will and interests. This perception, which is of an almost religious nature, is as perfectly sincere as it is naïve. The USA thinks of itself as the world's 'Nation-Guide', whose orders must surpass all international institutions and whose motivations may result in legitimate violations of international law, including the various treaties that the Americans themselves have fostered and signed.

Michael Leeden, an ideologist of the 'new world order' proposed by George H. W. Bush, believes that by opposing the unilateral attack against Iraq, 'France behaves as though it were the USA's strategic enemy' and thus deserves to be 'punished'. In other words, any objection to American decisions, however illegal they may be, implies contradicting the American will, thus placing the culprit into the position of a strategic enemy, which, in turn, renders the latter's behaviour illegitimate. American legitimacy has thus replaced all legality.

James Woolsey, the former executive director of the CIA, has stated calmly:

> What we criticise France for is not the fact that it exercises its right to freedom of expression, but the fact that it has ventured too far by organising the "no to America" coalition.

An interesting statement: from the American perspective, the freedom of expression and action enjoyed by other countries is thus limited, and it is the prohibition to say 'no' to the USA that constitutes this very limit. All one can do is remain neutral and abstain from asserting their position — no more, no less. Moreover, France has displayed '*insolence*' towards its tutelary mentor and must pay the price for its misconduct. The French veto '*has disrespected the memory of the GIs who fell defending France in 1944 and whose bodies are now to be repatriated to the USA*', says Ginny Brown-Waite, a Republican Representative from Florida. The 'allies' thus owe the USA, i.e. the land of the Good, an ethical and almost religious sort of allegiance and respect. Every irreverent nation is guilty of committing an act of blasphemy. The *rogue states* belonging to the Axis of Evil and suspected of having an anti-American terrorist or military agenda are hence not alone to be subject to punishment; all the countries that contradict American endeavours are to be punished as well. The USA is thus expanding its notion of legitimate self-defence in a manner that enables it to target any country that would dare oppose it. Defending oneself against American ambitions or attacks is therefore synonymous with aggressing the US.

The NAI can no longer tolerate the slightest criticism or veto on the part of its allies, above all the French. The allies (or rather, the vassals) are no longer entitled to have their own interests or impede the American *hubris*, as demonstrated by the Iraqi crisis. 'Anyone who does not side with me, and unequivocally so, is completely against me': such is the new and utterly demented slogan. The interests of the 'allies' are meant to merge entirely with those of their suzerain. The slightest criticism is seen as an act of aggression.

What is advocated by the NAI (i.e. by the Bush administration) is, in all likelihood, the most incompetent attitude in matters of foreign policy ever embraced by the USA. It considers the French and German *rebellion* (which, in actual fact, is very limited and highly cautious) against American warmongering to be an act of *aggression*, an offence against the dignity of the sovereign American empire. This incredible intolerance and exaggerated susceptibility is rightfully perceived in Emmanuel Todd's book *After the Empire* as '*a sign of the breakdown of the American order*', at least in terms of what the latter is nowadays like. Philippe de Saint-Robert has made a statement in the same vein:

> The American aggression [against Iraq] is far from being a sign that validates the self-assurance of world power. What it denotes is, quite to the contrary, an urge to evade a profound domestic crisis by means of a foreign adventure. (*Le Figaro*, 16/04/2003)

Helmut Sonnenfeldt, head of the Brooking Institution, is Henry Kissinger's former advisor and a man who has replaced his support for gentle domination with the straightforward form of imperialism espoused by the fundamentalist Protestant *neocons* of the Bush administration. He goes as far as to assert that the mere fact of '*wanting to counterbalance American power*' through an expanded future Europe (in accordance with French intentions) is an inadmissible act of hostility, which is the equivalent of stating that the USA considers its current position of 'the world's sole superpower' to be definitive, one that is meant to establish a New 'Bushian' World Order and that views all those who oppose this notion as trouble-makers who are subject to punishment.

From this perspective, the will of this Empire of Good outclasses international law and reduces the UN and its Security Council to a mere rubber stamp that submits to American wishes. In Sonnenfeldt's eyes, the manner in which the Security Council functions nowadays is intolerable '*because thanks to its right of veto, Paris is on an equal footing with Washington*'. Confirming the American desire to legally become the only independent world power and thus govern others, he specifies that '*if the Security Council were to sabotage all American initiatives, it would turn into an empty shell the very day the USA decides to look elsewhere*'.

What is extraordinary is that this new American doctrine has completely abandoned the old Wilsonian vision of a world governed by morals and legality, a vision that rejected the power politics and warmongering that typified ancient European nations. Without any linguistic precautions, it re-establishes the European (and above all German) nationalistic principles according to which '*might is right*', as well as the cynical realism of the Machiavellian school of thought. In spite of its declared moralism and messianism, the NAI has restored the notion that force, and force alone, is the law that rules human History and that disembodied, abstract principles have no value whatsoever as long as they are founded upon 'pure legality', the fictitious weapon wielded by the weak and impotent. The NAI also embraces the 'reason of state' conception, a term that is to be understood in its 19th century European sense. Admittedly, Henry Kissinger, who was one of Metternich's disciples, did pave the way for such a development.

By embracing this kind of attitude, the NAI is obviously distancing itself from the Christian principles upon which America was established. However, is hypocrisy not the feature of every temporary power? The European states of the 19th century never abided by any evangelical principles, and neither did the princes.

With its decidedly imperial ideological appearance, this radically new position breaks with the Kantian naivety of 'pure law'. It embodies a sort of syncretism between ancient theories, medieval doctrines and Bismarckian ideas, a syncretism that advocates '*the right of the strongest*' and the Protestant messianism of 'God's emissaries', who the *neocons*, beginning with Bush the madman, mistake themselves for. The *Pax Americana* thus borrows some of its aspects from the *Pax*

Romana and *Pax Britannica*. With regard to its intentions, however, it unknowingly resembles the *Pax Sovietica* and *Pax Islamica* as well.

Thomas Donnelly, one of the most influential theoreticians of American neoconservatism, has actually written an article entitled *Pax Americana*, mentioned in *Le Figaro* (28/03/2003). In it, he states that

> Paris is under the false impression that the "soft power" enjoyed by middle powers and exercised through the United Nations is of similar value to "hard power", which can only be attained through economic wealth and military strength.

His theory asserts that the arm wrestling contest between the USA and France will end with the latter's defeat, since it lacks the necessary military and economic-financial power and only possesses 'moral strength' and a commitment to 'law'. It was Stalin who once asked: 'The Pope? How many divisions?'. Confirming the fact that, being the most powerful country, the USA is entitled to dictate international law, Donnelly adds: '*A link between the right to formulate international law and the fact of taking responsibility for its implementation will be re-established* [in the newly-defined UN]'.

Donnelly's theories are likeable. They have the merit of replacing naïve pacifism with realism. However, as pointed out by Patrick Buchanan's isolationistic American nationalists, there is a childish side to the power-drunkenness experienced by current American leaders. Might is right, true enough, but it must be combined with ruse and be genuine, which cannot be said in the case of the USA, a country that possesses neither the ruse nor the true power which it believes itself to have. America sees itself as a superpower, even though it is not.

The fact that it mobilised half of its military arsenal so as to overcome tiny Iraq (in a military campaign which required Great Britain's indispensable assistance) is proof of both its weakness and its inability to govern this occupied country. The new US administration's need to resort to injunctions, admonishments and open threats towards any nation that rebels against its hegemony is a sign of decadent power. For the authority of a man, empire or nation cannot be decreed. It simply imposes itself in a natural manner.

The new American strategy is akin to a child throwing a tantrum for not being able to control his toy universe. When facing the Tribunal of History, the USA might well be judged as a failed and ephemeral empire whose current power-drunkenness is synonymous with its decline.

D. The Murky Concept of a 'Pre-Emptive War'

Arthur J. R. Schlesinger, Kennedy's former advisor, is among the most lucid and most vigorous critics of the NAI. In his memoirs entitled *A Life in the 20th century*, as well as in numerous articles published in the overseas press, he resorts to veiled terms to castigate what he refers to as the 'Bush doctrine', i.e. that of the neoconservatives. He considers its warmongering and its brutal form of imperialism to be counterproductive and harmful to the USA.

His view is the following: during the Cold War, the USA displayed caution and used a *containment* and dissuasion strategy against Communism. The Bush doctrine overturns the whole approach and espouses the dangerous (and stupid) doctrine of *'anticipated self-defence'*, a euphemistic appellation referring to 'pre-emptive war'. The latter, which served as justification for the Iraqi campaign, authorises America to attack in advance all those who (would) threaten the US, Good and world democracy.

Schlesinger reminds us that in 1848, the venerable Abraham Lincoln condemned the use of 'pre-emptive war' in the defence of American democratic principles. Back then, it was a matter of attacking Canada, a British colony prone to initiating a potential act of aggression against the Union. Lincoln explained that war could only be considered in case of an actual invasion targeting the national territory and should not be used to counter an *alleged* threat. Furthermore, what Schlesinger reproaches Bush for is the fact of violating the Lincolnian principle, according to which the President does not have the power to declare war singlehandedly.

However, Schlesinger is somewhat naïve: the USA has always, more or less, practiced 'pre-emptive war', using vague moral or self-defensive pretexts whenever its real aim was either to eliminate economic rivals or to appropriate various riches.

The deceitful claims regarding the presence of weapons of mass destruction that could threaten both America and world peace are no different from the Lusitania and Pearl Harbor provocations, which served as an excuse for American involvement in the two world wars, nor are they different from the Gulf of Tonkin naval incident that sparked off the war in Vietnam. The only difference is that, nowadays, the NAI resorts both to methods that lack subtlety and to psychic-like lies and ill-prepared pretexts, all of which are within the mental reach of President G. W. Bush and his overzealous team.

***

I am however wary of siding with the righteous souls who, in the name of their declared respect for the UN and public international law, condemn pre-emptive war. If it were always necessary for a given state to place its security in the hands of the 'thingy' and await the latter's authorisation before actually defending itself, the state in question would have great cause for concern.

The main point is that pre-emptive war and anticipative strikes are both perfectly justified whenever a state is objectively threatened (as was the case in 1982, during the Israeli bombardment of the Osirak nuclear reactor which Iraq had obtained from France), and it would be utterly naïve for anyone to attempt to subordinate them to the authorisation of the vague ensemble known as the 'international community'. Yet the NAI takes advantage of this concept through[3] its own deceitful expansion, thus objectively jeopardising world peace without actually protecting the USA in any way against genuine threats.

---

3   TN: And for...

If I were a genuine American nationalist, I would be scandalised by the horrific sums that are being spent on pseudo-preventive military adventures in the Middle East, the objective of which is, among other things, to enrich the military-industrial and oil complexes controlled by the oligarchy currently in power, all to the detriment of American citizens. I would additionally demand the expulsion and consequent numerical reduction of the 8 million Middle-Eastern and Asian Muslims that have settled in the USA and turned it into a real breeding ground for terrorists; their presence would strike me as a more objective threat than the 'weapons of mass destruction' owned by one country or another.

***

Furthermore, to demonstrate the coarseness and falseness of the 'weapons of mass destruction' pretext used by the Americans to initiate the Iraqi invasion, it would suffice to point out that if a given country genuinely possessed such weapons (i.e. weapons that have the potential to threaten American and global security), neither war nor military occupation would be necessary; all it would take is a few aerial or ballistic strikes conducted against the military sites in question, which the sophisticated American wiretap and surveillance devices are perfectly able to identify.

E. The NAI's Watchword — 'Everything Is Allowed'

The NAI operates in accordance with the following watchwords: 'Everything is allowed now' and 'we have not had any major rival since the fall of the USSR'. The former prudence displayed by the US-Soviet condominium is vanishing, which is a severe mistake, since every kind of domination must be founded upon the virtue of *prudence* (Aristotle). This is of no consequence, however, because *hubris* has now taken over the situation. Ever since the 9/11 events, American leaders have been striving for a sort of *global coup*, in harmony with a tenet inspired by Jack Marshall.

Anything is allowed, and I mean literally anything: the USA proceeds to violate the rules of the WTO (which I myself have enacted) for the sake of its own personal profit; it allows itself to pollute the environment while tearing the Kyoto protocol to shreds; it continues to conduct nuclear tests after protesting vehemently against those carried out by France; it targets the EU with injunctions to organise the latter in harmony with its own wishes; it decrees unilateral 'punishments' to chastise those countries which criticise the US global policy or seem to want to hinder it; it wages war anywhere and against whoever it pleases without UN approval, targeting countries that are deemed 'diabolical'; it demands that no member of the US military is ever prosecuted by the International Criminal Court; it resorts to ammunition comprising impoverished uranium, whose ionising radiation levels are considerable; it imposes the sale of GM food all over the world in collaboration with bribed European authorities, although such food may well be carcinogenic; it foments large-scale electronic espionage, particularly at the expense of its own allies; it imposes blockages and embargoes upon whoever fails to meet its approval; and so on. This list could easily be a few pages longer.

***

However, American leaders are well aware of the fact that this 'global coup' has two disadvantages: first of all, American economic power is decreasing in relative terms, especially when compared to Asia. After the year 2020, China will become the foremost global economic power, a fact that everyone is conscious of. On the other hand, the USA lives off the credit of other countries, with its gigantic commercial deficit only balanced by the investment flux from the rest of the world to America. The USA is thus indebted to other countries, which places it in a rather uncomfortable position, a position that is comparable to that of the Roman Empire once it had reached its apex and thus also the wake of its downfall.

Therefore, Washington set out to develop a doctrine that lies discretely at the centre of the NAI, namely that of absolute military supremacy, a supremacy unheard of since the days of Charles Quint. Hence the American objective to considerably increase the US military budget (which had been diminishing since the end of the Cold War), even though the USA is no longer under direct threat from any world power. With more than half of all global military expenses, which it invests into hyper-technological warfare capacities rather than a massive army, the NAI has waged everything upon its military tools so as to establish a hegemony that its economic, commercial, financial and cultural power will no longer enable it to sustain.

This constitutes a revolution. American militarism had hitherto been conceived of as a defensive tool, a means to contain foreign threats, with direct offensives serving as the economic-cultural weapon of choice. This era seems to be forgotten now, as the Pentagon has taken over from Wall Street. Militarism is henceforth perceived as a means of intimidation. The process has just been used against Iran and Syria. The problem is that any major power that resorts to direct threats rather than reason and persuasion runs a huge risk, especially in our current world, where the notion of power is no longer what it used to be.

Owing to its intimidation effect, this strategy could end up succeeding. This would, however, only be a temporary development, for the American population is not ready to face the consequences of a genuine war, even against a middle power. The USA is thus attempting to delay its inevitable decline, a decline that will come to pass in no more than fifteen years.

F. Hyperpower and Schizophrenia

The Iraqi campaign has proven that the American administration has overestimated the power of its new armaments, which have been described as 'a revolution in military affairs'. The fact of taking a whole month to 'pacify' an already agonising country (an Arabian one on top of that, knowing how unskilled the Arabs are at manoeuvre warfare and how atavistic their disorganisation is), despite making use of approximately half of one's military potential and even paying off Iraqi generals and granting them safe conducts so that they may desert their posts (as has been widely confirmed), only to end up failing and shamefully calling one's allies to the rescue in the end, is not exactly a brilliant performance on the part of the 'sole superpower'. Patton must be turning in his grave...

However, beyond this Pyrrhic victory, this pseudo war, the USA has not been perceived by the international public opinion as the liberator of an oppressed nation from the clutches of a tyrant, but as an aggressor. The resemblance to Napoleonian imperialism is striking. Following the Revolution, Napoleon presented himself as the liberator of a Europe that had been oppressed by the monarchic-feudal system. He was nonetheless seen as a classic conquering aggressor. After a series of victories, along came the dramatic French downfall, the first stage of our country's decline. The fate of the American dominion will be similar to that of the ephemeral French empire, only on a more massive scale; for anyone who ends up alienating the whole world is doomed to perish.

The NAI arouses a worldwide sentiment of illegitimacy with regard to American hegemony, a sentiment that prevails not only in the Muslim world, but even within the American public opinion. The dream of a humanity guided by an admired, cherished and respected USA (following the collapse of the USSR) is falling apart, as is any utopian hope for a *Pax Americana*.

Just like the Ottoman empire, the USSR displayed far greater wisdom than the USA; it did not claim to have the vocation to achieve world domination and act as a global police force. It thus managed to preserve its *national heart* at the time of its fall, as did Turkey. The USA will not follow suit... The old American notion of a Manifest Destiny (i.e. the mission and destiny that God entrusted America with so as to have it lead the world towards freedom, justice and progress) is taking in water from all sides. The proclamation of its almost religious right to govern the planet has, paradoxically, diabolised the USA and portrayed it as an exploitative, brutal and hypocritical imperialistic force, while simultaneously reinforcing the very same Islamism that labels America 'the Great Satan'.

***

The Muslim *jihadi* ambition, that of a universal holy war to conquer the world in the name of Allah, is actually the inverted clone of the Christian-Protestant American plan. By attacking Muslim countries (and claiming, quite sincerely, in fact, that it is not lashing out at Islam, but merely striving to depose tyrants), the USA is logically perceived by the simple minds of the Muslim masses as a power that is attempting to proselytise them, meaning to enslave them. Islam versus America: such is the global watchword of all imams.

America's eternal flaw lies in its inability to understand others. It suffers from egocentrism and is under the impression that its use of military force could lead Muslim countries to adopt 'democracy', a notion that is utterly incomprehensible to the Muslims, who are brought up in a religious system of hierarchal theocracy. It thus makes perfect sense for the USA to be seen (against its will, of course) as the instigator of a 'crusade' targeting Islam, a crusade led by an alliance of Protestants and Jews, hence the term 'Judaeo-crusaders', which Muslims use to label the Americans.

Historically speaking, it is always very hazardous to be misunderstood: the USA intended to act as the friend, liberator, ally and protector of Muslim peoples. Nevertheless, it now finds itself accused of being the latter's sinister oppressor, which renders the cowboys tearful with both shame and fury. *Naivety* has always been the main characteristic of American global governance, since the Americans are unable to comprehend the world; with the new form of American imperialism, however, this naivety has taken on gigantic and unreasonable proportions. As a matter of fact, the American tradition merges two opposites together: isolationism, i.e. the will to an autarchic civilisation and an oecumene preserved against ravaging storms, and a need for messianic interventionism. This contradiction is fatal when it comes to having a clear understanding of the world around. American culture is thus trapped between self-centredness and the need to expand itself, which robs it of any and all potential to understand others. At the core of the American mentality, one finds a very thick carapace of psychological incomprehension, regardless of the passion that Americans harbour for psychology. Despite its narrowmindedness and its dogmatism, the Muslim mentality is, by contrast, far subtler, calculating, perverse and Machiavellian, a fact that is due to the typical Arab temperament.

What is noteworthy is the presence of a moral contradiction from which the American nation has never managed to free itself: the chiasmus of violence and good will, which remain incompatible. Its existence constitutes a lesion that scars the American collective unconscious, one from which it will never recover: there is no denying the fact that the puritanical land of 'God's Peace', where human rights were invented (before France plagiarised the concept), was founded upon the eradication of American Indian tribes, as well as upon the agricultural enslavement of Blacks, not to mention the countless bombardments that targeted civilian populations in the wars of the 20th century. In no way is this a question of my condemning such behaviour, which has plagued the actions of all peoples (History is, after all, a river of blood and a state of eternal war); I am merely making the observation that the above-mentioned behaviour casts doubt upon the American desire to establish the USA as the land of virtue. Hence the American schizophrenia: in order to impose Goodness, does it not, in fact, spread Evil? Hiroshima, Nagasaki, Dresden and Vietnam are among the numerous examples....

Poor America. Although it is truly kind at heart, there are moral and economic factors that leave it with no choice but to wage war and, through 'collateral damage', slaughter all the peoples that it longs to liberate, offering them presents and humanitarian aid in addition to a bombardment bonus. America is a Santa Claus that kills unintentionally. In the long run, this contradiction is hardly manageable. America's psychological frailty might well be its Achilles heel.

G. The New American Imperialism's Cinematographic Imagination

In the NAI's vivid imagination, not only does one encounter the traditional form of American messianism (the Protestant ideology of combatting Evil, the assimilation of the USA to a *True Israel*, the theory of the latter's 'Manifest Destiny', etc.), but one resorts to more recent American myths as well. The first is that of the sheriff, whose duty it is to maintain order whenever confronted with bandits in the 'global village' that the Earth has now become, just as he once did in the Far-West itself. Next on the list is the spell-binding, repetitive reminder about the war waged against Hitler and the American intervention during World War II, an intervention that is the founding act of American hegemony. Akin to revolutionary France (only on a larger scale), the USA awards itself the recurrent role of world liberator from the clutches of tyrants. It is therefore necessary to maintain a constant, yet not too massive stock of *demonic tyrants* that are subject to termination and replenishment.

As a rule, imperialism is justified through the imperative of 'rushing to the aid of the oppressed', an imperative that has been highly typical of war justifications ever since the French Revolution. It is certain that westerns, with their image of the cavalry charging the savage American Indians in order to liberate the beleaguered settlers, play a certain role in the mental impregnation of American leaders, who have gorged on countless Hollywood films and television series.

Furthermore, let us not forget the desire to avenge the humiliation suffered in Vietnam, which has left a profound impression upon the

Americans. The latter would love to re-experience *Apocalypse Now* and claim victory this time around. The aim is also to alleviate the immense vexation endured by the GIs in Mogadishu, which was the focus of the film *Black Hawk Down*. What is equally worth mentioning is the impact that the Rambo character (played by Silvester Stallone) has had upon the minds of current American leaders: a ferocious boxer and a solitary warrior, Rambo is the incarnation of the *legitimate killer*. Donald Rumsfeld thus mistakes himself for Rambo, an attitude that is even felt in his choice of words.

Above all, however, the NAI feeds upon a sort of morbid and contradictory fascination for the notion of an 'Empire' as depicted in the *Star Wars* cinematographic saga: this Empire is simultaneously the embodiment of an Evil that must be eradicated and an invincible and fascinating power which the USA would love to resemble. How sinful... What serves as evidence for this is the entire industry that has surfaced around the 'negative' characters portrayed in the saga, whose uniforms and overall posture are inspired by the Third Reich, including the worldwide sale of *Star Wars* Bakelite figurines. We should also point out that shortly after the huge success achieved by the above-mentioned saga, American troops were equipped with helmets bearing a strange resemblance to those of the Wehrmacht and... those used by 'Death Star' troopers.

One thus delves to the core of American schizophrenia, which the NAI has adopted and raised to the point of paroxysm. 'We are the Good ones. As for those snakes that tempt us and obsess us, they are an Evil lot'. The biblical theme of Adam's temptation at the hands of the serpent is of course highly present. The same schizophrenia is also encountered in the American attitude to sexuality, in which puritanism merges with pornography, and in environmental matters, where radical ecology and the right to pollute without restriction entwine.

The NAI finds itself entangled in a mixture comprising a culture of brutal and cynical military force ('imitating the tyrants who we strive to defeat'), with all its mediatic attributes, and a humanistic and democratic discourse which is just as naïve and sincere. It is no longer in books and the teaching of history that American neoconservative leaders find their inspiration (as was the case in the days of Henry Kissinger, a German Jew endowed with a long memory), but in the clichés of a superficial, audio-visual imagination. Any form of imperialism that lacks *spirit* is doomed to be short-lived.

In addition, American filmography is haunted by the spectre of Rome. The amazing *Gladiator* (the best Hollywood *peplum*) is evidence of this. Through the NAI, the American leaders in Washington now believe themselves to be part of the Roman Emperor's court. Forgive me for calling *Baudrillard* to my aid here, but his notion of a travesty applies perfectly in this regard. Washington thus considers itself the extension of Christian imperial Rome in its struggle against the Barbarians. The issue is that Christian imperial Rome was a giant with feet of clay, even if it did come across as the culmination of the Empire. By founding its power upon emotional images and self-representative myths instead of an objective analysis of its own position and situation, the NAI reveals its persistent weakness.

H. The Inanity of 'International Law'

In order to counter American warmongering, France has called for the implementation of 'international law', in accordance with the latter's absolutistic definition. In a formulaic fashion, it has armed itself with both the vague concept of the 'legality of the international community' and the UN's authority, as if the latter were a global government. This is bizarre, especially coming from a country that sees itself as the precentor of the '*European superpower*'.

Despite the disastrous blunders that characterise their poorly-constructed pretexts to justify wars, the neoconservatives have, unlike the French, fully grasped the fact that, beyond the hypocrisy of an '*international legitimacy*', which they contrast with 'legality', the 'international community' is but a myth, as confirmed by those principles that were first defined by Bodin and Richelieu, then by Talleyrand and Metternich. They have also comprehended the following truths: that balance can only be rooted in the conflictual-cooperative relations of effective statist powers, regardless of any universal morals and in harmony with the law of interest (even when it is masked with moral values of Good); that a planetary central power erected into a Republic of Justice could never come to pass and that international order can only come about through a concert of powers in which the strongest one will obviously always have the final word; that international relations relate to the *'natural state of affairs'* (to use Sorel's words), a state that is tempered by ephemeral contracts between sovereign powers that will never recognise anyone or anything else to be superior, be it the Greater Good of mankind or the UN; that it is material power and not a legality or ethics that has been agreed upon peacefully which dictates international behaviour; and that no 'principle' (especially a moral one!) is ever eternal, and all precepts are based on temporary voluntary agreements, which is how *sovereignty* is actually defined.

Hence the reason why, when one implements this classic political philosophy, whose essence is of purely European origin and completely at odds with the universalistic and judicial dimension of American abstractionism, the USA has been absolutely right all along (from its own perspective) when affirming its sovereignty, refusing to allow its nationals to appear before the International Criminal Court, not ratifying the treaty that prohibits nuclear tests (a treaty that it nonetheless attempts to force upon others), surreptitiously violating the WTO's regulations while still practicing the very same protectionism it condemns elsewhere, unilaterally denouncing the second SALT treaty signed with Russia, maintaining in power the despots that suit it and overthrowing the ones who do not, and so on...

So as to counter this American policy, a policy that can be likened to that of European nations during the 19th century, moralising sermons will be to no avail. It is, instead, the establishment of a sovereign power with a correlative political will that represents the sole efficient means. Chirac's France has failed to realise this: it espouses various 'ethical' and 'anti-war' positions within the UN, while simultaneously allowing B52s to fly over its own territory, remaining without response when confronted with American boycotts and protectionism, allowing its industrial jewels to be purchased through American pension funds, remaining idle-handed when watching its junior executives and researchers emigrate in large numbers overseas, agreeing to finance the humanitarian aid and reconstruction of Iraq in the aftermath of the devastation wrought upon the country by the US Air Force, and so on. And let us rather not mention the Italian, Spanish and British attitude towards the USA, of course: their approach is that of serfs who seem to delight in being humiliated and cheated by their suzerain.

Although quite weak, it is only Putin's Russia that has displayed a consistent attitude in the face of American hegemony, simply saying *niet*, without any sanctimonious preaching.

I. A Desperate Aggressiveness

What is it then that sets this *New American Imperialism* apart from its classic American counterpart? It is not their respective roots, ideologies or profound legitimations, in fact, but their methods. For more than a century now, a puritanical and naïve sort of messianism has been at the source of American imperialism, an imperialism which has served as a moral justification for the strategic and (especially) economic-commercial stranglehold that the USA has had the world in.

However, as a result of the 9/11 attacks and the neoconservative coup following Bush's rigged election, American imperialism has recently distanced itself from its previously restrained and skilfully justified aggressiveness, embracing an unbridled and barely, if at all, justified form of hostility. In comparison with traditional imperialism, the NAI has replaced calculating behaviour and well-thought-out hypocrisy with crude lies and straightforward aggression validated through highly questionable arguments. What the classic kind of American imperialism resorted to were legitimated power and *force*, whereas the NAI utilises *violence*, supporting the latter with pretexts that lack credibility.

Compared to its traditional counterpart, the NAI has bitten off more than it can actually chew, since its ambitions are unreasonable. Instead of manipulating the UN (a practice that once paid off from the Israeli perspective) and taking advantage of NATO (an organisation which is a mere tool of strategic domination disguised as an alliance), the USA has little use for both, preferring to take advantage of various 'coalitions' shaped in accordance with its own wishes. The new American administration is no longer content with the USA being the *foremost* world power, as was once the case; the aim is now to make America the *sole* superpower. The USA does not strive to achieve a major global influence, but simply to dominate the *Rest of the World*, using direct warfare whenever necessary.

The NAI is sinking into utter unrealism and exacerbating the grave and disabling American tendency to ignore, underestimate and despise the 'rest of the world'. How can one govern other nations when one persistently fails to understand them? By convincing themselves that the USA represents a social and civilisational model which the whole world will end up embracing, the Americans have taken the flaws of the French Revolution to a higher level. They thus consider all other civilisations and cultures to be temporary, fleeting and illegitimate.

Let us, however, not blame America. The French notion of things is hardly different, and French anti-Americanism is but an expression of the rage felt by a competitor consigned to a position of inferiority. This is because the universalisms that characterise the American and French revolutions (the former having served as inspiration for the latter) are of a highly similar nature. By contrast, German anti-Americanism is of an utterly different kind. It is rooted in a 'nationalistic' vision of the world, in which all peoples enjoy their own norms, their own specific moral codes.

The NAI's approach is surprisingly similar to the French revolutionary and Napoleonian attitude of exporting 'liberty' using military force, while simultaneously taking advantage of the situation to impose the dominance of the Great Nation, of course. There is a difference, however: the 'French civilisation' established by Napoleon in a certain part of Europe was of a different substantiality, quality, demeanour and cultural profoundness than the neo-primitive American value system and *way of life*.

***

What dictates the behaviour espoused by a cornered USA and provides an explanation for its disrespect of all international law regulations is the fact that it has chosen, in the aftermath of the 9/11 attacks, to act in accordance with a state of emergency and exception; the problem is that the latter is not meant to be temporary and short-lived, but permanent! Owing to the struggle between Good and terrorist Evil, a struggle that is as present as it is resurgent, this state of exception is destined to become a normal state of affairs for American leaders, which generates a sort of infernal spiral, one that may well guide the USA towards despotic forms of domestic power and international behaviour. This is bound to ruin not only the USA's image, but also the reality of its position as the world's foremost democracy and the free world's beacon, both of which constitute the moral basis of its dominance.

A unified dynamic driven by a twofold engine thus emerges: the first is the NAI, which fuels the other, namely Islamic terrorism, in a headlong rush and build-up that will soon become uncontainable. What we may end up witnessing is the spectacle of an America that is falling prey not only to an ever-growing global hostility, but also to permanent terrorist acts, responding to the latter with warmongering

military actions whose uncontrollability can only be exacerbated. The
state of Israel will be dragged into this downward spiral, of course.

***

The NAI has also taken to the extreme its support of Israel, a country
that has found itself cornered. Numerous American analysts are horrified by the enormous, direct financial aid and unconditional assistance
that the USA grants the adventuresome Ariel Sharon.

Edward Luck, an international relations professor at the University
of Columbia and a man considered to be a 'falcon' himself, has expressed scepticism with regard to this policy, a policy that breaks
completely with Clinton's:

> Our President is under the impression that he has increased Israel's security
> by overthrowing Saddam Hussein and exerting pressure upon Syria, the
> Palestinians and their leaders, and that this factor has furthered reconcilia-
> tion more than any other. It is, however, a risky venture on his part. (JDD,
> 20/04/2003)

The NAI's wager to turn America into the sole, long-term superpower
is unmanageable and betrays an extremely severe historical naivety.
China and India must be having a good laugh. The theory of absolute
unilateralism does not correspond at all to a genuine American hegemony over the rest of the world, whether on a military level or in the
economic sphere.

Only the Atlanticist European milieus — particularly in Great
Britain and Eastern Europe — believe this tall tale. The ambition to
govern the world on one's own, which is the NAI's central ideological
precept, is a ridiculous objective. It betrays a fatal flaw that has always
hastened the downfall of great powers: the overestimation of one's
strength. This is what befell Alexander the Great when he believed he
could conquer Asia, Napoleon and Hitler when they thought that they
would rule a Europe stretching from Lisbon to Moscow, etc.

America lacks the necessary means to bring its velleity of universal
domination to fruition. It does not have a single ace up its sleeve in

this poker game. The American setback will occur when the USA finds itself alone, facing the rest of the world. This situation will thus be unmanageable from its perspective. Admittedly, the NAI does manifest a will to power whose aspects are often likeable and which breaks with the pessimistic attitude that typifies European policies, policies that remain confined to a constant cult of weakness. This will, however, is only built on sand. Instead of anticipating the USA becoming the *foremost* global power (in harmony with the viewpoints embraced by Kennedy, Kissinger and Nixon), Bush's neoconservatives long to turn it into the *sole* superpower, an endeavour which is as infantile as it is impossible.

***

The issue of military 'legitimation' within the NAI resulted in incredible feats during the Iraqi campaign. The USA went as far as to dismiss international law and ended up admitting, in an almost explicit fashion, that its will to wage war was in and of itself a source of legitimacy: the latter, whose essence is both of an ethical and religious nature, no longer requires the legal mechanisms of a signed treaty. This 'legal obsolescence', which was already noticeable during the American denunciation of the SALT II treaty on nuclear weapons signed with the USSR and in the American refusal to ratify the prohibition of nuclear testing, represents an interesting return to the kind of practices that Woodrow Wilson wanted to eradicate back in 1919.

The justification of warfare has always been conducted on two levels: that of genuine motivation (usually the country's expansion or the elimination of a rival) and that of pretexts or 'legitimacy'. The Trojan War represents the foundational model of this kind of warfare: the Greek pretext was Helen's abduction at the hands of the Trojans, but the real purpose lay in the necessity to weaken their competitors, who, from their headquarters by the Dardanelles, rivalled the Greek commercial ambitions in the Aegean Sea.

The NAI has introduced a new type of war legitimation: that of pre-emptive war. But is it truly a new notion? The answer is no. It is, in fact, the very same mechanism that was employed by the declining Roman Empire, which consisted of attacking the dangerous Barbarians that were gathering on the other side of the *limes*. The current American doctrine of 'pre-emptive war' is that of an equally declining power. Unable to persuade others using threats or diplomacy, the USA can only intervene directly.

***

Despite the fact that the new global American strategy has adopted the principles of 'power realism' advocated by Richelieu, Bismarck and Napoleon and that the Americans have espoused the new imperialistic theory of 'deficient sovereignty', the USA tirelessly perseveres in its holy war, its crusade, in a display of utter naivety. This crusade is being conducted in the name of Good, which makes it akin to Islamic holy war, which, likewise, embodies a straightforward attempt to conquer the world.

During the Cold War, Eisenhower believed himself to be opposing Communism in the name of God and demanded that prayers be said in schools. Nowadays, the puritanical G. W. Bush expects his Ministers to pray before the start of every single council meeting, thinking of himself more or less as God's sword arm, with America being the Lord's 'blessed' nation. This stupid attitude obviously exacerbates the *jihadist* tendencies of the Muslims, who are thus convinced that the USA does not target terrorism and despotism, but rather Islam and the Arabs, which in turn leads to an increase in Muslim ardour and their desire for vengeance. In the minds of all Arabs worldwide, even those who were once moderate, anti-British-American and anti-Jewish terrorism is now legitimated, all thanks to Bush's stupidity.

His *neocon* administration is the most mediocre in a hundred years and the least well-informed concerning the global state of affairs, validating clichés and caricatures at the expense of infantile and simplistic Americans. It has failed to comprehend that its approach is bound to trigger an upheaval among entire ominous masses in poor countries, most of whom are Muslims and will thus turn against the USA in a tidal wave of hatred. This is not only true of the various public opinions, but also of the elites and an ever-growing number of governments whose members will not always be open to bribery. In its entire history, never has America, a country that longs to be 'loved' and portrays itself as a global ethical civilizational model, been the target of such hatred. For the first time ever, anti-Americanism has become the dominant 'global sentiment', which has even had a cultural impact, since Afro-Maghrebians now refuse to wear jeans, watch American films or drink Coca-Cola. In Europe, which was once the sole part of the world where anti-Americanism was both contained and fought, the latter is soaring in public opinion polls, especially among the young. In Germany, for instance, as much as 75 % of all respondents espouse anti-Americanistic stances.

This situation is extremely dangerous for the USA: it increases the risk of a terrorist attack on its own soil and, on a global scale, against both its nationals and interests. Above all, however, the USA may well end up facing a worldwide boycott targeting its material and cultural products, a development that would deal American power an unbearable blow. As for us, we can only rejoice at this situation, of course, a situation through which the USA will undoubtedly incur the world's wrath.

***

A mixture of religious messianism and hegemonism, the NAI is deeply enrooted and garnered its first political expression during Senator Robert Kennedy's 1968 presidential campaign. Although a renowned alcoholic (just like G. W. Bush), Kennedy must have been completely sober the day he stated that the USA had the right to govern the world spiritually.

Just like Patrick Buchanan, there are Americans who are lucid enough to realise that, from the American perspective, this economic and messianic imperialism will lead to suicide. What follows is a warning issued by U.S Senator Fullbright in April 1966:

> The Vietnam war has paralysed the great American society and arouses a power frenzy in the United States. America betrays certain signs of the fatal presumptuousness, the excessive power expansion and the ambitiousness that brought ruin upon Athens, Napoleonian France and Nazi Germany. The process has barely just begun, but the war we are currently waging can only increase its pace. (*Le Monde*, 20/12/1966)

Fullbright was endowed with the power of foresight. The defeat suffered by the USA in the Vietnamese open terrain (the first of its kind) was a huge shock, a wound that has left America scarred.

And the Bush administration is at it again! High on power, it has forgotten the lessons that America learnt during the Vietnam war. Here is my personal prediction: having come out victorious from the Iraqi campaign, in which it outnumbered the enemy 100 to 1 (a Pyrrhic victory), the USA will be dragged into a dreadful Middle-Eastern quagmire. The war in the Middle East is just commencing and will go on for years; America will suffer a disastrous defeat, which will mark the beginning of its final decline and the collapse of the state of Israel.

The American debacle during the Vietnam war was a warning that the NAI pays no heed to and whose consequences were counterbalanced in a matter of fifteen years, since the Vietnam campaign was merely a major geostrategic endeavour when compared to the Middle East (due to the country's remoteness and lack of oil) and its only purpose was to combat Communism and the USSR in an indirect fashion, which is less of a challenge than the Muslim-Arab cauldron that has emerged from the depths of the ages. The Middle East may well entomb the American superpower and act as the latter's Russian campaign.

CHAPTER II

The Bible and Business

A. The Return of Biblical Messianism to the Core of American Politics

The NAI has re-established the biblical messianism of the Founding Fathers, a messianism that had been curbed for more than a century. This constitutes a naïve return to the sources. America is thus seen as the new Israel (hence the neoconservative alliance between Protestant and Jewish fundamentalists), a land that must simultaneously pacify and dominate the world. This self-righteous good conscience, one that aims to govern all other nations in the name of both Good and God, was castigated by British political scientist George Monbiot in an article entitled '*America is a Religion*', published in *The Guardian* (29/07/2003). He states: '*Nowadays, American leaders consider themselves to be priests with a divine mission — that of ridding the world of its demons*'. He adds that '*America is no longer a nation, but a religion*'. In this regard, it is obvious that the NAI is highly similar to the ideological conformation espoused by Islamism, in which Good struggles against Evil.

Monbiot points out that the entire American foreign policy is no longer defined by intelligence, the reasonable exploitation of information and the logical prediction of future developments, but by a sort of ideological, para-religious and irrational passion that causes the USA to scramble forward chaotically. This passion thus prevails over the technological and analytical means which America has at its disposal. How else could one account for the Iraqi quagmire? The NAI has gone insane, because it has attempted to reinstate the old doctrines advocated by Machiavellianism and Bismarckism (the prevalence of the strongest and the most cunning) without masking the latter with any skilful pretexts, all in the name of its messianic naivety.

Monbiot believes that

> American soldiers no longer restrict their actions to waging terrain warfare; they have now become missionaries. They are no longer there just to kill the enemy, but to drive out the demons.

The mistake made by both America and Islam is that of attempting to *convert* the world. It is a utopian endeavour that China does not share, which is precisely why it will emerge victorious in the course of the 21st century. The Chinese alone have learnt their Machiavellian lesson.

***

In actual fact, the NAI's use of biblical legitimation is ancient, and all that the neoconservatives have done is reactivate it. In his book entitled *Chosen People* (2002), Clifford Longley reminds us that the Founding Fathers were convinced of the fact that God had bestowed upon them a *divine purpose*. As for Thomas Jefferson, he equated the Americans with 'the new Hebrews'. On his part, George Washington claimed that the American independence was a sign of God's divine intervention in human history. The Lord Himself had allegedly decided to turn the new American people into His own instrument and herald, thus replacing the Jewish people, in accordance with a logic that is highly reminiscent of the one adopted by the Roman Catholic Church when it envisioned itself as the Judaic faith's rightful successor and thus the new 'true religion'.

The American neoconservatives, whose ranks comprise an equal rate of Protestants and Jews, subsequently decided to make a 'biblical compromise', which accounts for the unconditional American support granted to the state of Israel. Neoconservative Protestants (such as Bush himself) feel that there is not much of a difference between the USA and Israel with regard to the accomplishment of divine purpose. Bush is the only president in the entire American history to expect a kind of prayer to be said before every governmental Council. He has made the following declaration, in which he basically quoted the words of Woodrow Wilson: '*America is endowed with a unique spiritual power to liberate the human species, a mission that no other nation could ever contribute to*'. Never would Kennedy or Nixon have dared utter such nonsense. Ronald Reagan, who, just like Bush, was hardly considered a man of intelligence, had already set out to inaugurate this neo-messianism when he declared America to be '*a shining city on a hill*', in a reference to the biblical Sermon on the Mount. Back then, America opposed the existence of the '*Empire of Evil*' (Communism), which was then superseded by Bush's '*Axis of Evil*' (terrorism).

The 9/11 attacks only served to exacerbate this neo-messianism. On the very same day, Rudolf Giuliani, who was the mayor of New York at the time, declared: '*You must believe in America; America is a religion*'.

In his book entitled *No Man's Land* (Green Books, 2003), the above-mentioned political scientist, Monbiot, depicts the neoconservatives' deepest conviction, a conviction that is as infantile as it is fanatical:

> The USA does not need to preach God's will because it is His very embodiment, and the Americans who travel abroad do so in order to spread the light of the celestial domains. The American flag has become as holy as the Bible itself and the nation's name as holy as the Lord's. The American government has been transformed into a clergy.

Anyone who criticises Bush's foreign policy '*is anti-American and therefore a blasphemer*'. The countries that attempt to negotiate with Washington are drawing a blank, since '*negotiations are possible when dealing with politicians, but not priests*'. In a classic English manner, he also points out that the deifying attitude towards the American nation, which has led Bush to assert that America is *'defending the hopes of all mankind'*, has a fetid aspect to it, since, beneath the surface of those grandiose humanitarian and messianic proclamations, one also encounters an element of doom: *'Woe betide those who hope for something other than the American way of life'*.

It thus goes without saying that for Monbiot (a man renowned for being repulsed by Antlanticism), the NAI's neo-messianism can only have a tragic outcome. Let us then quote him one last time, as he expresses his thoughts in a most inimitably British way: *'Those who seek to drag heaven down to earth are destined only to engineer a hell'*.

***

This last remark is the source of yet another clarification on the kinship that ties the neo-messianic NAI to Islamism. Both are driven by a desire to impose Good upon the whole planet, and both are drowned in a similar sort of chaos. However, one should not assume that the NAI and its neoconservatives are 'anti-Islamic' and long to wage a holy war, i.e. a crusade, upon Islam, as imagined by countless Muslims and the Islamophilic and hysterical anti-Americans of Europe. Bush's 'Axis of Evil' also includes North Korea and virtually every rebellious country that rejects the new American world order. Although Islamism does indeed manifest a blatant hatred for the USA, the latter is not mutual. To emphasise this fact, Bush went to a mosque in Chicago the day after the 9/11 attacks in order to pay his solemn homage. The tragedy is that, as a result of the strategic imbecility displayed by the American elephant, the Muslim world interprets the US policy as *'a war waged by the Judeo-Crusaders upon Islam'* (to use the consecrated expression), which is anything but true.

In an article entitled *How Religion Influences the President* published in *The International Herald Tribune* (19/05/2003), Bill Keller explains that, having come out of rehab, former alcoholic Bush became a born-again evangelistic Christian zealot. Under his rule, the distinction between state and religion is gradually vanishing. According to Keller,

Bush, a former Methodist now turned Evangelist, is characterised by a fanatical and romantic sort of faith, one that demands that he strives to do Good, without however specifying the latter's exact ethical definition. It is a faith that lacks any *'precise agenda'* or well-defined moral programme. Hence the risk of drifting into an unscrupulous good conscience while simultaneously believing that, regardless of one's behaviour, one is acting in the name of God and the Greater Good, even when committing horrendous atrocities. Keller also highlights a novel ambition among Republican politicians: the desire to become the political party that represents all those who abide by the Bible, thus bringing together, for the very first time, American Catholics, Protestants (including the Mormons, who are often rich and influential) and Jews.

B. The Militarism of Good

Power, power! Such is the keyword of the American culture. The NAI pushes this syndrome to its limit, basing its stances on Hollywood movies. America thus holds a fascination for power.

The American 'will to power' is not subject to criticism in and of itself, since it is founded upon realism and obviously comes across as being more intelligent than the blunt and self-righteous pacifism currently advocated by Europeans. What we are facing here, however, is a trivial and low-end modality of the will to power, one that the NAI has taken to unheard of extremes and is thus akin to plain and simple suicidal stupidity. A good example of this is found in the manner in which the Americans allowed themselves to sink deeper into the Iraqi quagmire only to show off their muscles, violating international regulations in the process and ultimately asking the 'international community' for military support so as to maintain order.

The contradiction between the fascination for military power and the 'zero killed' imperative demanded by the American public opinion is blatant. And there is yet another, often emphasised contradiction:

a mixture of power quantitativism (a desire for things to be ever larger, more expensive, stronger, higher, richer, more violent, etc.) and ethical-religious justification. Do not assume the latter to be dishonest and a mere vulgar pretext. Biblical dramatics and a messianic sort of spirituality have, to a great extent, been internalised by the 'militarism of Good' and thus partake of it.

***

The NAI is reinvesting itself most intensely into the American puritan tradition. One cannot possibly imagine G. W. Bush having sexual relations with one of his secretaries, as Clinton once did. There is a huge difference between the neoconservatives and the Kennedy (Irish Catholic) clan, whose history is soaked in scandals, mafia-like assassinations and tragic drinking binges, always sailing across the murky waters that lie between the *jet set*, the *showbiz* world, the criminal underworld and politics. The Kennedy era was that of the Borgias.

The Bush era, by contrast, is of an entirely different nature and constitutes a unique development in American history. Although it cannot be classified, it is characterised by two striking features:

1) Following a rigged electoral process, G. W. Bush took over from his own father. This marked the rise of the Texan 'petropolitical' dynasty, whose members seized power; one would think this has taken place in Syria or Korea, the lands of dynastic presidents.

2) The involvement of the Bush clan and its neoconservative entourage in the signing of armament contracts indicates that the American foreign policy is in a state of confusion between serving the personal interests of American leaders and the alleged interests of the USA itself.

***

The financial / oil motivations behind war do not seem sordid at all to the American politicians that wage it. As part of their Protestant ethics, any and all profits are allowed provided that the cause is just. The same applies to rewards. The Bush family has liberated Iraq and is thus entitled to take full advantage of its oil reserves. Such are the American ethics of *vigilantism.*

C. Israelism?

What accounts for the pro-Israeli attitude embraced by the Bush administration? Everyone knows that the Sharon government enjoys the full support of the current Republican administration, which favours it above all others, and that one of the reasons behind the war in Iraq is a pro-Israeli stance unequalled in the entire course of recent American history, when, traditionally speaking, the Republicans have always been less inclined to support Israel than the Democrats. So why such a reversal?

The first explanation is that conservative Christians, who were all once rather hostile towards Jewish milieus, have recently proceeded to rally behind the Israeli cause. This constitutes a genuine political earthquake in the USA. *The Washington Post* clarifies this:

> For decades on end, Jews looked upon Christians with a mixture of suspicion and fear. [...] However, the crisis faced by Israel has repeatedly demonstrated the simple truth that evangelical Christians are currently Israel's stoutest supporters.

Indeed, a total of 62 % of conservative Christians are pro-Israeli, compared to 26 % of secular American Democrats! (These rates stem from a poll conducted by the Pew Research Center in June 2002. This is quite the novelty, since anti-Jewish attitudes are traditionally encountered among Republicans). The reasons for this convergence between the Jewish *establishment* and the Christian Right are religious in essence for the Christians themselves, who have been moved by the civil war that has been tearing Israel apart, but political from the Jewish perspective. These Protestants are (re)discovering their biblical and

Hebraic roots. In an article published by *The New York Times* on the 2nd of May 2002, Christian chronicler Ralph Reed remarked that there was '*an undeniable and strong spiritual connection between Israel and the Christian faith*'. James DeLoach, who works as a pastor in Boston, has established The Jewish Temple Foundation in his desire to destroy the esplanades of mosques in Jerusalem and rebuild the Temple of Solomon! Doctor John Walvoord, a Protestant theologian from Dallas and a professor at the Southwestern School of Bible Studies, teaches his followers that '*God only cares for his Sons, the Jews and the Gentiles, but is indifferent to Muslims, Buddhists and all other faiths*'. Some of these 'Zionist Christians', as they are typically referred to in the USA, have established a syncretism between Protestantism and Judaism (the theory of 'the Return of Christ') and, just like Jerry Falwell and Randall Price (the founder of the World of the Bible Ministries Protestant lobby), venture even further than radical Zionist Jews by advocating the existence of a Jewish monotheistic state free of any and all Arab presence and stretching from the Euphrates to the Nile (*Eretz Israel*), in accordance with Abraham's alleged wishes.

On their part, American Jews (and especially the famed and power-ful American Israel Public Affairs Committee, the AIPAC, which acts as the principal transmission tool for Israeli interests to the American authorities and is regularly accused of being 'the real US government' in the anti-Jewish press) have not signed this pact with the Protestant Republican Right for religious or emotional reasons, but because of their cynical political realism. Abraham Foxman, who runs the Anti-Defamation League (one of the most influential Jewish lobbies), has made the following public declaration:

> The differences between them [the Christians] and us are insurmountable. This does not, however, mean that we are to reject their support, which we are grateful for, especially since the Christians do not ask for anything in return for their aid.

This is where we can make perfect sense of the new strategy adopted by the Bush administration when granting Sharon its unconditional support and taking military action against the diabolical and anti-Jewish Saddam Hussein:

1) One must appeal to the now Zionistic conservative Christian electorate, whose members represent the very pillar of Republican electoral support.

2) One must attract Jewish voters and flatter the powerful mediatic networks of this 'community', as the latter have always been inclined to support the Democrats. Traditionally, Jewish voters have always been in favour of Democratic candidates, as has been the case with nearly all influential, mediatic and financial networks, to such an extent that a great number of Jews actually endorsed Al Gore against Bush, whose Justice Minister, Ashcroft, had a widespread reputation for being anti-Semitic... The Bush administration is thus trying to turn the tide. Religion, electioneering and petropolitics are all closely interlinked...

Nevertheless, several Jewish intellectuals have criticised this 'historic compromise' between the Jewish and Christian Rights for being fanatical and suicidal. The Republican pro-Zionistic attitude has equally been targeted. Allan C. Brownsfeld, the director of *Issues* (the quarterly published by yet another Jewish lobby, the American Council for Judaism), states:

> All of this constitutes a dangerously confused mess of religious, electoral and foreign policy elements. Such bed-sharing and unnatural embraces can only yield the most bitter fruit.

***

How and why has the Bush clan become pro-Israeli? Indeed, this represents quite an upheaval in the American domestic policy. Bush Senior was actually renowned for being anti-Israeli, and the Jewish

He decided to turn a blind eye to the colonisation of the occupied territories
and to become entirely pro-Israeli, since he wants to be re-elected in 2004.

Only the future will tell whether this calculating behaviour will be
fruitful, because there are many other 'influencer' groups (a Canadian
term meaning 'lobbyist') currently on the rise in the USA.

There is a constantly repeated cliché, one that is due to an incom-
plete awareness of global political events, as well as to a pro-Palestinian
passion fraught with victimhood: if the USA were to retract its support
for Israel and the latter ceased to oppress the poor Palestinians, Islamic
terrorism would simply go up in smoke. Islamophile Alain de Benoist
expressed this very platitude in an undated online communiqué entitled *American Hegemonism or the Genuine Meaning of the Iraqi War*:

> Obstinately, Washington refuses to acknowledge the fact that the neo-colo-
> nial situation faced by the Palestinian people is the essential cause behind
> global Islamist terrorism.

This is a most absurd remark for anyone who knows that the Saudi
terrorists who carried out the 9/11 attacks were, above all, 'protesting'
against the US military presence in the Arab peninsula, as they themselves admitted. And what about the Iranian attacks that shook Paris
in the 1980s? And the hundreds of terrorist acts that have taken place
on 3 different continents over the past 15 years? Is it all the result of
the Palestinian situation? In truth, the problem cannot be accounted
for on the sole basis of the attacks conducted in Israel. On the contrary, terrorism is an inherent part of the global conquest with which
Islamism targets the non-Muslim world, the very same Islamism that
uses all possible pretexts to claim that it is being persecuted and ag-
gressed when, in actual fact, it is the Islamists themselves who are the
only aggressors.

CHAPTER III

The Militaristic Option

A. The Realistic and Insane Aspects of American Imperialism

So as to confirm what has already been stated, here are some excerpts taken from a document published in September 2000 by the Republican think-tank known as the *Project for the New American Century* and drafted by G. W. Bush's team, namely Dick Cheney, Donald Rumsfeld, Paul Wolfowitz and Lewis Libby. The document is entitled *Rebuilding America's Defenses*. Interestingly enough, it was written prior to the 9/11 2001 attacks, which seems to imply and prove that these attacks merely served to accelerate an already established plan. So, hold on tight!

We must seize power in the Persian Gulf region, whether Saddam Hussein is there or not. The American presence on this soil is more important than the question of Saddam's regime. We must anticipate a plan that would allow us to maintain global American pre-eminence, preventing the emergence of a rival power and shaping an international security policy in accordance with American principles and interests. The USA's main mission is to claim victory in several wars. The American forces present in foreign countries are the "cavalry" of the new American frontiers. Peace missions must be headed by the USA, not the UN. Admittedly, Iraq, Iran, North Korea, Syria and Libya are all potential enemies, but we must watch out for Europe, which could become a power rivalling the USA. We must reinforce the American military presence in South-East Asia, which should pave the way for China's "democratisation" (in the Orwellian Newspeak, "democratisation" does not mean "democracy", but rather "Americanisation"). We must also dominate the Internet and cyberspace, and despite international prohibitions, the USA should develop new non-lethal weapons, especially electronic and biological ones, as well as new and advanced microbial forms that could exclusively target specific genotypes and thus become highly interesting weapons.

***

Ever since the Vietnam war, the American foreign policy has, unlike cultural imperialism, been unable to achieve its objectives and is turning out to be counterproductive for the USA itself, especially in relation to Islam. Let us give a few recent examples.

1) Supported by Giscard's France, the USA contributed to overthrowing the Iranian Shah and establishing Khomeiny in his place. As a result, Islamism was provided with an ideal launch pad.

2) Believing itself to be playing a winning card, the USA granted Afghan Islamists its full support against Brezhnev's foolish Soviets and their moribund Communism. It 'reared' Bin Laden, established the Taliban and reinforced Wahhabism, which betrays utter historical ignorance.

3) During the Gulf War of 1991, the undeclared American objective was to reclaim the Kuwaiti oil resources confiscated by Saddam Hussein. The secondary and unexpected outcome, however, was that the USA lost its Saudi ally, whose oil reserves are of an entirely different size compared to the Emirates'.

4) The Kosovo war and the military aggression against Serbia, which were meant to establish allied Muslim states at the heart of the European continent, facilitated the founding of uncontrollable governments and powers in Bosnia, Albania and Macedonia. The latter are prone to Islamism and *jihad* and are violently hostile

to Washington. They will thus become terrorist bases that fight American interests in Europe.

5) Not only does the USA's virtually unconditional support of Israel only serve to victimise Palestinian Arabs and reinforce global combative *jihad*, but it ultimately paves the way for Israel's inevitable defeat.

6) The attack against Afghanistan has fortified Muslim terrorist networks and their recruitment bases, which constitutes a full-scale strategic setback. Barzai's puppet government only controls Kabul. The military campaign's true purpose (to grant the USA control over Central Asia's resources and oil flows) has not been achieved. Bin Laden, Emir Omar and the *mujahid* elites are still as active and elusive as ever, and the international financial networks have either remained intact or been reinforced.

7) Islamist terrorism has gained in intensity as a result of Bush's clumsy 'anti-terrorist' struggle, a struggle that was triggered by the 9/11 attacks, which the CIA and FBI probably allowed to unfold, just like Pearl Harbor. The USA has been acting like a sorcerer's apprentice. On a global level, it has thus bet everything on Islamism so as to weaken Europe and Russia. However, this calculating behaviour has backfired against it like a boomerang. The Americans have contributed to the propagation and aggravation of the 'terrorist contagion'.

8) Last but not least, we have the icing on the cake: the military attack against Iraq, an alleged effort to overthrow Saddam Hussein, a micro-Hitler of sorts who was said to possess nuclear and chemical arsenals, despite the fact that his country is as poor as Mali (shortly before the onset of the Gulf War, the Pentagon had actually presented the Iraqi army as being 'the fourth most powerful' one. Yeah, we noticed…). The international press has pointed out the facts: the issue of the alleged 'weapons of mass destruction' owned

by Iraq does not hold water when the dangerous countries that *do* possess such weapons are actually Iran, Pakistan and North Korea, with the latter having admitted it openly.

***

Here is the most paradoxical aspect, however — both the Anglo-Saxon press and the American administration have acknowledged the following problems: first of all, it is not clear who should supersede the current regime. The gloomiest likelihood is that of having the Islamists replace the secular Baath Party. Secondly, while it is common knowledge that the Bush clan's ambition is to appropriate the Iraqi oil reserves (which may be the world's second largest) in anticipation of the failure of the Saudi resources should the ancient local monarchy be overthrown by an Islamist regime, how could Anglo-American companies ever be expected to peacefully exploit the oil wells of a country that has been plunged into chaos? There is, however, something even more troubling: if a conflagration were to occur in the Middle-East, everyone knows (and particularly Mr. Greenspan, the president of the Federal Reserve Bank) that oil prices would skyrocket on a worldwide scale, soaring at around 35 Euros a barrel. The attack against Iraq substantiates the Islamist conviction of an ongoing western aggression targeting Muslim-Arabs, which increases the global number of *mujahid* legions and terrorists. The Bush clan is well aware of these objections, but finds itself cornered and cannot back down without becoming the focus of mockery. It has no choice but to tackle the problem head on. Let us not forget that the American military industry needs to function somehow. The Iraqi campaign resulted in increased orders of sophisticated materials, which had been exhausted in Afghanistan. Just like its oil counterpart, this industry finances the Republican Party. And G. W. Bush longs to be re-elected...

In short, what is happening is that under G. W. Bush, the American foreign policy is losing its grip and taking some of its recent characteristics, namely its counterproductive militarism, its twisted alliances/

overthrows (which always end up backfiring against the USA) and its globally destabilising activities (which represent the very opposite of pacification), to their utmost extreme. The *Pax Americana* is akin to a bull trudging through a china shop. It was back in 1945 that the USA truly embodied a superpower, with 40 % of the world's GDP compared to its current 20 % rate. In 20 years' time, America will be reduced to a mere middle power on all possible levels and will obviously be overtaken by China.

Bush will have also pulled off the feat of cutting the USA off from its two principal European vassals: Germany and Great Britain. Never since 1945 has anything like this happened — both the German government and the British public opinion are openly opposed to the American ambitions regarding Iraq. The USA is basically isolating itself.

As for Europeans, they have been mentally emasculated (especially the British, who, in the name of a decadent set of democratic values, are allowed to shelter with impunity the worst possible green totalitarian scum) and fail to grasp the fact that the best means to protect themselves against Islamist terrorism (whose philosophy reflects the Koran's very essence) is to ban any and all Muslim immigration on European soil, rather than to participate in the bombing of Muslim countries (once again, with utter impunity) at the behest of NATO. The Americans have, in fact, adopted a stupid foreign policy, but they at least have one, unlike the Europeans, who have none whatsoever and allow the tide to carry them away as if they were on a drunken boat[4].

The USA overestimates its own power and has chosen to take the fatal path of harsh imperialism, the very same kind that caused the demise of Alexander the Great, the Spanish empire, Napoleon, William II and Hitler.

---

4   TN: This is a reference to Arthur Rimbaud's work.

The consequences may well turn out to be very grave for the Americans, who will thus be confronted with repetitive giga-terrorism (in a hyper-fragile society that lives in dread of death), the destabilisation of oil economy (which acts as the pillar of American power), the overthrow of 'allied' Muslim regimes at the hands of their own exasperated masses (who will then call for the establishment of Islamic republics), the growing hostility of European public opinions (despite the americanomorphic cultural plugging), etc. The belief that all issues can be resolved through Dollars (and the simultaneous use of bombs) is a huge historical mistake. Whenever the trading option replaces a country's sovereign function and governs its military operations, as in America's case, a disaster is unavoidable.

The so-called American 'empire' is actually nothing of the sort. It is but a 'business', one that is ephemeral by essence. No one could ever dominate the world by turning everyone against them, nor could they do so by imagining themselves mere customers in a supermarket. What the USA would have needed is a Talleyrand of its own. His name was actually Henry Kissinger, but no one listened to him. All the Americans now have is thus G. W. Bush, who is nothing but a poor man's version of Texan oil tycoon J.R from the *Dallas* TV series. The 'Empire of Good' which the Americans long for has only led to the emergence of a wall that now surrounds the USA and arouses sheer hatred for it. Let us then hope that a large number of American people of European descent will choose to adopt the *southern spirit* and attempt to halt America's race to the bottom.

***

Conservative Patrick Buchanan wrote an article entitled *American Roots of 21st Century Wars* in which he covered the topic of independence and secession struggles (*World Net Daily*, 05/06/2002). He states:

> Not only Israel, but India in Kashmir, China in Sinkiang and Serbia in Kosovo confront independence movements by Islamic peoples who are throwing in our face our own hallowed principle of self-determination, as

Hitler did in the 1930s. And there is the same perplexity and moral confusion among Western elites now as then. Are we hypocrites who only believe in self-determination when it does not threaten our own or allied interests? And if we are true believers in self-determination, was Lincoln right to send a million-man army to crush a people's rebellion to break free of his Union, as our forefathers had broken free of the British Crown? If America was a "union of free and independent states," why was the South not free to depart? So, today, in Chechnya, Putin invokes Lincoln as Islamic rebels invoke Wilson and the young slave-owner Jefferson. And so we all stumble toward a war of civilizations in which the atomic bomb may be the ultima ratio.

Let us once more remember that in all cases where Muslims demand new territories and secessions, they represent a majority (or have become one) thanks to immigration and childbirth (Kosovo, Macedonia, Russia, and Kashmir). Indeed, historically speaking, territories are always claimed by those whose people is dominant and not by those who, like the Israelis, assert that this right was bestowed upon them by God, as Buchanan says, or even those who, akin to the Serbs, base their claims on long foregone 'historic rights'. In France, where the French are now a minority on their own ancestral soil, we will soon face the same secessional issues and a subsequent attempt at conquest. For it is not so much the vague problematics relating to Corsica, Brittany, Catalonia or Scotland that will have to be resolved in the next 20 years, but the independence of Muslim enclaves located at the very heart of Europe, enclaves whose size is constantly growing. In their mosques, the Muslims are already speaking of 'reclaiming' Andalusia and the South of France.

***

How many atomic bombs does North Korea have? And why does Bush remain silent on the topic?

William Perry, a high-ranking official at the Pentagon and a man who, at one point, was both Clinton's special envoy in North Korea and the American Defence Secretary, made the following declaration on the 21st of July 2003 when interviewed by the American PBS channel:

> If North Korea perseveres in its current programme, it will, by the end of 2003, have a total of 8 nuclear heads in its possession and be able to manufacture 5 to 10 of them per year.

The North Koreans use their Taopedong missiles to threaten both South Korea, where 38,000 GIs are stationed, and Japan. In Perry's eyes, the principal danger lies in selling either plutonium or bombs to terrorists, who may subsequently choose to detonate the device in an American city. He believes that potential buyers are now lining up. On the other hand, according to *The New York Times* (20/07/2003), the massive presence of Krypton 5, a gas released during the fabrication of plutonium, has been detected along the border that separates the two Koreas. What is extraordinary, however, is that while the American State Department did not hesitate to accuse Iraq of possessing 'weapons of mass destruction' without any proof whatsoever, it casts doubt upon such information in the case of North Korea, although the latter is very convincing. In other words, Bush chooses to retreat when confronted with the evidence that points to the existence of North Korean nuclear weapons. He may be brave, but not fearless... Had Saddam Hussein been convicted of having just one nuclear warhead, he would still hold the reins of power in Baghdad.

***

What accounts for the USA's easy victory in Iraq? *Le Journal Du Dimanche* had already indicated that one of the Iraqi chiefs of staff, General Al-Tikriti, had opted for treason and, having been bribed by the Americans, chose not to defend Baghdad in exchange for a safe-conduct for himself and those closest to him. An article published in the *Defense News* weekly (19/05/2003) specified things further. When questioned by journalists, General Tommy Franks himself had allegedly confessed to having paid off the executives of the Iraqi republican guard. The corruption of enemies is unflinchingly presented as a weapon of war:

> In order to overthrow Saddam Hussein's regime, the USA has, according to
> both numerous high-ranking officials at the Pentagon and on-site military
> officers, made use of a wide range of weapons, including pay-offs meant to
> convince various Iraqi generals to keep their forces out of the conflict.

In fact, in the rare cases where resistance and confrontations did take place, American troops made a fool out of themselves (in an effort to minimise their casualties, most probably).

B. The Madness Pervading the Iraqi Campaign

The Iraqi campaign embodies a rather comical violation of international law, one that points to the fact that the USA feels cornered. The Bush administration is dragging the USA into adopting a risky approach unlike any other in its entire history, an approach comprising the use of vulgar pretexts for unilateral acts of aggression that discredit the legitimate right of this 'superpower' to police the world. Rooted in bad faith, such attacks and contradictions only serve to deride the American administration.

This 'pre-emptive war', waged upon a small country that has already been bled dry (a country with a population of 24 million inhabitants that the Americans have chosen to invade because they know perfectly well that it does not actually have any weapons of mass destruction), is evidence of the USA's immense weakness and decline, and not of its power, as nowadays understood by the entire world.

The fact of mobilising six nuclear aircraft carriers and 200,000 soldiers before begging the British and the Turks for help, in an effort to overthrow a regime that has been under embargo and bombarded for a whole decade, demonstrates that the USA is utterly incapable of taking on a middle power (especially after the openly acknowledged fiasco resulting from the Afghan operation). In a state of delirium, the sheriff can no longer dissuade nor frighten the 'scoundrels' (as witnessed during the Korean provocations); all he can manage to do is to open fire upon the weak and unarmed.

***

We have already highlighted all the goals behind the neoconservative warmongering. What they strive to do is: to appropriate Iraqi oil — in case the Arab peninsula falls into the hands of Islamists — and reoccupy Mesopotamia so as to ensure Israel's protection and keep Iran at bay (while making sure that they never actually attack the latter, which would be a completely different kettle of fish); to establish themselves in the Middle-East and Central Asia to outflank Russia from the south and neutralise it, preventing the birth of a Euro-Russian axis; and to keep the military-industrial complex that finances the Republican Party in motion. We have also mentioned the private (and oil-related) dispute between the Bush family and Saddam Hussein, who was once rearmed by Bush Senior; the domestic electoral operation which aims to reassure a public opinion that has been traumatised by the 9/11 attacks and convince the American people of America's invincibility; and the American nation's irrepressible need to 'combat Evil'. Additionally, we have covered the topic of the naïve, yet sincere American desire to 'democratise' the Muslim Near-East. This is the basis of Ivan Roufiol's view, who wonders *'why democracy seems so inaccessible from the Muslim perspective'* (*Le Figaro*, 07/03/2003). The reason, my dear friend, is that everything in Islam, beginning with the Koran and the Hadiths, condemns any notion of democracy.

In short, all of these factors play a certain role in the Bush clan's motivations. The Bush administration crystallises the worst, most improvised, most irresponsible and most naïve and cynical attitudes embraced by the American foreign policy during the past century (including the effort to restore freedom and happiness in a country whose population has been brought to the brink of starvation and bombarded for ten long years by the Americans themselves…), while simultaneously incorporating every conceivable American flaw and excluding any and every quality. Let us not forget, furthermore, that all declining world powers are prone to waging war without good reason.

***

The consequences of war are obviously very harmful to the USA. Let us now enumerate them: regional destabilisation; the reinforcement of Islamic and terrorist prestige (America is Islam's ideal impresario — they have been playing an insane game since the 1980s, a game in which the USA first allied itself to Islamism before arousing its hatred and fighting against it and ultimately strengthening it on a worldwide scale); the moulding of Bin Laden into a global *jihadi* hero; the Islamisation of Iraq, a country that has sunk into chaos instead of being democratised; the unexpected birth of a French-German-Russian continental axis challenging the Anglo-Saxons, which is precisely what the Americans sought to avoid; the unleashing of both Western and Muslim public fury against an 'American Imperialism' considered to be synonymous with genuine 'Evil'; and, last but not least, the definite risk of facing a very severe form of economic depression and financial/budgetary crises as a result of this military campaign and the quagmire that stems from occupation.

***

What is most necessary at this stage is for us to reason in a completely Machiavellian and cynical manner, only taking into consideration European interests (including those of Russia) and avoiding any sort of moral indignation. Let us rejoice at watching the Americans sink into crocodile-infested backwaters. Following Hegelian dialectical reasoning, let us hope that both this war and the global reaction to American naivety can, however inadvertently, serve as *History's midwives* by actually triggering the dreaded 'civilisational clash' between us and Islam, the very same Islam that acts as the banner of the Third World menace. For this is how everything will, at long last, become clear. Objectively speaking, the American hubris has sparked a global confrontation and increasing disorders that represent our only hope of awaking. The Americans, who, following the fall of Communism, longed to preside over the 'End of History' and their 'new world order' (as imagined by Bush Senior), have actually set off a historical devolution (through Bush Junior) which is as detrimental to them as it is advantageous to us!

In connection to this remark, I would like to make another: let us not forget that one of the main reasons behind Jacques Chirac's opposition to the American expedition lay in his (sincere) Philo-Arabism and his concern to treat the millions of Muslim-Arabs living in France with utmost care, and not in an alleged anti-American and Gaullist stance that he never espoused. All one had to do was to look at the physiognomy of all those who participated in French 'anti-war' manifestations and the banners they carried, and everything became clear… The European position must, in fact, follow a 'third path' — that of resisting the American *adversary* as well as the far more dangerous enemy gradually occupying our land.

***

It is perfectly logical for an Arab or Muslim to mobilise passionately against this American imperialistic intervention, but it remains an utter waste of time and energy from the European perspective. Why should Europeans ever have to defend the Muslim-Arabs against the American *imperium* or rise up in support of the Palestinian cause? What does this struggle have to do with us?

American imperialism should only be resisted whenever it targets Europe (by having the courage to take retaliatory commercial measures, for instance). We have no duty whatsoever to show solidary towards the Muslim-Arab world, a world that has done us no favours since the 8th century CE. It is normal for a '*good European*' (a term proposed by Nietzsche) to systematically strive to impede American imperialism, especially since the latter exerts itself tirelessly to wage a merciless economic and industrial war upon us and subject us to political enslavement (which is in its interest, naturally). This is not really the point, however. What is crucial is for us not to lose sight of what is vital, namely our own survival, as well as Europe's.

It would be too easy and too convenient to consider America our chief enemy. It is but an intellectual reflex that betrays one's refusal to acknowledge the actual invasion of Europe through the construction of mosques and the wombs of Muslim women. American power is factitious, temporary and far less dangerous than the Third World / Muslim ethnic and religious bulldozer. Why should we do the USA (a country that is, in fact, losing face in this crisis) the favour of overestimating it? Just like the Chinese, we too should display cynicism and indifference in the face of the war that Bush has been waging.

Last, but not least, the USA has suffered three setbacks in Europe: firstly, owing to their clumsy insolence and their scornful attitude towards the UN, the Americans have alienated the European public opinion and thus enabled the exacerbation of anti-American sentiments, regardless of their efforts to bribe the governments of Eastern and Southern Europe; secondly, by viewing the British government as a vassal ever at its disposal, the USA has robbed itself of British solidarity for good; thirdly, the Americans have managed to shape a Paris-Brussels-Berlin-Moscow (-Beijing) axis in the course of the current crisis, the very axis that has been the stuff of nightmares to them. Furthermore, the Iraqi crisis has highlighted the huge importance of sovereign states, which living-room intellectuals have declared '*obsolete*' as a result of their own geopolitical ignorance, believing that such states could be replaced by some international or local 'networks'.

***

Let us now conclude our study with the remarks made by certain American analysts. In January 2003, nationalist Patrick Buchanan stated the following in his magazine entitled *The American Conservative*: '*The American army that has been deployed in Baghdad provoked an automatic appeal for jihad spreading from Morocco to Malaysia*'. Buchanan predicts the outbreak of a religious and civilisational war that will engulf the entire planet. He criticises the American neoconservatives who practice small-scale anti-Iraqi imperialism in order to smooth the path of immigration in the USA itself:

> The conservative movement has been abducted and perverted to the point where it has become a globalist and interventionist ideology, one that is favourable to the opening of borders and unrestricted immigration.

In the same issue of the above-mentioned magazine, Eric Margolis expresses an identical opinion when speaking of the 'pirate-like' attitude embraced by the New American Imperialism, an imperialism that pays no attention to the domestic problems faced by White Americans.

On his hackworth.com.USA website, Colonel David Hackworth, a man considered to be a great American military figure, advocates the notion that the current US administration has adopted 'mafia-like' behaviour and is driven by false morals and sordid financial interests. In *The Washington Times* (02/02/2003), Craig Roberts expresses the view that, instead of containing Islamic terrorism on Western soil, Bush's warmongering policy will only serve to increase it.

Even when thinking beyond any Vietnam-style neo-pacifism (all of Hollywood is actually against Bush), there are many people in the US who feel that it would be wiser for Bush to control the Muslim-Arab communities that have begun to proliferate in Michigan (their numbers total 1 million already!) and put a stop to the immigrant waves originating from Mexico. This American intellectual current, which is either indifferent or hostile towards Zionist lobbies and strongly opposed to Islam, implicitly advocates 'an alliance comprising the entire White race on our planet', thus transcending any notion of a 'Western world'.

***

Why did the USA invade Iraq, then? The first answer, one which has every chance of being correct and is repeated everywhere, is that the Bush administration (with its 'petropoliticians') aims to take control of the country's oil resources (which are the cheapest to exploit) in case those of Arabia become inaccessible. This explanation is advocated by all those Anglo-Saxon media analysts who do not appreciate the current Republican policy. They denounce the new and illegal theory of 'pre-emptive war', the violation of the UN charter and the counterproductive impact that this unbridled imperialism has on America itself (including the stimulation of Islamic terrorism and global anti-Americanism, the destabilisation of the Middle-East, the disastrous increase in oil prices, etc.), while generally condemning the harmful naivety displayed by the Bush administration. What is interesting to point out is that this position is not only espoused by the 'Democratic' Left, but also by traditional conservatives, who consider their country's current aggressive militarism to be harmful to both its prestige and its leadership role. Paradoxically, the most solid criticism of 'American imperialism' has not been coming from French (or rather Parisian) Americanophobes of the *Monde Diplomatique* type, but from the Republican nationalist milieus located overseas.

There is, however, a second possible explanation which is just as convincing. Some American leaders, including those who surround and manipulate the indigent G. W. Bush, namely Wolfowitz, Rumsfeld and Perle, are truly convinced that had Saddam Hussein (who was Bin Laden's secret friend and a new Hitler in his own right) actually remained in power, he would have developed his own weapons of mass destruction in the medium-term (even if he did not possess any at the time) as part of a desperately fanatical strategy that would have ultimately targeted Israel, perhaps even the USA itself. Therefore, what accounts for the American military velleities against Iraq is not merely the hypocritical cynicism that characterises petropolitics, but also the Israeli desire to avoid a '*second holocaust*', to use the American press' favourite terminology, and the pressure exerted in this regard by Israel. Hence the pertinent concept of a 'pre-emptive war' embraced by the NAI.

To put things differently, one cannot exclude the possibility that the American aggression against Iraq is the result of the current

Republican submission to Israeli strategies and fears, since the latter now finds itself cornered and in demographic decline, feeling ever more assailed by its Arab neighbours. American nationalists are convinced that the American imperial eagle is being instrumentalised on a geopolitical level (and directed like a hunting falcon) by the Jewish state and is thus not, strictly speaking, genuinely independent, unlike perhaps China and India, for example.

Is the American imperialistic fury a sign of strength or one of weakness? The answer is obvious. The *Pax Americana* was once founded upon persuasion, muffled threats, diplomacy and the benevolent prestige of a protective world power. The war against Iraq, a small, impoverished country against which the Americans mobilised colossal resources, may well turn into another Vietnam. In the eyes of the whole world, the USA is *making a fool of itself* and losing the very moral leadership that it holds so dear. This is why China, its challenger, has misled it into making a mistake in a most discrete and gentle fashion, by using the UN Security Council to grant America permission to attack Iraq, in a typical Chinese 'encircling game' ploy[5].

***

Through its Iraqi campaign, the USA has managed to disrupt the flow of sympathy that it enjoyed following the 9/11 attacks, when *Le Monde* published its very servile '*We are all Americans*' headline. However, a recent electronic survey conducted by the American magazine *Time Europe* (which gathered a total of 700,000 responses) revealed that when asked which country represented the greatest danger to world peace in 2003, 5.8 % of all respondents opted for North Korea, 6.4 % for Iraq and as many as 87.9 % for the USA.

***

---

5   TN: The Chinese play an abstract strategy board game known as 'Go' or 'encircling game'.

One may of course feel indignant at the sight of the small Iraqi boy whose entire body was burnt and whose arms were severed by an 'intelligent' bomb, or the Iraqi tradesman wearing a keffiyeh and screaming in agony after his entire family were slaughtered by a gratuitous shot fired by a Bradley Fighting Vehicle (as seen in the international media); especially considering how American casualties are subject to highly mediatised funerary ceremonies or wakes and how lightly injured prisoners of war enjoy a 'hero's welcome' upon being brought back to the USA. The (truly numerous) Iraqi military casualties of the American attack are never mentioned, for they were all just pawns to be eliminated, human material to be neutralised, their deaths equated to the destruction of an armoured vehicle. Massacred Iraqi civilians were worth slightly more, playing the part of semi-human *mediatic objects* and offering viewers a visual spectacle. As for the American victims, their importance was of an entirely different calibre, for they were all considered very real indeed.

We witnessed the same thing in World War II, during which European and Japanese civilians were never the focus of a special kind of commemoration, even though they had been decimated in the millions.

Are we to feel indignant about it? Is it just an American specificity? The answer to both questions is a negative one. The demonisation of one's enemies has been constant throughout human history. The fact of considering enemy casualties to be equal to one's own, in a display of sportsmanlike conduct, is beyond human rationality. The Athenians only paid homage to their own dead, never their Persian enemies. The cemeteries where the fallen belong to both sides of the conflict, particularly those of France, remain a historical exception. For in no way is war a sport, and never could it become 'civilised'.

This is precisely why the indignation uttered by Parisian intellectuals from the depths of their troubled hearts and living rooms at both the 'massacres' resulting from American bombardments and the devastation of US 'collateral strikes' has had no effect whatsoever. For in no way is it all an American specificity. The Russians, from Berlin (1945) to Grozny, have done the exact same thing.

One may also notice that the terror bombardments against civilian populations practiced by the British and Americans from 1943 to 1944 and targeting both Germany and Japan (the inspiration for which originated in Great Britain, by the way) no longer take place these days. For the NAI takes public opinion into account and has adopted the following calculating behaviour: the imperative of having 'the lowest possible number of casualties' among the 'boys' is balanced by the necessity to predetermine a maximal number of civilian victims. Compared to the conventional form of American imperialism, the NAI claims fewer civilian lives (Saddam Hussein murdered a larger number of Iraqis than the Bush family), which highlights its skilful ability to keep a veneer of moral semblance while simultaneously implementing puritan cynicism in the most unflinching fashion.

C. Could American Imperialism Ever Be Successful?

I have repeatedly advocated the theory which states that the American 'hyperpower' is actually nothing of the sort; that Europe overestimates the USA's power and thus becomes the latter's consenting vassal; that the American economy has fragile foundations; that the military expeditions conducted in the Gulf, the Balkans and Afghanistan were counterproductive from Uncle Sam's perspective; and that any act of aggression against Iraq would lead to disaster, particularly for the USA itself. In short, one could indeed say that America is both a 'toothless tiger' and a 'colossus with feet of clay', a country that has surrendered to a power delirium which is becoming ever more chaotic, as America gradually becomes aware of the fact that it no longer controls global happenings as it once did, having aroused a growing sentiment of worldwide hatred.

This viewpoint is shared by American political scientist Gabriel Ash, as expressed in his article entitled *The Coming crisis of American Imperialism* (Yellowtimes.org), which we shall now summarise.

America's global domination has vanished into the distance, having typified a time when its army was 'an international policing force' and its rule over international institutions (the UN, the IMF, the World Bank, the Group of 7, etc.) remained uncontested. American power reached its peak during the period that spanned from the fall of the USSR to Bush's reaction to the 9/11 attacks and then decreased, thanks to the manner in which Bush managed to unsettle the balance with his simplistic unilateralism and nationalism. The USA no longer *dominates* the ROW (Rest of the World); instead, it *confronts* it. The latest setback suffered by the US took place in the UN, where the Americans failed to obtain an immediate blank check that would allow them to attack Iraq. It is not the UN that they have discredited, but themselves, since excessive imperialism is harmful to one's imperialistic ambitions. The *Pax Americana* is dead, '*having lost all of its legitimacy*'.

Meanwhile, American economic imperialism is being challenged on a worldwide scale, since it advocates absolute liberalism for others and protectionism for itself.

> Bush's imperialism is no longer "imperial", but constitutes a regression towards nationalism and the pre-war forms of British and French intervention. "America first" is the primary slogan espoused by a selfish foreign policy that violates arms control treaties, refuses to sign the Kyoto protocol, etc.

The disastrous G. W. Bush has instrumentalised anti-terrorism so as to indulge in plain and simple acts of aggression, which has robbed his diplomatic endeavours of both their prestige and their authority. Bush comes across as '*the most hated tyrant of all*', surpassing Saddam, Bin Laden and their consorts. '*It is Bush and his administration that actually embody the Axis of Evil*'. Furthermore, everyone has realised that Bush and his 'falcons' (Cheney, Rumsfeld, Wolfowitz and Perle) only intended to appropriate other people's oil resources in a highly clumsy and brutal fashion, without actually managing to do so! One could truly question the efficacy of this enormous army, which, bombardments aside, has never succeeded in claiming control over any country's soil.

Ash draws the following conclusion:

> The policy adopted by the Bush administration undermines American global hegemony. It has awakened anti-American patriotism everywhere. Its clumsy imperialism has jeopardised American capitalism and given worldwide anti-Americanism its wings. Soon, investments may well cease to throng to the US. Historically, Bush's presidency will be remembered as the one that initiated our hegemony's destruction.

***

American imperialism is counterproductive. *Times* reporter Anthony Browne, who is stationed in Baghdad, published an inquiry entitled 'Radical Islam Is Beginning to Fill the Void Left by the Collapse of the Iraqi Government' (04/06/2003), in which he showed that the entire Iraqi civil society had been reclaimed by Islamism, a claim that he supported with numerous examples. On his part, (anti-Bush) nationalist Patrick Buchanan argues (*World Net Daily*, 02/06/2003) that the American intervention in Iraq will drive several countries towards the acquisition of weapons of mass destruction and increase the terrorist threat: '*With the War in Iraq, the USA seems to have succeeded in accelerating the proliferation of nuclear weapons which it was supposed to prevent*'. Everyone knows that Iran has resumed its nuclear armament programme, a programme that was originally initiated by Akbar Etemad before being put on ice by the Shah in his desire not to indispose the USSR.

***

Kennedy's former advisor, Arthur J. R. Schlesinger, explained in *Le Figaro* (23/06/2003, *The Limits of the Bush Doctrine*) that the 'preemptive war' doctrine used to justify the Iraqi campaign contradicted the principles promulgated by Abraham Lincoln in 1848, when he was pressured into preventively attacking Canada, a country from which a British aggression could come about at any time. Lincoln rejected this approach. From Schlesinger's perspective, the doctrine of pre-emptive war has been discredited by the blatant lie regarding Saddam Hussein's alleged 'weapons of mass destruction':

> This credibility deficiency could destroy the foreign policy founded on pre-emptive war. [...] It is doubtful whether Bush, who has lost all credibility, could ever lead his people to wage war against Iran or North Korea through the mere virtue of his presidential assertions.

Overall, the author is convinced that the 'Bush doctrine' is weakening and discrediting the American empire.

***

In an article entitled *On to Baghdad — And Beyond*, Patrick Buchanan develops the idea that a warmongering America may temporarily end up winning wars while simultaneously losing any hope for peace. *'Following our victory, our problems are just about to begin'*. In other words, the NAI will result in a chain of military conflicts, which is somehow reminiscent of the unjust 1918 peace agreement that led to the next conflict. In Buchanan's eyes, the *Pax Americana* will not bring about peace (especially in the Near-East), but simply *'paves the way for a coming war'* (*The American Conservative*, 21/04/2003).

***

Highlighting all the lies, diplomatic blunders and neoconservative mistakes made during the invasion of Iraq, American military historian and geopolitician Gabriel Kolko wrote a *Counterpunch* article entitled *The Age of Unilateral War* (29/04/2003), where he not only expresses the same feelings as Emmanuel Todd and Patrick Buchanan with regard to his country's inane and absolute hegemonic will, but also his conviction that this attitude will hasten the decline of American power. He says:

The fact is that the world is becoming increasingly multipolar, both economically and technologically, and that the American desire to maintain
absolute military supremacy over the world is a delusion. Russia remains a
military superpower, while China is in the process of becoming one.

In order to put a stop to the proliferation of weapons of mass destruction during the next 20 years,

> … there is no other solution but to sign international accords and support
> such organisms as the UN, both of which are rejected by the USA as being
> an impediment to its power. America has no alternative but to accept the
> world as it is, or prepare itself for a tragedy.

***

For Caroline Meyer, a columnist at The Magazine of Future Warfare,
hypermilitarism and the massive increase in the current American
administration's military expenditures are a sign of panic and weakness. In an article entitled *The cost of Empire* (May 2003), she adopts
the views of *New York Times* editorialist Paul Krugman according to
which the American Defence budget (which officially totalled 400
million dollars in 2002) is actually as high as 500 million dollars from
the 'black budget' perspective, including secret expenses that were
never voted into effect. This could be compared to the 1.4 billion dollars spent by the Iraqi government on military expenditures before the
start of the war. Meyer also reveals that more than 100 US marines
were killed during the battle of Nasiriya and that the commander
of the first marines regiment has been sacked. Furthermore, she denounces the fact that the current budget relating to the 'anti-terrorist
war' is greater in size to that of the Cold War, which was intended to
contain the USSR. She identifies with the opinion advocated by political scientist H.-L. Mecken, which states that if the USA does indeed
spend more money on protecting itself from a new terrorist attack
(akin to the one conducted on 9/11) than it once did on the prevention
of a Soviet nuclear attack (which seems absurd), one reason for this is
that the neoconservatives are eager to maintain a general atmosphere

community had little love for him. His Secretary of State, James Baker, was both known and hated for having made the following remark: *'Fuck the Jews! They don't vote for us anyway!'* Furthermore, the Jews used to consider the Republican Party to be hostile to their cause. When Bush defeated Al Gore in the American presidential elections, American and Israeli Jews felt very worried, especially considering the fact that the Bush clan has been a linchpin of the Texas oil business, a sphere in which Arabs feature very prominently. Then came a divine surprise: 'Bush Junior' turned out to be the most pro-Israeli American President of all!

What we are thus witnessing is a political revolution: traditionally, it was always the Democrats who the Jews (and the various ethnic minorities) voted for, while the Republicans were suspected of being latently anti-Jewish; nowadays, however, it is the latter who come across as being more Judeophilic and pro-Israeli than anyone else. A survey conducted by Gallup in June 2002 revealed that more than 66 % of Republican voters sympathise with Israel rather than with the Palestinians, compared to a mere 40 % among the supporters of the Democratic Party. This is due to the 9/11 shock that has stricken the versatile American public opinion, where a reconciliation has taken place between conservative Christians and Jews, who now stand united against 'Islamic terrorism' (although their relations were once characterised by very intense mutual hostility). Bush has jumped at the opportunity: he intends to be the first American President to rob the Democrats of Jewish votes and prove James Baker wrong: 'By giving Sharon and the Israelis our full support, we will attract the Jewish public opinion and its mediatic and financial power', he must have thought to himself. As explained by analyst Fatty Kay (in *Times Online*),

> … in the past, the Bush clan cared very little about Jewish voters, who represented a mere 2 % of the overall electorate, but it has now taken heed of their mediatic and financial influence.

Bush therefore proceeded to turn his coat.

of danger and threat, so as to impose their power upon a terrorised population.

***

Is the USA the new embodiment of the Roman Empire or a pseudo-superpower founded upon a *bluffing* technique? What follows is an analytical synthesis based on diverse sources.

In *The Globalist* (19/06/2002), Michael Lind, member of the New America Foundation, expressed the opinion that America's power is highly exaggerated and, on a global scale, inferior to what it was like back in 1945. In his view, in no way is the USA a 'new Roman Empire', and Bush's arrogant militaristic supremacism (baptised 'the Wolfowitz doctrine', in accordance with the American Deputy Defence Minister) is not founded on sufficient military or even economic means. This doctrine aims to dissuade Europe, Russia, India and China from developing excessively powerful military forces and from abiding by foreign policies that are not dependent upon American directives. In exchange, the USA is to commit itself to protecting them and resolving their disputes. This ambition is untenable. With 20 % of the world's GDP, the USA lacks the importance it had during the 1960s; it is losing ground on the demographical level; Asia may well catch up with it in the field of high technologies; in time, the USA is bound to find itself geopolitically disadvantaged as a result of its insular position; and the deployment of military forces is costlier for the Americans than for Eurasian countries.

There is yet another troubling sign from the American perspective: the Hispanics inhabiting the American South-Eastern states (especially Texas) have been demanding autonomy and their own political parties, which may eventually lead to pure and simple secession. During the 1990s, the number of Texan Hispanics increased by 2.3 million, which equals 60 % of the overall population growth in Texas.

James Caroll, a chronicler at *The Boston Globe*, explains (in *America The Fearful*, 22/05/2002) that the current American mentality is dominated by pathological anxiety and paranoia, which renders it fragile and prevents it from overcoming severe crises, whether in the sphere of economics or that of terrorism. He predicts that in the event of another giga-terroristic attack, the USA would be brought to its knees for a long time to come.

Numerous articles published by the American and British press have highlighted the following evident truth: the USA has suffered defeat in the face of Islamic terrorism, Bin Laden (who is not to be found anywhere) and the various networks such as Al-Qaida, none of which have been dismantled and are now even more menacing than they were prior to the Afghan campaign. The interrogation of prisoners in Guantanamo Bay (all of whom played a secondary role) has not yielded any results worth mentioning. Additionally, the Iraqi military expedition has given Islamic terrorism both a new target to strike at, namely the American army (now in open terrain), and a new holy war territory that had hitherto been preserved — Mesopotamia.

Moreover, according to *Times Online* (14/05/2002), Bush got fleeced by Putin during the Russia-NATO negotiations, thus allowing the Russians to exercise a right of veto upon the organisation's decisions.

In short, the sabre-rattling manifested by the American 'hyperpower' and its Bush administration is akin to the Coué method. In Europe, hysterically anti-American milieus have fallen for it (as have those who worship the USA) and acknowledged the alleged colossal power enjoyed by an America that arouses both their hatred and their unjustified fascination. If Europe had any will to speak of, it would surpass all others in terms of power…

***

Despite the Airbus A 380 claiming to be the largest aeroplane ever built, this honour will instead be claimed by the 'Pelican', currently under review at Boeing. It is a true colossus with a wingspan of 166 metres (70 metres in the case of a 747) and a length of 84 metres (only 42 metres for the 747), driven by 4 enormous turboprops equipped with 8-blade propellers. It will be capable of transporting loads of up to 14,000 tonnes over a 19,000-kilometre distance, thus surpassing the Russian Antonov 225, a giant that can only carry a quarter of such weight over a mere distance of 5,000 kilometres. It will be incredible. Its aerodynamical profile (wings that curve downwards and a chassis whose breadth exceeds its height) will allow it to make use of an 'air cushion' and fly at an altitude of 18 metres above sea level, at an approximate speed of 400 kilometres an hour. Each hour on board the Pelican will be twice as cheap as on any high-capacity aircraft currently available.

But what purpose will this airborne leviathan serve? It will, of course, transport enormous quantities of cargo over very long distances, but according to the statement made by Boeing project manager Blaine Rawdon in an interview with British newspaper *Metro*, the Pelican will, above all,

> ... be very interesting to military decision-makers. Each aircraft will be able to carry thousands of soldiers and a total of 17 50-tonne tanks over huge distances, all within a reduced time scale and at lower cost compared to ships.

It will, furthermore, be virtually undetectable by radars thanks to its ability to skim the ground or the sea like a cruise missile.

So, what is the point of such a gargantuan programme? Is it meant to rejuvenate the military-industrial complex a little more? Yes, but there is more to it than that. The real reason, in my view, is that Pentagon strategists have realised that the USA, the 'Empire of Good', is targeted by such global hatred (stemming from peoples that fail to comprehend the American military-civilising mission) that the countless US bases on foreign soil will not remain there forever, especially when it comes to Asia and the Middle-East. The states that have allowed such bases to be established on their own soil (ranging from South Korea to Saudi Arabia) may, at any given moment, shut the latter down, especially when we consider how volatile history has become at the start of the 21st century, a century fraught with brutal and unpredictable changes.

The USA is thus considering the medium-term deployment of massive forces from its own territory, without the necessity of investing large sums of money into maintaining expensive military bases on the soil of its rather unreliable 'allies'. This attitude is a mixture of isolationism and interventionism. It constitutes, however, a worrying development, since it betrays the fact that the Pentagon has deemed it necessary for the USA to undertake global military campaigns over the next two decades for the purpose of maintaining order in a manner that serves its own interests. It is obvious that the Americans will not emerge victorious, succeeding only in destabilising the world a little further. The 'super drone' programme, involving the use of pilotless aircrafts capable of carrying out long-distance bombardments from the American territory, reinforces this hypothesis.

A secret inquiry conducted by the Pentagon at the behest of the White House has predicted that the USA will be compelled to undertake numerous military operations over the next ten years, across every continent, regardless of whether the UN endorses them or not. Those who oppose this strategy fear that the USA will suffer utter defeat and trigger a retaliatory giga-terroristic response. The future is likely to prove them right.

CHAPTER IV

A Pseudo-Empire

A. The Historical Utopianism and Stupidity Pervading American 'Unilateralism'

In the eyes of any serious historian, the objective of the neoconservatives heading the NAI (meaning unilateralism or 'unequal bilateralism') cannot yield any success. Regardless of American power and without falling into the excesses embraced by Emmanuel Todd (a man who tends to mistake his desires for reality when announcing America's imminent and brutal collapse), no power has ever managed to exercise absolute hegemony, especially not the Roman Empire, a fact that becomes clear when one studies its history. The ambition of accomplishing rapid and complete world domination, which the NAI's neoconservatives strive for so as to impose the 'American paradise', is a utopia whose naivety exceeds that of the communist paradise. This is due to conjunctural reasons (America's current weaknesses, which are discussed elsewhere and are not impacted by its enormous techno-military effort), but above all historical and structural ones.

The fact of having one single people, nation and civilisation indefinitely dominate all others is unheard of. Current American leaders are sinking deeper into the Founding Fathers' evangelical messianism than their predecessors ever did, the very same messianism that once longed to turn America into the prefiguration of God's absolute reign on Earth. Islam and Communism would subsequently espouse the same attitude, though with a greater degree of subtleness.

The NAI is founded upon utter historical ignorance, which constitutes a mere exacerbation of a highly characteristic American trait. For the first time ever, the leaders of a single nation (one that has been the most powerful one for a short period of time and will remain so for an equally limited timespan) are earnestly imagining that they could claim dominion over the Earth, i.e. global domination, using a mixture of moral theodicy (low-end theology), techno-military supremacy and generalised mercantilism. Such an objective is as foolish as the claim that one could have five aces in hand during a poker game. This dream of absolute hegemony is a completely unattainable historical chimera that may well turn out to be a fatal wager for the Americans, since their versatile and fragile public opinion will plummet into despair, contrition and panic as soon as the USA tastes its first defeat, as already witnessed in the past. There is nothing wrong with a desire to be one of several 'superpowers', but the dream of being the 'sole hyperpower' embraced by the NAI may well lead to an utter nightmare.

***

The Iraqi quagmire is the perfect illustration of this fact. How on earth were the Americans stupid enough to believe that pacifying Iraq would be a labour of love? The level of naivety displayed by Bush's neoconservative administration in this regard is confounding and surpasses any other such attitude in American history, a history that is nonetheless particularly rife with blunders and enormous diplomatic and geostrategic mistakes. As stated by Patrick Buchanan, what we have here is, in all likelihood, the worst government the USA has ever had.

America's defeat and powerlessness is combined with the ridiculous: following the repetitive tall-tale regarding the Iraqi WMDs (weapons of mass destruction) and the claims that the USA could manage things on its own, Bush's and Rumsfeld's boastful and infantile sword-rattling was exacerbated by the humiliation of turning to the

UN and NATO for military assistance so as to either relieve or support the impotent Americans; the pathetic spectacle which the world's allegedly 'most powerful army' offered us all through its inability to bear a few casualties a day or endure harsher living conditions than those in California only served to make matters worse.

What follows is a statement made by an American Marine sergeant during an interview with *Le Journal du Dimanche* (20/07/2003), a statement that would have been unthinkable in any other army:

> Iraq makes me sick. When, a week ago, we were told that we would have to stay here longer, there was dead silence. That's when I understood what it meant to lose hope. [...] When I think that I've actually missed the release of Star Trek and The Matrix... As soon as I close my eyes, I think of my future honeymoon. Once I leave Iraq, there's only one thing I want: to go to Alaska.

A so-called elite army whose members confide in the press using such words has obviously no military value to speak of.

***

In actual fact, the paradox regarding all of this is that, at a time when the NAI intends to turn the American military power into the central pillar of its unilateralism (while particularly basing its attitude on the untenable notion of 'pre-emptive war'), it is blatantly visible that the US army is not genuinely operational, which is probably even truer now than it has ever been. Its only strength, which is a considerable one, of course, is exclusively founded upon a fantastic technology of aerial and ballistic strikes conducted from a distance; but it turns out to be incapable of holding its ground on the battlefield or even of conquering soil through traditional warfare (so as to defeat an already exsanguinated Iraq, for instance, the USA had to bribe its generals). Unless the new form of American militarism employs android robots to keep the invaded lands or monitored zones under its control, one can hardly see how it could ever achieve palpable success.

One thus has the impression of being faced with an oneiric sort of warmongering, whose 'Rambo-esque' nature is solely rooted in spectacle and does not reflect the reality of things, thus automatically collapsing upon itself like a bellows. Its purpose is to leave public opinion in awe using a muscular (and budgetary) demonstration of force. However, just like the cicada in La Fontaine's fable, the US will find itself deprived of power once the north wind begins to blow. It made use of enormous means to vanquish a tiny power that is presented as being a menacing monster, only to find itself unable to restore order. Remember the comical episode where Bush, as under-skilled as ever, proceeded to play 'Top Gun' as he got off a military plane on the Abraham Lincoln bridge and announced America's glorious victory over Saddam-Hitler? This kind of theatrical production is typical of powers that are completely overtaken by the events.

B. The 'Declinist' Theory

Even in the USA itself, the opponents of this new neoconservative imperialism are often labelled 'declinists'; they explain the American military fury (which resorts to vigilante-like pretexts) through America's awareness of its own waning power, an awareness that one seeks to deny in a most half-hearted manner. It seems that following the collapse of the USSR, American leaders became convinced that the US superpower would easily manage to dominate the entire world on a permanent basis. It was, however, not to be: the 9/11 terrorist attacks (the very first act of war to take place on American soil since the British aggression in 1812) came as a bolt from the blue and were followed by further anti-American attacks around the world, all of which were Islamic in origin. Faced with such disillusionment, a certain part of the Protestant Republican elite appears to have rejected this impotence and chosen to counterattack through warmongering acts (as witnessed during the Iraqi and Afghan campaigns), even at the price of contravening international law.

The declinists consider this attitude catastrophic, since it precipi-
tates an even greater decline. They point out that all waning empires
which no longer enjoy a natural *authority* founded upon *power* resort
to straightforward violence where once mere menace sufficed. The
NAI is thus seen as the embodiment of a desperate and irrational reaction in an effort to impose American domination in a most thunder-
ous and callous fashion. Its endeavour is undoubtedly doomed to fail,
because it is fraught with countless blunders not only in the field of
communication, but also in its onsite military and political strategy.

✱✱✱

Emmanuel Todd, author of *After the Empire: The Breakdown of the
American Order*, develops this 'declinist' view (often encountered in
the US), according to which current American imperialism is not to
be understood as a powerful type of imperialism, but as a mere means
of concealing and offsetting a severe military, financial and even
techno-economic decline. He states: '*America is attempting to mask its
own waning through theatrical military activism targeting insignificant
countries*'.

The belief in the existence of an American hyperpower that has
had no match since the fall of the USSR is but a myth. The USA may
actually be on the brink of a systematic 'imperial' collapse, just like
the USSR during the first Afghan war. '*Military posturing is the last
display of a declining empire's waning power*', says Todd (Le Figaro,
05/04/2003). His opinion is based on the Roman example.

America's weaknesses are blatant: an enormous commercial deficit
(1.5 billion dollars a day), an insufficient amount of domestic oil resources, the deterioration of US diplomatic credibility in the aftermath
of the lies that served to justify the Gulf War (in its second version),
the failure of the melting-pot, the domestic Latino invasion, endemic
poverty, etc. According to Todd, '*the American society is falling apart
on all levels, which leads the USA to project its inner disorder upon the
world*'.

It would seem that America is becoming geopolitically isolated in the face of the immense Eurasian continent and feels overlooked compared to the 'old world'. As Robert Steuckers and I already sensed back in the 1980s, America is no longer the 'new world', but the old one, while Europe and Asia are becoming the new. As a result, the USA feels the irrepressible and pathetic urge to flex its muscles in order to come across as being indispensable; hence its attack upon Iraq.

America has moved on from being a global force of order to one of disorder. Todd says: '*There is something horrifying about watching Doctor Jekyll turn into Mister Hyde right before our very eyes*'. Bush Junior has brought radical destruction upon the 'New World Order' established by his father. He has alienated himself from France, Germany, Russia and even Turkey, without having any means of economic response against these countries. Militarily speaking, the USA is powerless not just against China, but also against North Korea, Iran, Syria and others. With a deficit of 500 billion dollars a year, it no longer has the necessary means to pursue its global imperialism.

Although a country of propaganda, publicity and communication, the USA has suffered a crushing defeat in the face of the international public opinion: it is no longer perceived as the empire of 'Good', but that of Evil, warmongering, bombardments, blunders, disorder, and oil mischief. The Americans, whose administration denounces the existence of *rogue states*, are looked upon as mobsters and gangsters and suspected of being the worst of all thugs (Al Capone), when all that they longed for was to be seen as virtuous puritans. The USA's image has undergone a sort of 'Chicago-isation'. This represents a terrible ordeal for the Americans: the cowboy pastor is weeping because people take him for a vile bastard that holds up banks. 'Why have we, those who embody the Good, become the target of such negative sentiments?', the gullible Bush cries to himself. The King has been shamed.

***

In Emmanuel Todd's opinion, even the American victor never ceased to grow weak following his defeat of the USSR at the end of the Cold War, which applies to the technological sphere as well. Boldly, Todd states:

> The USA has a lot of credentials, but these are typical of declining powers. A technologically dynamic industry would never worry about showing off its credentials, since it remains aware of the fact that its advancement is so rapid that none could ever manage to equal it. If America persists in its tendency to "seek out" its researchers abroad, this is due to its own population's inability to reproduce itself in an intellectually and technologically efficient manner. It does produce solicitors, financial experts, etc., but as far as industry is concerned (an industry which lies at the very heart of technological progress), America does not fare too well.

Such remarks are heart-warming and reassuring, and we would love to believe them… Todd has, however, ventured a little too far there. Is he not rather oblivious to the formidable effort made by the American federal state in matters of research?

There are of course other declinist views: that American society is crumbling from within, that its social contract has been breached, that it faces ever-increasing poverty, etc. All of this may well be true, but is it all not a means for us to readily forget the decline of Europe itself?

Whatever the case, the collapse of the USSR led the whole world to believe that the USA was actually the power that had emerged victorious (from the Cold War) and was thus meant to gain in importance. However, it is all but an illusion. Indeed, the USA is growing ever weaker in relation to the rest of the world, despite the mythological assertions that render it the world's 'unique superpower' and which Europeans are alone to believe. American contribution to the global creation of wealth has decreased from 40 % in 1945 to a mere 25 % today.

***

There are of course other entreating opinions espoused by the declinists: owing to its intense and clumsy imperialism, the USA is said to have reactivated the Paris-Berlin-Moscow axis and awakened a resistant European political consciousness. The American military apparatus, conceived as the sole diplomatic solution, is thought to be overly expensive and the American economy is thus unable to withstand the weight of a gargantuan Defence budget. The victory that the USA has claimed in Iraq is bound to trigger inextricable strategic complications for the American global police.

Nevertheless, our optimism concerning the American decline and the reawakening of a dynamical Euro-Russian power must not succumb to the Coué method, however likeable and well-intentioned it may be. We must not mistake our desires for reality. No matter how harmful it is for us to overestimate American power, it is even more detrimental to underestimate it while over-embellishing European and Russian capacities.

As a result of their own ideological conformism, the 'decadentists' who, just like Todd himself, herald Europe's final victory over its American rival, pay heed neither to our disastrous demographic situation, nor to the colonising immigration that Europe is being subjected to at the hands of the Third World, which embody the worst threats that we have ever faced in our long history. For what value could Western Europe and Russia ever have if they were robbed of their very substance? This inner anthropological collapse afflicting Europe is precisely what Washington is counting on.

C. The Bush Doctrine's Middle-Eastern Impasse

Since 1945, the American approach to the Middle-East, a perfectly legitimate one for a major power to adopt, has been focused on securing its own oil supplies. The US geostrategic imperative has been rooted in ensuring the proper functioning of the Middle-Eastern *service station*,

i.e. the plethoric provider of 'Arabian light' (the best oil of all), as well
as in preventing other powers from depriving the USA of it.

In order to achieve this, it was capital for the Americans to court
the Arabs in a cynical manner, even those who were enthusiastic nationalists or those governed by tyrants and despots from long bygone
ages. Hence Nasser's CIA-funded coup in 1952, the brutal fashion in
which the British-Israeli-French Suez intervention was terminated in
1956, and the massive financial aid given to the 'Guardian of the Gulf',
Iranian Shah Pahlavi. This strategy was known as the 'Eisenhower
doctrine' and had previously been elaborated by Secretary of State
John Foster Dulles. At the time, the USA was very careful not to support Israel, so as to avoid displeasing the medieval or 'socialist' potentates that governed the region. This support would only see the light
of day after 1967 (the 6-day war) as a result of the pressure exerted by
American Jewish lobbies.

This initial pro-Arab strategy, however, turned out to be disastrous,
as it was founded upon a flattering and benefit-based form of 'anti-
colonialism' and 'anti-Europeanism' that was not reciprocated. In the
name of a vague 'Arab socialism', the ungrateful Gamal Abdel Nasser
turned towards the USSR instead, as did for example Algeria (a country
ruled by Islamist-Marxist Boumedienne), thus completely disregarding the pro-FLN stance adopted by the State Department. The year
of 1973 brought yet another shock: following the Kippur war, Saudi
Arabia proceeded to quadruple its oil prices — leaving the Americans
helpless and unable to do anything about it — and to exploit its newfound wealth to finance the revival of global Islamism and *jihad*.

Trapped by its own desire to preserve its petrol station at all costs,
the American foreign policy dodges, enmeshes itself and swallows one
insult after another. It plays the slippery card of Islamism, turns a blind
eye to the Saudi activism that funds the *mujahideen* everywhere, openly
grants the latter its assistance against the Soviets in Afghanistan (since
both the Taliban and Bin Laden were fed with the American manna),
and remains idle-handed and without any vengeful intent whatsoever

following the unpunished terrorist attack which took place in Beirut in 1982 and slaughtered 241 marines (even though the CIA was perfectly aware of the fact that the strike had been ordered by Iran and Syria and carried out by Hezbollah and the PLO, an organisation headed by slimy Yasser Arafat). Despite all this, the Eisenhower doctrine still prevailed — despotic monarchies and the various barbaric Muslim-Arab 'republics' still enjoyed blind American support in accordance with Dulles' formula which says: '*He's a bastard, but he's our bastard*'. All of this in order to achieve the supreme imperative: that of controlling the oil pump, thus securing the mandatory supplies, not the prices.

It is obvious that this policy presupposed the presence of a major chasm (which became increasingly difficult to bridge) between the American support of Israel demanded by the AIPAC (the American-Israeli Public Affairs Committee founded in 1950, which, having traditionally been favourable to the Democrats, suddenly became pro-Republican once Bush was elected) and American petropolitics, i.e. the USA's 'petro-friendship' with the Arabs. Befriending two mutual enemies is a difficult endeavour...

***

Soon, three facts would render the Eisenhower doctrine untenable and trigger its implosion: the collapse of the USSR at the end of the Cold War, which kept the USA sheltered from the need to maintain the Muslim-Arabs in the Western camp at all costs; the 9/11 attacks, in addition to all the other anti-American *jihadi* acts that either preceded them or have followed since 1994; and the resumption of the Israeli-Palestinian civil war, exacerbated by the intransigent attitude adopted by the 'Israeli lion', Ariel Sharon.

The neoconservative American administration then proceeds to change direction completely. It relinquishes diplomatic caution and replaces the latter with a military policy and unilateralism, all in the name of a protean war against 'terrorism', which now supersedes 'communism' in an extremely costly and risky strategy. The Afghan and

Iraqi campaigns take place, serving as a prelude to the American desire to have Syria, Iran and Wahhabi Arabia toe the line, not to mention Lebanon. It is no longer a matter of negotiating, but an intention to impose oneself through force. Any and all contradictions are resolved from above in the hope of remodelling the Middle-East into a pro-American, multi-state protectorate (thanks to the benefits of 'democracy') that would neither threaten Israel nor impede the smooth functioning of the *service station*, using direct and heavy-handed military intimidation, brutal intervention and interference to achieve this.

Numerous American analysts are sceptical about this imperialistic attempt at equilibristics, this 'equilibristic imperialism', if you will. Others, however, namely European Americanophiles, strongly believe in the geostrategic aptitude of the Texan cowboys, who remain completely ignorant of the mentalities that typify the 'rest of the world'. Exemplifying such an attitude, Lauren Muraviec writes:

> One now speaks again of a free Lebanon [following the war in Iraq] instead of just pretending that all Middle-Eastern problems relate to the "Palestinian issue", which embodies the dictatorial antiphon that allowed despots to conceal their exiguous governance and tyranny. The collapse of Saddam Hussein's house of cards has highlighted the extent to which Middle-Eastern despotisms are but toothless tigers. (*21st century war*, Odile Jacob editions, 2000.)

***

We must reject both obsessional anti-Americans and the gullible enthusiasts of the new American order. Overestimating the virtually inexistent capacities of the Iraqi defensive forces (who turned out to be mere pretend soldiers) and paying little attention to the despotic, criminal and pathetically incapable aspect of the tribal clique that surrounded Stalin's small Arabian admirer, the former predicted the US army's defeat. The latter, by contrast, have lulled themselves with illusions regarding the alleged efficacy of the 'moral' and unilateral strategy embraced by the New American Imperialism. Although the

USA did claim a rapid military victory, its performance was, in fact, not much of a feat.

In the medium term, it will be an entirely different matter. The above-mentioned 'pro-Western and democratic remodelling' of the Islamic Middle-East is bound to come up against insurmountable obstacles. The 'Bush doctrine' is even more reminiscent of an engine that is fuelled by sheer utopia than the now defunct 'Eisenhower doctrine' ever was.

1) Despite the hyper-medialised Kurdish and Shiite coalescence towards 'American liberation', the USA has killed or maimed a large number of Iraqi civilians, a fact that will not be forgotten. The global anti-American hatred that has thus been aroused will certainly not abate, especially among those Middle-Eastern Muslim masses, regardless of their 'liberation'. The protectorates whose humiliated public opinions abhor their own protectors are never viable ones.

2) There is another fact that one rarely mentions: Afghanistan, whose pacification was a complete fiasco, is still in the throes of an ongoing war. In this chess game, the pawn that should have been the first to be taken is still standing.

3) The American administration is utterly ignorant of both the Islamic nature and the Arab mentality, which are equally restive towards the Western kind of 'democracy', and underestimates the power of the anti-American global *jihad* that it has just awakened. It has triggered a 'clash of civilisations', even if it casts doubt upon the latter's pertinence.

4) The persistent civil war between the Israelis and the Palestinians and the American inability to put an end to it will prevent the birth of a stable protectorate in the Middle-East.

5) In the medium term, the financial costs of a long-lasting regional takeover are unattainable for the USA and its limited economic means. Military operations against Syria and (a fortiori) Iran do not

come into serious consideration, which is not only due to financial issues and the averse international reactions that this would kindle, but also to the fact that the US army is not in a position to vanquish any other military forces but those of small, depleted powers.

***

The USA's sole hope of transforming Arabia, Iran and Syria into protectorates and puppet governments lies in acts of bribery and corruption: the Americans would have to pay off local leaders to purchase their obedience. Account taken of the currently seething global context, however, such a solution will turn out to be absolutely impossible to apply.

The USA is guilty of grossly overestimating itself. The new Bush doctrine is not only a fascinating imitation of British Victorian imperialism, i.e. the splendid *Pax Britannica*, but also a disorganised reproduction of the different forms of interventionism embraced by Napoleon, Bismarck, Hitler and even Stalin, who all longed to create buffer zones for themselves using plain and direct force.

Unfortunately for Rambo and his mentally childish neoconservative advisors, who have rediscovered the imperialistic strategy espoused by the Europeans during the 19th century and the first half of the 20th, the latter no longer reflects the objective conditions of our planet in any way. Compared to the rest of the world, the USA does not embody the 'crushing force' that characterised Napoleonian France when the latter faced a European coalition (a confrontation that France lost in the end), nor is it in the same position it occupied in 1945, when it enjoyed a monopoly of military domination that other powers lacked.

The American plagiarism of ancient European imperialism (which was once scorned) is doomed to fail. The callous unilateralism practiced by the Americans has encountered a hurdle — that of the objective power balance. Soon enough, the ever-growing Chinese and Indian giants will bring the USA back to reality. On a global scale, America's relative economic weight keeps decreasing, not to mention the Russian defiance and an emerging Euro-Siberian project that is still in its infancy.

Furthermore, when faced with Islam's fanatical power, rapidly increasing demographics and *jihad* (a *jihad* that arouses admiration as a result of its archaism and furious desire to invade the world *from below*), the USA and its naïve, hymn-chanting Christians have failed to comprehend that their loophole strategy is inappropriate under the circumstances. Instead of targeting Islam with Western conversion, it would have been wiser to revert to the *containment* strategy that the Pentagon once implemented against Soviet communism. This is, by the way, the opinion that I advocate in this book, an opinion that is obviously founded upon the swift eradication of *any* Islamic presence on both American and European soil.

***

Last but not least, Bush's 'new imperialist' or 'unilateralist' doctrine is subject to the vicissitudes which stem from the versatility of the American public opinion, since the latter changes its convictions at the slightest setback. The current American administration is not eternal. The triumphalism pervading the minds of the neoconservatives, who are all high on the Iraqi campaign, may well evolve into a state of clinical depression at some point. New leaders embracing isolationistic, minimalistic and pacifistic views may end up seizing control of Washington. Let us bear in mind the fact that the federal state is not really the guide of a nation, people or 'empire'; its behaviour is rather that an international, political-military-industrial company (in which culture is but a mere industrial sector). It thus could, at any given moment, proceed to completely alter its strategy in a display of incredible flexibility.

In the world of the 21st century, the USA will no longer be the main hyperpower. As I have already stated in *Archeofuturism*, America lacks the archaism and rootedness that the peoples of the Great Continent possess. The New World is doomed to remain peripheral forever, a mere Luna Park on its huge island. The USA is probably experiencing its zenith right now, or rather the end of it, as the last embers of its factitious power burn out. The Americans were admittedly the first to land on the moon, just like professor Calculus. They did in fact end up claiming dominion over the moon, but the Earth is a completely different matter...

As for Europe, it is very ill indeed. Yet it remains Europe, because *its soil speaks to it* and it has its own underground and unconscious dimension. I am thus convinced that in less than 500 years' time, one will still speak of the Europeans, Muslims, Chinese, Japanese, Indians, Jews, and Christians, but the world will have forgotten what the term 'USA' ever meant.

D. The Right of Might

All of those who felt scandalised and surprised to see the USA marginalising the UN and violating international law by attacking Iraq are utterly naïve. They all forget (especially the ones who constantly quote Carl Schmitt without having grasped his ideas) that de Gaulle himself once labelled the UN a 'thingy' and that the latter is founded upon a ridiculous sort of utopia: the notion of a Kantian international law, one which is both abstract and egalitarian and so disconnected from any concept of a power balance that, in the eyes of the Security Council, Guinea is just as important as India.

The Iraqi campaign, which was conducted without the consent of the above-mentioned council, was not the first of its kind. For everyone has forgotten that India once proceeded to sever Bangladesh from Pakistan without bothering to consult the UN; that the Soviet army intervened in Hungary, Czechoslovakia and Afghanistan without the support of the UN; that the Korean and Vietnam wars were waged despite the Chinese and Soviet vetoes; that Egypt, Syria, Lebanon and Jordan first attacked Israel in 1967, with a further Egyptian aggression taking place in 1973, in a show of utter disregard for the UN; and so on.

Ever since its creation, the UN has always failed miserably in all its endeavours, which is especially true of all its attempts to interpose itself and pacify others using its ridiculous 'blue helmets'. In its newfound cynicism (which is definitely new, since the Americans, who should be seen as the genuine founders of both the UN and its predecessor, the League of Nations, did not think this way at a time when the UN still served their interests), the USA is absolutely right when attempting to limit the role of the United Nations to a strictly humanitarian one and striving to govern global affairs. The main issue, however, is finding out whether it actually has the means to achieve this.

When Gary Schmitt, the director of the 'Project for the New American Century', points out that '*the USA has every right to act as the principal referee in matters of* [global] *security, because it is the only civilised power that has both the ability and the will to do so*', he reverts to a sound political philosophy, one that is founded upon the right of the strongest, or rather upon the idea that might is right and not the other way around. Such an attitude was embraced by Sparta, the Roman Empire, the kings of France, Napoleon, Bismarck, the British Empire and many others.

Ever since the fall of the USSR, the USA has ceased to believe in the ridiculous and naïve fictions relating to some 'international community' and the existence of permanent alliances (which only serve to restrain foreign policies). Instead, the Americans intend to form and lead coalitions whose exact composition is shaped by current events. Robert Kagan, himself a neoconservative theoretician, mocks the new Europe that desires to exist in a '*post-modern paradise*' governed by the '*principle of moral conscience*', a principle that is as unrealistic as it is devoid of any will to power. Explaining things in a leisurely fashion, Kagan gave *Le Nouvel Observateur* the following statement: '*Military power and the logic of force will be the decisive factors in the world we are now entering. America's long hegemonic era has barely just begun*'. The first sentence mirrors a remarkable lucidity. The second, by contrast, is mere wishful thinking and a sign of a very naïve state of mind. From a Machiavellian perspective, the mistake made by the American leaders is that they are playing their cards with such blatant naivety. The Americans have always been *bad liars*: they resort to lies at the worst possible time and whenever the world is well aware of their deceitfulness (as witnessed through their use of the 'weapons of mass destruction' pretext against Iraq), yet tell the truth at a time when they should actually be lying or, at the very least, not saying anything. By displaying the true nature of their imperialism for the whole world to see, they weaken their imperialistic position by increasing the world's resistance to it.

***

In addition to American oil endeavours, there might also be an additional (meaning real) explanation behind America's military adventurism in Iraq, an adventurism that has had disastrous consequences for the USA itself.

In Alain-Gérard Slama's view, '*the only explanation for such an amassment of mistakes is that the USA itself is undergoing a crisis*' and that its universalistic model is no longer effective: '*As vigorously highlighted by Emmanuel Todd* [in *After the Empire*, Gallimard editions, 2002], *it is the decline experienced by the universalism of old that has channelled the American people's traditional flaws into a state of distorted identity*' (*Le Figaro*, 31/03/2003). In other words, it is apparently through its military crusade that the American administration is trying to re-solder a society whose values and legitimacy are now collapsing.

Indeed, the signs that point to such an 'American crisis' are accumulating: an invasion at the hands of the Latinos; the utter failure of the melting-pot; the domestic decline of the Anglo-Saxon model and even that of the English language itself; the establishment of a segregated racio-social society characterised by a rapid increase in poverty; an ever-growing demand for a welfare state; an overpopulated prison system; the emergence of a badly tolerated police state, as freedom of information gradually dissipates and a wave of intolerant 'political correctness' spreads; the astronomical and ever-increasing debt of the USA's external deficit combined with the devaluation of stock market assets, burdening a country that thrives on the stock market (a worse crisis than that of 1929 is to be feared); a growing budgetary deficit; America's rapidly diminishing hold over a world economy which it no longer dominates as a result of Asia's increasing power; and the USA's dread of being overtaken by China in the medium term and outperformed on every possible level including the military one.

Furthermore, the granite lump embodied by America's judicial and constitutional institutions is now being challenged for the very first time in American history. G. W. Bush is the very first American president who, despite only being supported by a minority, was elected as a result of electoral fraud, as if the USA were some vulgar banana republic.

***

The USA has no notion of what it means to be deeply rooted, and its identity is akin to a sand castle that could collapse at any given moment. This is precisely why an *artificial sort of patriotism* is constantly necessary so as to prevent the potential crumbling of the amnesiac and kaleidoscopic American society. It is not a nation in any way, thus lacking any sense of history or common tradition and remaining devoid of social and ethnic unity. Even the English language now fails to unite this society, whose strongest cementing element lies in economic materialism, an element whose adhesive properties are very weak; for what characterises the American society is consumerism, punt-taking, and money worship.

So as to maintain this crumbling edifice in place and re-federate an immense society undergoing an identity and value crisis, the neoconservative administration has taken advantage of the 9/11 shock in order to implement the most classic recipe: a mixture of pseudo-patriotic militarism and superficial religiousness, amounting to puritan bibli-cal deism, i.e. a sort of simplified Christianity. For what also accounts for the second Gulf War is the desire to reinvigorate a crisis-stricken American patriotism.

**

The problem is that, in the course of the 20th century, American minds were increasingly branded with a contradiction which the war in Iraq has now clearly highlighted: on the one hand, a callous and martial sort of voluntarism, one that is ever arrogant and domineering, and, on the other, an immense mental frailty, meaning a propensity for discouragement, fear and doubt (in Mogadishu, for instance, Clinton ordered the expeditionary corps to retreat following the slaughter of 18 American soldiers in an ambush). Americans may threaten others, but still lack the tenacity enjoyed by the British. At the slightest setback, they sink into depression and are volatile. If what they undertake is not immediately channelled into a *success story* (particularly in the military field), they begin to despair and simply give in. Both American society and the *dreamworld* upon which it has been established (the American Dream model being the embodiment of the paradise that the USA strives to impose upon the Earth) thus lack the necessary readiness to face the 21st century, whose harshness is bound to be pitiless.

We may yet witness the disappearance of the American imperial republic during the current century, simply because, when it comes down to it, it is but an *enterprise*, a company, being neither a society, nor a nation or people, a fact which sets it apart from Europe, China, India, etc. Akin to a company, the USA is bound to be ephemeral, having only experienced its moment of glory and its peak in the brief course of the 20th century. Moreover, the destruction of the World Trade Center (its headquarters, so to speak) at the hands of fanatical Saudi Wahhabis on the 11th of September 2001 may have marked the beginning of its end.

E. A Western-Like War

The reason why the NAI lacks efficacy and remains counterproductive is that it has reinforced the very menace that it claimed to be able to eradicate. Following the 9/11 attacks, the Iraqi and Afghan '*anti-terrorist*' campaigns (in addition to America's unconditional support of Ariel Sharon) increased the numbers of the *mujahideen* volunteering to commit acts of terrorism. The devastating consequences will not come to light immediately, but will all be felt in good time.

Due to their mental simplicity and attempts at electioneering, the neoconservatives are only able to combat their invisible and underground adversaries using the mediatic and spectacular method of the cowboy that takes out his gun and opens fire in all directions. They deploy their army and bombard the enemy in an effort to reassure themselves and their people. Their 9/11 lesson has not been learnt at all.

The tragedy that has stricken the USA lies in its mental frailty. America's sole understanding of war is that of a western film, in which the cavalry charges towards its enemy and takes the American Indians prisoners. It assumes that sophisticated weapons can somehow replace fieldwork and shadow warfare, remaining forever 'modern' in the 19th and 20th century sense of the word and never becoming 'post-modern' in the 21st century understanding of things. Having adopted 'communication' and promotional propaganda as its credo, the USA, strangely enough, lacks any and all know-how in this field. Even before the Iraqi war started, it became clear that America had fallen miserably short in the mediatic struggle that was meant to legitimise its intervention. The USSR was far more capable in matters of propaganda, having, for as long as 70 years, managed to mobilise a certain part of the European intelligentsia and media in support of its totalitarian system.

The struggle against terrorism can only stem for a counter-terrorism effort conducted by an equally terroristic state. In the face of Islamic terrorism, the only possible response must come from the appropriate secret services and lead to direct and discreet operations during which the targets are eliminated physically, without ever having to resort to a tribunal or court. The fact of detaining the Afghan and Arab warriors captured in Afghanistan under illegal circumstances that violate the Geneva conventions, as part of an attempt to 'loosen their tongues', is a pointless act of intimidation, one that, in fact, soils America's image, sharpens the anti-American desire for vengeance and strengthens the recruitment capacities of terrorist networks, without any productivity on the part of the US military intelligence. This counter-terrorism effort must not founded upon the open elimination of terrorist leaders using missiles (as practiced by Israel), but on a discreet infiltration into the networks in question. Unfortunately for the USA, its extensive and bureaucratic secret services seem to lack the aptitude to keep the American government well-informed, despite their immense technological means. Dealing with terrorism as if it were a traditional military threat, while resorting to conventional military means, is a sign of astonishing stupidity on the part of the world's main superpower, a superpower that is endowed with enormous intelligence services and filled with 'specialists', experts and think-tanks.

***

Ever since the 9/11 events, the NAI has been attaching great importance to *spectacle*. It is an old tendency that is becoming ever more pronounced. American power is more spectacular and televisual than genuine. The purpose is to intimidate the adversary through a mediatic demonstration of power. In practice, unfortunately, the USA lacks the ability to follow through. A mere image cannot replace reality. It is hardly sufficient for an empire to resort to financial incentives and attempt to convince others of its power through audio-visual propaganda in order impose itself. Although dominating peoples and their territories is mandatory in this regard, Washington is incapable of doing so. American leaders lack the slightest notion of what a 'people' actually is.

F. The End of American Democracy
— A Path towards Soft Despotism?

The NAI embodies the decline of American democracy; it is not a decline in a Caesarist or tyrannical sense, but rather one where the regime of what could be labelled *'an authoritarian and mercantile oligarchy'* is reinforced, in accordance with the analysis conducted by Michel Bugnon-Mordant in *The USA — A Global Manipulation* (Favre editions). This trait had long been present before the neoconservatives took control of things. The NAI is founded upon this new form of power, a power that exploits electoral democracy as a mere facade.

There are two striking characteristics on this level: first of all, the American leaders are deeply implicated in financial schemes surrounding the military-industrial and oil complexes, sometimes taking advantage of their family ties and their belonging to the right clique. The Iraqi campaign was not organised solely due to 'American' geo-political or geo-economic interests, but also (or most of all, perhaps) those of the petropolitical governmental elites (Bush, Cheney, etc.) or those of the prominent members of the military-industrial complex (Rumsfeld, Perle, etc.) It is thus not the USA's 'strategic oil provisions' that acted as the decisive factor during the Iraqi war, but rather those petropoliticians' desire to increase the provisions of their own bank accounts.

Furthermore, it must be said that Bush, who was elected President following an electoral scam, is not the true American leader at all (since his intellectual level prevents him from assuming such a role), but merely an influenceable head of state, a puppet that has been granted his position by the lobbies to whom he owes his obedience. Paradoxically, the new American regime sanctifies the decline of the presidential function. This notion is the focus of Warren P. Strobel's brilliant demonstration (*The Charlotte Observer*, 29/03/2003), in which he states that G. W. Bush is 'the toy of a machinery' that enabled him to become President, although he obviously acts as its accomplice because of his family's interests.

This leads me to make the following remarks:

1) American nationalists (meaning the neoconservatives' enemies) claim that US militarism is in complete contradiction to American interests and only protects those of a certain oligarchy. From this perspective, the issue is not 'American patriotism', but rather the protection that lobbies are granted.

2) The NAI relies on a sort of regression towards a nepotic form of power that actually resembles that of oriental monarchies. Nothing is more reminiscent of the attitude espoused by current American leaders, whether those involved in petropolitics or the military industry, than the despotic practices of their Middle-Eastern counterparts, whose behaviour mirrors their own attachment to their family, clique and financial interests. Bush is actually the first American President to have taken over from his own father, just like Bashar Al-Assad in Syria.

3) It is not to be excluded that the neoconservatives will resort to every possible means to maintain themselves in power, including the rigging of elections. Never before has anyone seen a government make use of such a huge number of lies and such clumsy cynicism in its endeavours. In this respect, Roosevelt, Kennedy and Johnson cannot even begin to compare. The USA may therefore end up facing a severe political and constitutional crisis, one that is unlike anything it has experienced since the Unionist victory.

America no longer enjoys 'political sovereignty' in the traditional sense, but is instead governed through an agreement involving different clans with diverging interests, all of which are ultimately financial in nature. Venturing even further, William Pfaff believes that, thanks to the Iraqi campaign, the NAI has led the American government across the Rubicon of 'totalitarianism' (in *Which Country Is Next on the List*, *The International Herald Tribune*, 10/04/2003):

> When it comes down to it, the neoconservatives are fanatics. They think it worthwhile to kill people in the name of unfounded views. Traditional ethics posited that war was justified by legitimate self-defence. Totalitarian ethics justifies war through the intent to make peoples and societies "better".

This view is a powerful one and deserves to be granted attention. However, it seems to be stricken with 'something' that draws it closer to the realm of science fiction. The unresolved question is whether the neoconservative effort is a footnote that will quickly be forgotten or the beginning of a lasting phenomenon.

***

The American paradox, which concerns both the various US governments and the American public culture, lies in the mixing of contradictory attitudes that cannot coexist harmoniously in the long term and will undoubtedly lead to domestic breakdown. These conflicting attitudes include idealistic messianism and low-rate pragmatism; philanthropic lyricism and a fascination for brutality; the praising of democracy and the practice of plutocracy; an emphasis on patriotism and the failure of the melting pot to the benefit of a society divided into impervious ethnic beehives; and, last but not least, an ambition to achieve global economic domination contrasting with the acceptance of the structural (and colossal) deficit of the American trade balance.

CHAPTER V

Europe — America's Nightmare?

A. The NAI's Anti-Europeanism and Francophobia

In an article published by *Historia* in March 2003, political scientist Rémi Kaufer demonstrated that the American secret services had initially financed both the construction of Europe and European federalist notions through the American Committee on United Europe. They believed that the USA would find it easier to manipulate a united Europe than to bring separate states under its control, thus achieving ideal conditions for the containment of Communism. Henceforth, the Americans never relinquished this vision, for while they live in dread of a 'European power' stretching along a Paris-Berlin-Moscow axis, they are thrilled at the sight of Europe's current state, especially considering the perspective of Turkish EU membership and the emergence of a 'new Europe' in the east, a Europe that is as pro-American as it is dear to Donald Rumsfeld. However, this opinion is not shared by numerous neoconservative imperialists. The fact is that if Washington exerts all this effort to neutralise, divide and weaken the 'European power' through the WTO etc., it is because the Americans fear a *European awakening*, a transformation that would transfigure the current soft ideology embraced by Brussels into a vision that would rival the USA's. Let us not forget that the NIA is characterised by the ideological (and stupid) novelty of refusing to tolerate any other genuinely global power than the American one.

In order to measure the magnitude of the American fear of a European rebirth, let us turn our attention to the report published in June 2003 by *The New Republic*, a neoconservative weekly paper. Despite the stagnation afflicting the European economy and regardless of our global weakness, demographic aging and the mass immigration weighing us down, etc., the headline was '*Europe, a Superpower*', followed by two central articles entitled '*Why America Should Fear the European Economy*' and '*Why America Should Fear the Construction of Europe*'. In fact, as remarked by Pascal Riche in *Libération* (20/06/2003), '*something has changed*' since the Franco-German refusal to support the war against Iraq:

> Washington had previously considered Europe to be a loyal and harmless ally. The neoconservatives were convinced that this peaceful continent, whose military capacity seemed to be virtually inexistent, was not only experiencing a demographic decline, but also stricken with economic weakness and did not therefore merit excessive attention. However, the European Union has suddenly become the source of a potential threat.

***

What follows is the very core of the NAI's neoconservative and unilateralist doctrine regarding both Europe and France. In the above-mentioned weekly, neoconservative ideologist Andrew Sullivan states:

> The power that stands to benefit most from the construction of Europe is France. And as we have learnt through bitter experience, French intentions are essentially hostile to the US, whether culturally, economically or diplomatically. The current challenge faced by our American foreign policy lies in finding a way to prevent the new European configuration from taking shape, courting and maintaining the loyalty of pro-American governments and states and saving the European continent from ancient Europe's smothering embrace.

What is noticeable is that neoconservative ideologists are no longer willing to handle the world with kid gloves. With a sort of rabid naivety, they have shown their hand and revealed their intent to callously interfere in the affairs of others (*'to prevent the new European configuration from taking shape'* while *'courting'* governments that are expected to remain loyal).

In the aftermath of the French opposition to the irreproachable legalism pervading the Iraqi campaign, the threat of targeting France with 'punishment' corroborates Sullivan's ideological point of view and confirms the fact that Washington has relinquished indirect imperialism for the sake of a straightforward and openly acknowledged imperialistic approach reflected in an American return to a suzerainlike attitude towards Europe, an attitude which the Americans have now explicitly disclosed and which obviously constitutes an enormous blunder in terms of diplomatic psychology.

In June 2003, Robert Bradtke, the Deputy Assistant Secretary for European and Eurasian Affairs, poured his soul out to the American media, explaining that the White House was going to put Europe and particularly France *'under observation'*. This notion of a *counterweight*, which Europe may well end up developing under French leadership, embodies the bane of all neoconservatives, including Bradtke himself.

***

One of the reasons behind Washington's animosity towards France is perhaps also the fact that our country represents the sole independent nuclear power in the western world, for, as demonstrated elsewhere, Great Britain cannot be perceived as one at all, since its small arsenal (totalling 30 % of the French nuclear potential in terms of genuine striking capacities) is completely dependent on American 'double-keying'.

In short, the NAI perceives our potentially ailing Europe as a pebble in its cowboy boot and France as the flint's sharp tip. Imagine that Europe were to regain its health and will... Many of the friends with whom I have shared this hypothesis have told me that if such a development ever came to pass, the USA would find itself compelled to wage war upon us, in harmony with the restored logic of World War II. I personally have severe doubts about this scenario and rather believe that our awakening would trigger a Euro-American 'cold war', but definitely not a genuine conflict.

***

According to Tom Waisse, the USA must *'increase its efforts to dilute the European Union'* by integrating subservient eastern countries into the latter, countries that no longer belong to the diabolical Soviet Empire of Evil, but are controlled by the beneficent Uncle Sam, while simultaneously ordering the EU to grant Turkey membership before incorporating the Maghreb as well. The French vision of a 'European power' that is perhaps allied to the US, yet still autonomous, is a scandal in the eyes of the new American notion of the world. Waisse says: *'Eastern countries will reject Chirac's project of turning Europe into a counterweight to American power'*. In a display of calm cynicism, he then makes the following confession: *'The White House wants* [not even 'wishes' or 'would like'] *Europeans to share the military burden through NATO, but rejects* [instead of 'deplores'] *the idea of a common diplomacy or defence that would, one day, turn cooperation into rivalry'*.

In other words, Europe is expected to participate in the American military effort and obey Washington at all times, without having a legitimate right to its own strategic policy. By contrast, the USA has every right to monitor the shaping of the EU, which is required to function similarly to NATO and, above all, grant Turkey membership. The European Union must never have a foreign policy of its own; such a policy is only acceptable if it abides by American definitions (and thus never sees the light of day). The emergence of a common European diplomacy and defence will result in sanctions should this attitude be hostile to the US (which is logical), even in the event that European countries create a simple alliance while remaining independent. The simplest rivalry cannot be tolerated by this 'liberal' America, an

America that allows itself to rival others without giving them the opportunity to reciprocate.

***

In his essay entitled *American Power, European Weakness*, American Robert Kagan points out that, as a result of their weakness and rejection of military efforts, the Europeans have turned towards a moralising and utopian vision of a legalistic and consensual world order inspired by the philosophy of the Enlightenment. He says that the USA has, on the other hand, espoused the realism of Thomas Hobbes. Even Atlanticist Wolfgang Schäuble, the CDU-CSU vice-president at the Bundestag, acknowledges the fact that Europe must make a military effort to equal the USA and that moralistic speeches regarding 'international law' could never replace power.

The NAI is right to believe that in our current world, where menace is henceforth protean and *globalised* conflict leaves no region unscathed, a sovereign and unilateral power to strike (without UN involvement) cannot be contested and the lead-footed legalism of international legislation has become naïve. The problem is that the Americans are, as ever, implementing this sound philosophy with horrific clumsiness.

During the 21st century, war will take on every conceivable shape but that of a sport with applicable rules. Just like Alain Juppé and his concept of '*global governance*', those who believe in the birth of a global state (and there are many in France who do) are completely mistaken. We are heading straight towards a jungle where all political coups are allowed. The notions of respect for the sovereignty of the weak and the prohibition of preventive military interventions, which embodied the very foundations of international law following the Treaty of Westphalia (whose ideology was first adopted by the League of Nations, then by the UN), already failed miserably back in the 19th and 20th centuries and will certainly be impossible to implement during the 21st.

***

This is precisely why the French position, which claims to be able to counter American unilateralism through the reign of law and consensual multilateralism, clearly relates to both a Kantian sort of unrealism and a vision worthy of the Third Republic. In this regard, Chirac is the faithful successor of Aristide Briand and his judicial pacifism, as analysed by Éric Zemmour. The European power advocated by Chirac's France through mere lip service and meant to counterbalance American hegemony can never be founded upon a UN world order presided over by elderly wise men. Instead, due to the resumption of Islamic *jihad* (a *jihad* that knows no law but that of a fanaticism legitimised through superstition) and the NAI's equally fanatical attitude, a European power could only see the light of day through Europe's genuine sovereignty as part of an alliance with Russia, meaning through an approach that is free of both pacifistic utopianism and the cosmopolitan naivety that typifies the religion of Human Rights and rooted in a considerable military power surpassing America's, which is within our reach from a technological and financial perspective. What certain American milieus are counting on is the Third-Worldisation of Europe, as this constitutes the ideal means to radically weaken their economic and strategic rival. However, it is not Washington that is at the source of Europe's Third-Worldisation, but the indigenous forces of European decadence, as the USA contents itself with watching these events unfold. The American insistence on Turkish EU membership, which would serve as a major decomposing factor, will not be sufficient on its own should European governments be strongly opposed to such a step. In no way does the USA force Europe to Third-Worldise and Islamise itself by putting a knife to its throat. It is we who are completely responsible for what is afflicting us. The European opposition to geostrategic American imperialism, especially that of France, Belgium and Germany, would gain far more credibility if those countries' politicians dared resist the economic and commercial war waged by America upon Europe; but they all lack such courage. One is often under the impression that this emotional sort of anti-Americanism is but a façade, relying on empty words and enragement, on inconsequential clawing in an attempt to justify and overshadow Europe's incredibly complicit passivity in the face of America's economic and technological grip on our own lifeblood. What seems far graver to me than the fact of breaching the Security Council's rules or the aggression against Iraq is that 40 % of France's private high industry is in the hands of various American pension funds. Europe's anti-Americanists are only preoccupied with one aspect of US imperialism: its effect upon the Third World. Rarely do they worry about its weakening impact on Europe. As for me, I am hardly moved by the fact that the USA exercises a merciless hegemony upon southern countries; the only thing that matters to me is our ability to defend our continent against the American sway.

***

According to certain analysts including Italian political scientist Giorgio Agamben, the main purpose behind the Iraqi campaign was to weaken and divide Europe. In *Le Figaro* (07/04/2002), Agamben stated:

> It is above all a war against Europe. The moment Europe became an economic power that threatened American supremacy, the USA set out to prove that Europe lacked any political existence. [...] The American diplomacy has openly and systematically strived to destroy European political unity. Its endeavour has unfortunately been successful. It is one of the secret and unspoken motivations behind this war. [...] In addition to demonstrating that Europe did not have any political power, the USA has also proven that the UN is not a genuine political entity, but a humanitarian one at the most.

Indeed, in a display of sheer cynicism, America entrusts the UN (which it considers subservient) with the partial task of bringing humanitarian relief to a post-war and devastated Iraq, whose situation the Americans are primarily responsible for after 10 years of embargoes and bombardments, not to mention the impact of the latest campaign.

***

Through the Iraqi war and its effort to govern Mesopotamia, for instance, one of the NAI's primary objectives is to trigger Europe's neutralisation and enfeeblement, as well as to seize control of local oil fields. The NAI is fixated on the notion of preventing Europe — or rather what I have termed Euro-Siberia, which includes both Europe and Russia — from emerging as a counterpower. It all began with the American intervention in Kosovo and the war in Serbia (i.e. long before the 11th of September 2001), where, as demonstrated by Alexandre Del Valle, the Americans were intent on founding Muslim states now located at the very heart of Europe. Divide and conquer: the USA thus advocates Turkish EU membership so as to disfigure our continent and set the 'old' Franco-German Europe (Donald Rumsfeld) against a 'new' vassal Europe rooted in former communist countries, while simultaneously exploiting Great Britain as a permanent source of discord and a staging post for its own imperialism.

In this respect, there is a subtle difference between the NAI and traditional American imperialism. The latter was meant to enable the containment of both the USSR and Communism, in accordance with McNamara's renowned doctrine. Following the collapse of the USSR, Washington was quick to realise that Europe was no longer in need of military protection and that it would soon become a fearsome strategic rival. Europeans thus lost their sympathetic and harmless protégé status and became dangerous vassals that covet emancipation. And yet Europe is so weak! It has neither military power, nor an assertive will to speak of; it suffers from a declining demography and allows both Islam and the Third World to invade it. Despite all this, it remains an ever-increasing source of worry for the ruling American political caste. The European cadaver may still regain its mobility. In the eyes of the American hegemonic ambition, Europe (and especially Euro-Siberia) is far more of a threat than Communism ever was, since it is perceived as a global adversary and a major obstacle hindering Washington's hunger for absolute hegemony. For this reason, the NAI has proceeded to apply the *principle of precaution*: 'even if today's Europe lacks the necessary will to genuinely defy us, we must resort to every possible means to prevent it from becoming a real power'.

B. A Europe Perceived as a Menace

What is it that actually motivates the NAI? Emanuel Todd is the author of *After the Empire*, a book in which he writes that '*the USA is attempting to mask its own waning by directing its military activism against insignificant states*'. He proposes the following interesting scenario: the Iraqi oil reserves were just the secondary purpose behind the attack against Iraq. The true aim was to '*send the whole world a message stating that the Americans were still the masters and that others had better behave themselves*'. According to the author, Saddam Hussein (a toothless tiger by any means) was part of a simulated piece of theatrical antagonism, the true adversary being none other than Europe itself, a continent that the Americans wanted to intimidate and drive out of the region. The Iraqi campaign thus targeted a certain 'European power'. Sensing that, after the fall of the Soviet Union and Communism, the world no longer required US protection and having taken heed of their own global economic decline, the American leaders in Washington are artificialising and willingly overestimating the threat posed by the 'Axis of Evil', a fabricated earthly Satan. The USA thus manifests '*a fundamental desire to remain at the very centre of the world*' by showing us that '*its role remains indispensable, when, in actual fact, the old world is ever less in need of its involvement*'. Todd clarifies that:

> … in order to remain at the centre of the world, the USA has developed a theatrical sort of micro-militarism and proceeded to attack military midgets so as to create an illusory impression of its own power.

***

In an article entitled *America's Divided View of European Unity*, Gerard Baker, a political editorialist at London's *Financial Times*, explains that if, following Eisenhower's presidency, various US business and political milieus looked upon European unification very favourably, things are far less evident today. He advocates the notion that current American leaders view with great suspicion the prospect of a united Europe acting as a counterweight to US influence:

> A Europe united under traditional Franco-German leadership would have constituted a catastrophe for America's political and military ambitions.

In Baker's view, the future establishment of such a European entity is frowned upon because it anticipates, however timidly, an independent security policy. The USA will simply not tolerate any European contestations against its own objectives. The only thing that it could condone is a discussion regarding the means. In the eyes of the current US administration, a genuinely independent European Union no longer acting in tandem with NATO would embody a true *casus belli*.

***

For Christopher Gérard, the fact that Washington is so intent on accomplishing Muslim Turkey's EU membership is reminiscent of the ancient thalassocratic strategy once embraced by Great Britain and nowadays by the US in an effort to sabotage the continental Union embodied by Europe. He writes:

> America's current hegemony allows Washington, which has taken over from the City, to pursue with an equal dose of coherence and patience an ancient strategy towards the weakening of Europe, going to any possible lengths to separate the latter from Russia. [...] Our geopolitical enemy has every interest in neutralising its potential rival by playing the Lebanisation card. This process began with the Iron Curtain and endured during the American expeditions in the Balkans, spreading from Bosnia to the Kosovo region. Once Europe has been paralysed, Washington will be able to turn its attention towards its other rivals, namely Moscow, Delhi and Beijing, and shatter the Eurasian axis. [...] Are we to accept the fact that Rome will thus

no longer be in Rome and that the banner of Muhammad will flutter above its toppled temples? (*La Libre Belgique*, 13/12/2003.)

This analysis reflects the author's belief in the existence of a secret alliance uniting Washington and Islam against Europe.

***

Charles A. Kupchan, author of *The Decline and Fall of the American Empire*, is a professor at the University of Georgetown and the head of a thought current according to which the neo-imperialism embraced by the Bush administration has, paradoxically, brought about the global enfeeblement of the American power:

> One of the real threats that lie ahead of us is the transformation of a "light" empire into a "heavy" one which, far from being a source of reassurance for other nations, will make us come across as hostile. Instead of giving the impression of being a beneficent hegemonic power, we thus appear as predators. In the eyes of the whole world, we seem to be losing the legitimacy of remaining a superpower, a legitimacy that was both our main asset and our most precious "product". If this situation persists, all of our ventures will fail. We may well witness several countries forming armed coalitions against the United States. (As stated during an interview entitled *The End of America's Reign*, published by numerous American newspapers in December 2002.)

Strangely enough, Kupchan believes that America's true '*challenger*' in the years leading up to 2030 will actually be the EU, not China:

> Europe is no longer a group of sovereign nations. Mirroring the United States of the 18th century, it has, instead, become a unified ensemble, a collective entity with a growing aptitude towards embodying a counterweight to our empire.

***

Having also authored a book entitled *The End of the American Era* (Knopf editions), Kupchan predicts that in 2030, the world will be divided among the following confederate blocs: North America (comprising the USA, Canada and Mexico), Latin America, Eastern Asia (revolving around a China that will have formed an alliance with Japan), an ever more impoverished Africa and, last but not least, a Euro-Russian partnership. What he actually foresees is a conflictual multilateralism or, at best, a cold war that differs greatly from the unilateral sort of American hegemony that current US leaders dream of. Summarising his viewpoints, he declared (in an interview with the Italian magazine *Sette*, 19/12/2002): '*For the time being, Bush is waging war upon Saddam, but our real enemy is Europe*'.

***

Let us imagine that, following an extremely severe future crisis, a new European power were to rise and, in the aftermath of a revolution ignited by the native masses and the necessary leadership of a providential personality, undertake an *ethnic Reconquista* (after all, history can only progress thanks to the alchemical combination of these two elements). As a result, the USA may decide to intervene militarily — in the name of human rights and democracy — and attempt to reclaim our continent, bombarding us and attacking us. I, for one, have serious doubts about this hypothetical version of our future history, simply because American strategists only attack the weak or, at least, those that the US believes to be so. Faced with a regenerated European power, the Americans would be inclined to compromise.

C. The United Kingdom, America's Mistreated Vassal

If there is any European country that has become subservient to the USA, especially since the Iraqi campaign, it is undoubtedly poor Great Britain, even more so under Blair than under Mrs. Thatcher. In *The Guardian* (17/07/2003), David Leigh and Richard Norton Taylor explained that their country was now '*the USA's client state, having lost its sovereignty to America's advantage*'.

The authors assert that American leaders have compelled Blair to go against British public opinion (for rather obscure reasons, as some people speak of a 'personal file'), which represents the peak of submission. They also claim that the British commanding officers stationed in southern Iraq are entirely obedient to the Pentagon. They point out that the Tomahawk cruise missiles purchased by Great Britain at Raytheon, USA, can only be used under American permission; the same goes for the British army's imaging satellites. The authors add that, owing to the 'double keying' principle, Britain is banned from using its own nuclear weapons (meaning those 58 Trident missiles carried by submarines and, once again, purchased at Lockheed Martin in the US) without American authorisation; that the American military bases located in the United Kingdom and at Diego Garcia (and financed at British taxpayers' expense) are not subject to British control in any way; and that British secret services act as America's dependants, follow US orders and are under the obligation to provide the USA with information without automatic reciprocity.

Washington shows no gratitude in the face of this wilful British submission, only a certain disdain. We all remember Donald Rumsfeld's words when he said that the USA did not require the support of British troops in order to crush Iraq. Great Britain has submitted to the logic of *unequal treaties* with the USA, as China did in relation to the West in the 19th century. In a display of utter masochism, successive British governments have expressed great pride at this '*superb cooperation*' (as once declared by Her Majesty's Home Secretary, David Blunkett). In a devastating analysis published by first-rate magazine *Prospect* in early 2003, Sir Rodric Braithwaite, the former director of the British secret services who had acted as the Crown's ambassador to China, stated that his country had practically become both America's lesser military proxy and its 51st state.

***

Commenting on David Kelly's suspicious suicide affair, William Pfaff, who served as the Defence Ministry's adviser on biological weapons, also denounced this subjection which, under Blair, has been taken to unheard of levels (*The International Herald Tribune*, 24/06/2002). What follows is British Defence Secretary Hoon's confession, dated late June 2003: '*It is absolutely inconceivable for the United Kingdom to undertake a large-scale military operation independently of the USA*'. Not only without American participation, that is, but even without US authorisation. Pfaff notes:

> In today's Europe, only France has massive independent military capaci-
> ties. All other non-neutral European countries simply watch as their armed
> forces are calibrated in order to become mere specialised units in a US-led
> NATO.

Blair ventures even further: by selling America the BAE Systems defence and avionics group, what he did was sell off his country's techno-military capacities.

> Blair endorses the American pretentiousness that drives the US to mock
> international treaties and obligations and grant itself the right to global
> military domination.

Blair has, however, made a major mistake when adopting this submissive attitude, for his NAI masters lack the necessary means to realise their pretentious and unreasonable ambitions. But why is it that Blair has proceeded to organise his country's suicide in this manner? Why display such servility towards an America that has become drunk on a power that it does not actually possess? Blair has not gained anything specific from serving the USA, if one does not count the *Congress medal* that he received for good services rendered. In Pfaff's eyes, the answer defies reason. He believes that if America's current foreign policy endures, regardless of whether Bush is re-elected or not, '*we will witness an American national tragedy*' worse than that the military defeat in Vietnam, one that will, in turn, '*inevitably lead to a British national tragedy*'.

***

There is a powerful and quite radical British-American Atlanticist clan which supports the NAI and its neoconservatives and feels that Great Britain must become a sort of American protectorate whose European role is to dissuade Europe from becoming a 'world power' and to drive the latter towards contenting itself with being a major market devoid of any and all political will. Thatcher and Blair both belong to this clan, and Clinton's electoral strategist, Dick Morris, is one of the ideologists behind this tendency. In an article entitled *Britain's Future Lies Over the Atlantic, Not the Channel* and published by *The Daily Telegraph* on May the 19th 2003, he states:

> The distance from London to Paris is greater than that which separates 10, Downing Street from 1600, Pennsylvania Avenue. [...] Britain's diplomatic future is neither connected to France, nor Germany, but to America. The British are an efficacious people, endowed with energy and positivity. Just like the Americans, they worry about their future. Unlike the French, however, they are neither eccentric, nor neurotic, and unlike the Germans, they have never tasted defeat and humiliation. [Classy, is he not?]

This American then proceeds to give his English friends some 'advice':

> Great Britain is free to trade and share its money with whomever it wishes; if it desires, it can choose to align its domestic policy to Brussels' continental bureaucracy and abide by it. Fulfil your economic destiny with the continent if you wish; but keep your political vows for a marriage with America. We Americans long for you, far more so than your European counterparts ever could, and our common future is far brighter than what they propose'.

His statement sounds like a dutiful wife's love declaration…

D. A Consensual Weakness

European countries, including France (regardless of its endless sabre rattling), always surrender to Washington's desires, because they overestimate both America's power and its means of action or retaliation. We are not to 'vex' our suzerain, you see. What everyone fails to comprehend is that America is neither a superpower, nor even a hyperpower. One abides by its injunctions for emotional and ideological reasons, but not as a result of practical and reasonable motivations. The entire European policy lacks any sort of will to resist American imperialism and is founded upon utter ignorance of the sole true words ever spoken by Mao: '*The USA is but a toothless tiger*'.

The British case is highly emblematic: they relinquish their whole national sovereignty, allowing America to exploit and enslave them (which only applies to their leaders, not their public opinion), all in the name of some fictitious Anglo-Saxon solidarity. As for eastern European countries, they have not fared much better either, which is true of Poland above all others. Following their misadventures under Soviet hegemony, they have thrown themselves into the arms of American 'democracy'.

***

One can doubt the fact that Chirac's objection to the American warmongering in Iraq is primarily due to his love of international law and a neo-Gaullist desire to counterbalance America's hegemony. For it is, above all, a pacifistic and Third World-like attitude that has been a constant for Chirac, who holds great admiration for the peoples of the South. He is a naïve preacher of interplanetary dialogue, horrified at the sight of the emerging 'civilisational clash', one that he strives to deny at all costs by embracing the delusion of a secular and democratic Islam as well as that of a successful Republican 'integration', just like the entire intellectual and political caste in France.

More than anything, he intends to treat the ever more numerous Muslim-Arabs with utmost care. The latter weigh our foreign policy down, reducing our independence through their neo-colonial presence, which is far graver than all the pressure exerted by American hegemony. In this respect, the headscarf affair is the latest example. Neither of the two woes is desirable, of course, but I would definitely rather live in a Europe dominated by an American commission than on a continent where mosques prevail and where we must submit to foreign Muslim control. Why? My position, however unbearable it may seem to those who espouse obsessional anti-American hysteria, is rooted in plain calculating Machiavellianism: for it is infinitely easier for us to liberate ourselves from an American hegemony that has been imposed upon us *from abroad* than to free ourselves from a Muslim-Arab occupation that has afflicted us *on our own soil*. In no way is the latter the result of the former, as the usual sophistic claims would have us believe.

✳✳✳

Jean-Louis Bourlanges, a European MP, is convinced that by heading the pacifistic and legalistic campaign against the American crusade, Chirac has put himself into a ridiculous position and, as a result of both Saddam Hussein's fall and America's military victory, suffered a political Waterloo. He implicitly believes that any Franco-German opposition to the NAI is but smoke and mirrors, since France and Germany both lack any and all will to attain power, unless one counts that of speech, i.e. that of powerless words.

He notes:

> In fact, the US government strived to achieve three objectives: to eliminate the Iraqi regime under the pretext of disarming it, to put an end to the UN's cumbersome guardianship, and to shatter the unity of a Europe that has turned into a commercial threat and is capable of teaching political lessons. The policy adopted by France seems to be tailor-made and especially suited to allow the USA to accomplish its triple ambition. (*Le Figaro*, 18/04/2003.)

Bourlanges sinks into partial confusion here: if it is indeed the case that France lacks the means to materialise its opposition, it is nonetheless absurd for it to be expected not to manifest the latter. On the other hand, what he fails to mention is that the American 'victory' in Iraq will ultimately turn out to be a plain and simple defeat.

✳✳✳

Having said this, is the French government's diplomacy not rather grotesque? Mr. Raffarin and Villepin have both made stunning declarations to the media: on the 31st of March 2003, at Clermont-Ferrand, our Prime Minister made a statement in which he declared himself to be in favour of an American victory and, criticising anti-war demonstrations, asked his audience '*not to fight the wrong enemy*'. How absurd. Are they thus siding with those whose war they have declared to be illegal?

Extremely annoyed by the poll conducted by *Le Monde* on the 31st of March 2003, which revealed that two thirds of the French population were anti-American (a figure that is especially due to the presence of French Muslims), and by the people carrying Saddam Hussein's portrait and chanting anti-Semitic slogans during anti-war demonstrations, Chirac is now attempting a stunning gymnastics effort. All of this indicates and confirms the fact that Chirac's anti-warmongering stances were more focused on mobilising voters for the 2007 elections than on actually opposing American hegemony. Politically speaking, he is thus doing the splits. While having lunch with several UMP senators on April the 2nd, he reminded them that '*the transatlantic alliance cannot be questioned in any way*' and openly wished for an American victory as well. What acrobatics! France is both in favour of the war and opposed to it, you see, and both pro- and anti-American. Hardly credible, is it? As I pen these lines, we must all wonder whether France will not end up sending its own troops to Iraq, under UN mandate, of course, yet under American leadership.

***

In order to be able to oppose the US, our words cannot rival the importance of power. This statement was confirmed by a recent alarmist report brought to us by the French Institute for International Relations (IFRI) on 07/02/2003, a report that warns of Europe's demographic, techno-economic and scientific decline in the face of the USA and Asia. Yves Messarovitch wrote the following in *Le Figaro Magazine* (15/02/2003), entitling it '*The Law of the Strongest*':

The inevitable truth is that the USA and Europe (that of France and Germany anyway) have chosen structurally diverging paths. America watches as its industrial, financial and even military potential increases day by day. It creates more working posts than it terminates, deposits more patents, works harder and, ultimately, grows wealthier. On their part, France and Germany are essentially struggling to evade a pattern of employment loss, innovation weakness and lack of working appetite. It is however only by curing these ailments that the re-conquest of our diplomatic and military sovereignty can take place. One cannot be achieved without the other.

Indeed, claiming to counter America's global policy and to resist its imperialism is all well and good, but one must first have the means to do so, meaning the will and power to rival its hegemony. The anti-Americanism embraced by the pacifists, ecologists, paleo-socialists, human rights activists, 'alter-globalists' and other overexcited Europeans will never be anything but ineffective pseudo-lyricism and a soft romantic attitude.

***

The USA is clearly alone in its rejection of a 'multipolar' world, which acts as a false nose in its efforts to mask a ridiculous and impudent claim to (hegemonic) *primacy*. The threat to Washington's power does not, however, stem from the pleadings which one hears from France and Chirac, but, as always, from China. Taking advantage of his visit to Moscow on May the 27th 2003, Chinese President Hu Jintao declared (in a report published by *The Russia Journal Daily*): '*The tendency towards a multipolar world is irreversible and prevalent*'. He then went on to mention a '*strategic partnership with Russia*'. During a speech at the University of Moscow, he implicitly attacked the USA and its unilateralist pretence, while simultaneously preaching Machiavellian pacifism: '*Peace cannot be attained through the use of force*'. In no way does this prevent China from aspiring to become the world's foremost military and nuclear power in the medium term, of course. Unfortunately for us, the Chinese dragon emerging from its ancient torpor must indeed be a greater source of worry to the Pentagon than the Franco-German axis.

***

How does the USA fight against cutting-edge European industry? The answer is: through European cowardliness and pusillanimity. Infuriated by the success of the Airbus and Ariane projects, the American administration has introduced an array of measures to weaken its European rival; not only by using political means to impose its high-tech (and especially military and technological) products upon the European market and attempting to undermine Europe's spatial programmes (notably its satellites, which often outperform American ones), but also by proposing a hypocritical policy of industrial cooperation known as a *'transatlantic relationship'*.

Let us give the emblematic example of the Joint Strike Fighter (JSF), a combat aircraft that can strike against several targets. It is a new generation fighter bomber developed in the USA. The Americans suggested that the Europeans join this project by abandoning their own combat fighter plane programmes. Except for the French, who still cling to their *Rafales*, Europe simply gave in. British Rolls Royce and BAE have thus taken charge of 8 % of the American project. Adopting the attitude of a consenting victim, Italy, the Netherlands and Germany have also joined in. Instead of investing more than 4 billion Euros into its own programmes, Europe is to spend it all on research and development to the sole profit of the US, which will subsequently proceed to sell Europe the JSF. As ever, it is of course voluntarily that our pusillanimous European politicians immolate their countries' sovereignty and independence upon the altar of 'transatlantic friendship'.

In *Critical Utopia* ('*The Sovereignty of Nations and the "Trojan Asses"*', July 2003), Claude Karnoouh and Bruno Drweski commented on the submissive stance espoused by Central Europe (meaning by former communist countries and the various candidates for EU-membership) with regard to the American empire, an empire that intends to force our continent into submission using its gullible Trojan horses, or rather its 'Trojan asses'. The authors point out that unlike Europe, '*the USA adheres to an actual statal policy*'. Implicitly criticising the lack of means and strategic will behind Franco-German 'multilateralism' and the rebellion against Washington (which is restricted to pure and simple rhetoric), they state:

> Globally speaking, there is thus no alternative strategy to that of the American hyperpower and the PESC project remains, at least for the time being, a mere passing idea that allows the EU to garner further sympathies, without however increasing the latter's efficacy as a counterweight. At a time when the EU (and most countries that constitute it) has not yet adopted a clear strategic approach allowing it to break with America's imperialistic hegemony, American imperialism has, by contrast, embraced a strategy aiming to take control of other nations through various means such as war, economic pressure, political coups, the bribing of "decision-makers", the creation of entire networks of influence agents and propaganda, and so on.

Their analysis is indeed a sound one, but it could never justify those nations' idle-handedness. Moral condemnations have no value whatsoever.

E. Cultural Imperialism?

The most hilarious attitude is the one that typifies those who stomp their feet while vehemently protesting against American cultural domination and the 'cultural war' waged upon us by the US, declaring themselves to be fighting for a French 'cultural exception'. Within this single opprobrium, they confuse the American *way of life* and America's 'mass subculture'. It would all be credible if their pious condemnations were supported with acts. Most of the time, however, the accusers themselves indulge in the American way of life, in a display of monumental hypocrisy, which is (particularly) true of the individuals that adulate Tradition and express contempt for consumeristic materialism. Their own lifestyle thus contradicts their imprecations.

On the other hand, before they proceed to scream out their protests at 'American cultural imperialism' (which is admittedly a blatant fact), Europeans had better avoid sinking deeper into cultural and artistic decadence. They have done this to a greater degree than the Americans, since Europe is truly a beacon in matters of degenerate art (my spreading of this expression is bound to make me incur the wrath of the *politically correct*), while America is but a modest semaphore. The utter depths of 'faecal culture' (plastic arts, literature, the theatre, cinematography, etc.), anti-aestheticism, pretentious worthlessness and masochistic subversion can unfortunately be found more in Europe than the US.

It is a tragedy when one determines that American culture resists decadence more effectively than our contemporary European culture. It is as if Europe held a fascination for 'stooping ever lower'. Under these circumstances, would it not be preferable to contradict and counter American cultural imperialism instead of merely denouncing it? Would it perhaps not be wiser to raise the level of our European productions and increase their appeal? Who else is to blame but us if American films dominate Europe? The same is true of television series and games.

The same rules apply in the field of cultural war as in matters of economic and technological warfare, for actions speak louder than words. The European brain drain towards the USA is not due to the Great Satan's 'imperialism', but the result of European incompetence (according to a report published by the Economic Analysis Council, the rate is as high as 50 % of all engineering and business university graduates).

As part of the competitive historical struggle opposing our world's civilisations, peoples and nations, it is all a matter of production efficacy and palpable achievements. Moralistic and anti-American imprecations are simply ridiculous and could never succeed in convincing the public to boycott Hollywood and preventing our creative minds from crossing the ocean.

Owing to subsidisation processes and ideological preferences, artistic and cultural dregs may well hold sway in Europe. In France itself,
it is our taxpayers that finance both low-rate films and pretentious,
morbid junk that will never find its own audience. This could never
happen in the USA. The dominance of the American culture stems
from its epic and popular aspects and its ability to globally evade the
blurry and unfounded intellectualism that characterises sponsored
European authors and artists. In the eyes of the masses, this is precisely
what accounts for its superiority. It gets worse, however: it is, in fact, to
American novels and films that we owe the popularisation of Europe's
ancestral sagas during the past 40 years, and not to our own European
productions. As for 'mass American subculture', as it is often called,
it challenges us and demands but one response: that of *outdoing it*,
attracting our own crowds and refraining from digging an impassable
divide between 'popular culture' and 'elitist culture'. The grandest cultural works have always been popular.

***

One of the leitmotivs characterising OHAA (Obsessive and Hysterical
Anti-Americanism) is the notion of 'American subculture'. Once again,
even if it is not a completely mistaken attitude, it is nonetheless still
an exaggeration. One thus proceeds through reductionism, as common sense is blinded by scorn. There is, of course, an audio-visual and
televisual discharge connected to mass bewilderment, especially in the
case of youths. It is channelled through everything that we are familiar
with, meaning everything that has been extensively denounced and
analysed everywhere (including the US) and founded upon sport
spectacles, TV programmes, music, video games, pornography, and
so on. Ultimately, however, both Europe and Japan participate in this
subculture as much as America itself. It is impossible for anyone to
demonstrate that the USA is the actual driving force behind this phenomenon or that it attempts to impose anything at all through force.
Crédit Lyonnais, Vivendi Universal and various Japanese banks all

lined up to finance Hollywood. Neither TF1's prime time programmes, nor those of private French music radio stations have been defined by American interests.

Furthermore, by criticising this subculture (one that has, in fact, been greatly inspired by America), one tends to quickly forget that the USA has also been, in a very broad sense, responsible for an elitist and high-quality cultural production. The fact of considering America to be a cultural desert that only floods the world with stupidities is not very wise indeed. Moreover, French intellectuals belonging to both the Left and the Right (with the latter imitating the former) have no other option but to increase their references to their American counterparts. How sad it is to notice that, on all possible levels, transatlantic cultural creativity is endowed with greater vivacity than the European one. This is not due to some cynical chokehold orchestrated by the USA; the real cause lies rather in a sort of anaemia that has stricken Europe's imagination.

When OHAA supporters explain that both the Muslim-Arab ancestral culture (with all the dogmas and narrowmindedness that Voltaire once mocked) and native African cultures are far superior to everything that America produces, it is no longer an analysis or an opinion that one is dealing with, but an imprecation. How extraordinary it is for us to listen to the babbling of formatted intellectuals telling us that Disneyland is a deculturating factor and a catastrophe (for our European identity, of course), but that the ever more rapid Islamisation of our lands is far less of a serious problem, an unimportant issue or even a blessing. I am not particularly fond of Disneyland, MacDonald's, or American television series, but let us not lose sight of our common sense here: they are not even remotely as harmful to our identity as the blatant invasion at the hands of Islam and the Third World; and the accelerating cultural impregnation which Islam and the various immigrant populations subject us to smothers our identities with much greater efficacy and violence than 'Americanisation' ever could, since the latter remains a veneer.

CHAPTER VI

Islamism and Americanism

A. The USA Versus Islam: The Weakness of a Factitious Power

It is obvious that the Iraqi Baathist regime was an absolutely classic and age-old example of oriental despotism disguised as a 'republic'; that Saddam Hussein modelled himself according to Stalin; that Saddam's power was of a tribal nature (that of Tikrit Sunnites); and that his two sons, Uday and Qusay (the alleged heir), would have been worthy of the court of Sardanapalus. As part of its numerous, successive and contradictory justifications of its Iraqi campaign (known as 'Freedom for Iraq'), the USA claimed that it was striving to ensure liberty and democracy in Mesopotamia.

Why does it not attempt to implement its messianic will to China, Kuwait, Algeria and especially Black Africa? The answer is too obvious to be formulated. However, beyond its interested cynicism, America is honest in its liberty- and democracy-motivated messianism. As understood by Giorgio Locchi, American imperialism is founded on the almost religious and global implementation of its civilisational model, which completely disregards the ethnic and cultural particularities that define various peoples. For the latter's sake, the USA intends to meddle in the affairs of others on a permanent basis, an approach which, from a long-term perspective, can only be a source of trouble for the Americans themselves.

***

In spite of having adopted Hobbes' principle of power, the ruling Republican neoconservatives have not gone all the way. They persist in their chimeric desire to *convert* other civilisations in a manner that would ultimately shape the entire world in accordance with the American system.

And this is precisely where one realises that there is nothing imperial about the NAI, since it is not Machiavellian at all. Instead, it is rooted in naïve utopianism. A genuine form of imperialism would tolerate differences and would not long to impose its own *morality* on a global scale. It would be content to dominate, without attempting to change political regimes for ethical reasons. The USA claims to be 'democratising' the Muslim Middle-East, which is an absolute impossibility, since the latter's ancestral traditions are autocratic, theocratic and tribal in essence and not democratic. The Romans had greater respect for the religion of conquered peoples.

Just like the French republic in its longing for the creation of a 'secular Islam', the American republic intends to compel the Islamic Middle-East to conform to its Protestant worldview. It is a purely childish, utopian attitude. Both the foolish cowboy and the French intellectual preacher pretend that they could actually model Islam — one of the most powerful human civilisations — in harmony with their 'democracy', which they believe to be both universal and timeless. Islam's entire socio-political philosophy and sacredness, however, rest upon totalitarianism (which is not to be understood pejoratively), unconditional obedience to immutable 'divine' precepts and the demonisation of any and all free will.

The American dream is to have the whole world reflect America's image and for cultures to restrict themselves to simple *folklore*, a folklore that is subordinate to the consumeristic and democratic *way of life.* Alas, there is nothing folkloric about Islam, which embodies a specific lifestyle and thought system whose roots go very deep.

The examples of Germany and Japan, both of which were forcefully 'democratised', remain embedded in the American unconscious. But this recipe cannot be applied to Muslim peoples, simply because, in its central concept of *Jamahiriyah*, Islam fails to comprehend the notion of general will and displays a preference for mobilising the masses of Muslim believers around a *Calif*, a leader shrouded in a halo of mysticism.

***

Faced with Muslim peoples, puritanical and naïve America has come up against both a granite boulder (represented by Islam's superstitious masses) and the oriental lime of local rulers, who are always willing to compromise and surrender to corruption. The Arabs obviously feel humiliated, especially following the military venture in Iraq. They have long been aware of their own material powerlessness and structural inability to even come close to Western techno-economic and military capacities (as have many peoples in Third World countries). However, the USA is delusional in its belief that the sole historical source of power is of a material nature. Muslim peoples are focused on an entirely different domain, one that will truly pay off in the long term: their own demographic dynamism and their simplistic religion's power to attract, a religion which can resolve any issues that may arise.

The USA seems to have claimed victory in the Iraqi campaign, as if it were a filmed spectacle. Nevertheless, it is losing the war against Islam, which is rapidly seeping into its soil (and the European one as well).

B. Islamophilia, an Inadequate Weapon Against America

At a time when many chose to embrace Americanomania (even though they have, in the meantime, submitted to anti-American hysteria), I was among the first people in 'Identitarian' milieus to warn against the dangers of Americanomorphic mass culture. I nonetheless feel that this 'American subculture', which was initially denounced by the neo-Marxists of the Frankfurt school back in the 1950s, is far less of a threat to us that the mental Islamism and general Muslim worldview taking root in Europe.

The first reason for this is that the Muslim worldview is literally (and not pejoratively) 'totalitarian', addressing all of society, from the elites to the commoners, from the educated to the uneducated, without any distinction. By contrast, American 'mass subculture' only affects those who are willing to succumb to it. Its impact is admittedly powerful, yet remains superficial and purely *distractive*.

The latter cause stems from the former: the Islamic worldview encompasses all aspects of life, regardless of whether they are spiritual, intellectual or material. It has an answer to everything, keeping the individual in a state of enslavement from which all notion of free will is excluded. It is therefore *deep*, since it enroots its dogmas into the utmost *depths* of the soul, which makes it similar to Marxism, but with a heavier and more permeating impact as a result of an omnipresent divine dimension. In contrast, mental Americanisation does not affect the deeper aspects of the individual, nor does it formulate any social and philosophical prescriptions. It is both disorderly and pellicular. It is akin to grime that is deposited upon a surface but can still be cleaned, whereas Islamic impregnation resembles indelible ink or blood stains that have been completely absorbed by a fabric.

Despite the global spreading of the Americanomorphic subculture, its 'non-lethal' character is due to its shallowness and inherent disorder, perhaps even to its stupidity. It renders imbeciles even more imbecilic, hardly affecting the elites, if at all. It does not convey any message, nor a coherent worldview, restricting its role to audio-visual *flashes*.

On the other hand, the spreading of the Islamic worldview has far more dire consequences. Islam's worldview is neither *stupid*, nor shallow, but merely *simplistic*. Manichean and binary (with everything having a Good and Evil aspect), it confines the mind to a sort of straightjacket that fully excludes all doubt, experience, free judgement and curiosity. Any and every form of reasoning is prohibited to the benefit of dogma and gnosis. Hence the impossibility to achieve any genuine mental creativity, a creativity that has been replaced with mental orbiting around the Koran and the Hadiths, i.e. the famed sacred texts which constitute an endless plugging of affirmations and imprecations proscribing any and all possible discussion. The result is that all entrapped minds end up like a group of asses revolving around the stake to which they have been tied.

Mental Americanism is devoid of such a dimension, limiting itself to the level of *fashion*. And we all know that no fashion is long-lasting. Cultural Americanisation is weed like and easy to outroot, never impacting the soil's fertility, whereas Islamisation is a source of pollution that seeps into the fertile soil, transforming the land into a barren desert.

***

The first stupid mistake made by Islamophiles (especially intellectual converts, who have succumbed to mental bedazzlement) is that they imagine their 'Islam' to be an anti-American weapon, when the truth is that:

1) The Manichean roots of the Puritan civilisation are close to Islam's;

2) In its geopolitical approach, the NAI does not attempt in any way to hinder the Islamic expansion, but, on the contrary, to facilitate the Islamisation of Europe.

In fact, the love which these intellectuals feel for Islam is not merely motivated by 'Islam' itself (a religion that even converts know little about), but also by anti-Judaism and a visceral and unfounded anti-American attitude.

The deception practiced by the Islamophilic milieu lies of course in the fact that, using a most scandalous type of historical manipulation, it claims that an alliance between Europe, the Third World and Islam against the Great Satan is absolutely indispensable. There is an allegedly profound affinity between the European continent and the Muslim-Arab world. This viewpoint is untenable and founded upon a blatant disregard for the following facts:

1) Ever since the 8th century, the relations between the above-mentioned world and Europe have always been sanguinary and conflictual. Islam has always acted as the aggressor (the Muslim invasion of Spain, the events in the Balkans, 800 years of bloody pirate raids, etc.). All Europeans have ever done is defend themselves. As for European colonialism, it was beneficial to the Muslim civilisation and a grave charitable mistake on our part. There is no need for me to demonstrate the obvious.

2) Islam's primary ambition is the conquest of Europe. In order to achieve this, the Muslims are willing to attune their efforts with those of the US. Islam will never accept a Euro-Arab alliance and scornfully mocks those brownnosing Europeans who swallow their Arab-Islamic friends' sermons whole, as these sermons only apply to those who abide by them.

3) Allow me to emphasise it all once again: *the adoption of an 'Arab policy' makes no sense from the European perspective*, since Europe does not stand to gain anything from such an approach, as the latter could only lead to problems. The only sensible anthropological and geopolitical attitude is one of armed peace, of a reciprocal exchange from a distance. As far as their oil is concerned, Muslim-Arabs have no other option but to sell it to us, and even if they did not, the Russian reserves are probably the largest anyway, not to mention the extensive and gradually indispensable use of EPR (third generation) nuclear reactors. Techno-scientific alliances, you say? We do not stand to gain anything from those. A military alliance? What a joke. And why should we ever involve ourselves in the

Israeli-Palestinian conflict? Let the Americans face this gruelling task. Our great Euro-Siberian entity must cultivate power neutrality (in this respect, Robert Steuckers used the term *'gigantic hedge-hog'*) and only show interest in reaching a friendly agreement with China and India, the rapidly growing colossi which must be taken more seriously than the 'Arab world', 'Muslim countries' or, worse, Black Africa. For despite their respective demographic growth, all three are doomed to remain pygmies in terms of techno-scientific achievements and strategic capacities.

It would be a fatal mistake for anyone to assume that we could ever counter American hegemony by forming alliances with the above-mentioned ensembles. It is a worldview worthy of philosophers and 'cultivated minds' that prefer abstract ideas to specific facts.

C. The Pest or the Flu?

One must be entirely blind, stupid or 'intellectual' (or perhaps even open to bribery) to believe that America embodies a greater threat to our specific European identity and integrity than the colonisation that afflicts our continent and is conducted by the Third World and Islam. In France, we witnessed the 'anti-war coalition' marching in the streets, bringing together Muslim Imams and their herds (shouting 'Allahu Akbar' and deploying Arab banners), pro-immigrant Trotskyites from the Leftist galaxy, undocumented migrants (who take advantage of every opportunity), neo-Stalinian syndicalists, 'alter-globalists', and many others. From our European perspective, the worst possible consequence of American neo-imperialism lies in the reinforcement of alleged Islamic martyrdom and the strengthening of pro-immigration Leftism. Since our intellectuals are essentially incapable of choosing a third path (one that is *equally* opposed to Islam, immigration and the American policy, and in favour of Europe), the ridiculous American administration has, as a result of its military campaign in

Iraq, managed to turn anti-Americanism, Islamophilia and Third-Worldism into dominant (and related) ideologies.

For there is something suspicious about this generalised anti-American coalition. In no way were those who demonstrated against the war in Iraq protesting against anti-European American imperialism, nor were they supporting the creation of a European power. They were definitely not in favour of increasing our assertiveness in the face of our overseas adversary and of setting European re-conquest into motion. What they supported was actually 'the oppressed Third World' and an Islam that displays great skill in manipulating them, thus granting our real enemy their support. They are therefore simultaneous accomplices of our American rival and our Islamic-Third-Worldist enemy, which is quite a feat.

***

Should we not consider the Arabisation and Africanisation of France a positive, a counterweight to the American television series that ravage our very souls? Since American soap operas rob us of our identity, doesn't the dialogical complexity that stems from the presence of the Third-World on our soil actually restore it? What matters in the end is that mass immigration, whose general consequences are favourable, forces us to question the metaphysics of subjectivity.

Such is the rigmarole that typifies collaborators, comprising an alliance of Leftists and neo-Leftists. They bemoan Islamophobia as the most severe of all ailments! Because one encounters it everywhere, right? What does it matter that the French state openly supports Islam and rolls out the red carpet for the Muslims to use by allowing the fundamentalist UOIF (Union of the Islamic Organisations of France) to take charge of Muslim institutional representation in France… Such is their utter stupidity.

***

Although I am well aware of the fact that it is apparently very difficult, what I would like people to understand is that the most urgent, absolute and lethal threat to Europe is not embodied by American imperialism (which I have always strongly resisted), but by our sub-replacement fertility and the invasion afflicting our continent. This invasion at the hands of Third-World migrants is obviously our own fault, for in no way could American imperialism be blamed for this deadly phenomenon, and neither could 'liberalism', since it is European Social-Democratic statism, and not the business community, that fuels the Third World suction pump.

Regardless of America's blatant imperialistic aspirations, any desire to turn it into the source of all our ailments relates to sheer intellectual temptation in which one readily absolves himself of any and all responsibility. It also constitutes an avoidance strategy. So as not to be held legally accountable for their actions, which is of course always the aim, some identify the US as Europe's absolute foe, thus avoiding the topic of the real invasion that threatens our continent. One does not run any risk by writing '*US go home*' on walls. In our republican and 'secular' country, however, one may well, for instance, be imprisoned or fined for having written 'Islam go home'.

***

I gladly acknowledge Islam's grandeur, for it is a foe worthy of interest. Americanism, on the other hand, is not an enemy because it does not merit any attention and will collapse of its own accord as a result of its rootlessness. Koranic schools are far more dangerous than American soap operas, or those propaganda shows that are broadcasted by various Islamist channels and watched all over France.

Islamic terrorism bears no relevance to the fate of the Palestinians. The advocates of hysterical anti-Americanism claim that the primary and unique cause behind Islamic terrorism lies in the fate suffered by the Palestinian people at the hands of the Jewish state and America's open support of Israel. According to them, Islam would otherwise be perfectly pacifistic, and we would face neither terrorism, nor violence.

This viewpoint is completely contradicted by both historical facts and current affairs. In Nigeria, the Sudan, Indonesia, and many other places, the exactions and terrorist acts perpetrated by the Islamists have nothing to do with the Israeli policy. The Islamic attacks conducted on European and American soil began long before the current Israeli government took power, and the new 'intifada' started well before American neoconservative imperialism ever emerged. Moreover, are Sharon and Bush to be held responsible for the acts of piracy and various atrocities committed by Barbary pirates against Europe for ten whole centuries, the conquest of Constantinople or the besieging of Vienna at the hands of the Ottomans?

Enough with this nonsense. I definitely do not sympathise with either of the above-mentioned political leaders, but anyone convinced that Bush and Sharon have somehow caused Islamist terrorism is clearly delirious. Admittedly, their respective policies do foment the latter. However, we can all rely on Islamism to use every conceivable and possible pretext to have its *mujahideen* plant bombs. Islam's inherent logic aims to expand the *Dar-al-Harb* (literally 'the abode of war') to include all countries ruled either by the infidels or by renegade Muslims, using all available means and resorting to every possible justification along the way. Islam actually presents its aggressions as acts of self-defence, as demonstrated by Islamologist Christian Marot in *Europe in the Face of Islam* (Eurasia editions, 2003).

Even if the state of Israel were to yield or collapse at some point, and even if the USA kept a low profile and readopted Jimmy Carter's moralising and crypto-Leftist doctrine, Islam would, regardless of circumstance, still not lay down its weapons, for it possesses its own internal dynamic of conquest, namely the *jihad*. It would still aim to conquer Europe and then subdue the entire world using every imaginable means, while resorting to its battalions of bleating useful idiots comprised of European or American converts and hysterical anti-American Islamophiles or Palestinophiles (belonging to both the Right and the Left).

***

Seriously now, what is more of a threat to our French and European identity? Hollywood or an ever flowing migratory tap? The American neoconservative infringement to international law during the invasion of Iraq or the violation of the right to asylum by the hundreds of thousands of fake refugees that come to Europe, 80 % of whom are Muslims? The American administration's vague threats of industrial and commercial retaliation against France or the insults targeting our country and the visa-related blackmail at the hands of the Algerian authorities? The headway made by British and American English in international seminars or the demands to make Arabic the fourth national language in Belgium? The girls dressed in T-shirts and jeans or those veiled, shrouded women? The technological and economic war waged against us by America or the birth-rate war launched by a conquering Third World on our own soil? The American attacks against our European cutting-edge industry or the destruction afflicting our domestic wealth as a result of the massive costs of untamed immigration? And so on, and so forth.

Admittedly, the future impact of *both* these kindred threats is very real indeed, but one must be utterly blind and succumb to ideological dogma to believe that we are dealing with a zero-sum equation and that the first menace could ever be equal to the second; for the former only results in illness, while the latter remains fatal.

It is not the Americans who are the reason for Europe's drowning, but the European political caste whose members have, for the past thirty years, been gleefully orchestrating our ethnocide. Who is responsible for the daily insecurity burdening our people, the collapse of our national education system and our sub-replacement fertility? The Americans? Who are the ones who cost France several billion Euros spent on the 'social curing' of criminality, civil inclusion, reinsertion, unrestricted aid, urban policies, etc.? The CIA, perhaps? The inability to distinguish a foe from an adversary and rival or absolute danger from temporary peril is truly a flaw that is exclusive to French intellectuals, who have always been characterised by their contempt for reality: let us not forget that they once embraced Stalinism.

Who is now wreaking insecurity and terror upon our cities and French countryside? American and Anglo-Saxon tourists, perhaps? Who is primarily accountable for the unemployment rates in France, Belgium and Germany? American multinational corporations, fiscalism, bureaucracy and anti-entrepreneurial regulation policies? Who prohibits France, Germany, Italy and Spain from endowing themselves with a reasonable defence capacity and constructing an autonomous and powerful armament industry in conjunction with Russia? Is it the pressure exerted by America, or rather the scornful attitude of European politicians towards all aspects of European defence (whose budget is considered an 'adjustment variable') and industry? I mean, seriously, one must be willing to take responsibility for their own actions before blaming others.

CHAPTER VII

OHAA or Obsessive and Hysterical Anti-Americanism

A. A Schizophrenic Line of Thought

OHAA is a neurosis that leads those afflicted to consider America to be our main foe and invader, as a result of their panicky fear of designating the real threat, namely our continent's genuine and massive invasion at the hands of the Third World and Islam. America is thus guilty by substitution. The Americans (along with Zionism and Capitalism) are at fault on all levels; Europe, on the other hand, is not to be blamed or held responsible in any way. We are therefore witnessing the intentional misidentification of the actual source of danger in various intellectual analyses, just as a patient chooses to disguise the cause of his affliction. And should you point this out to these advocates of Manichean thought, you would immediately be accused of being an 'Americanist' or a 'Zionist', which adds insult to injury. 'You see, ladies and gentlemen, the ailments that afflict us are due to a far more complicated reason than you think. Appearances are deceiving. In no way does the decline of our national education and our youth's cultural level stem from post-68 laxity and the impact of mass immigration on our school system, for it is clearly due to the debilitating impact of American soap operas. And as for endemic unemployment, it is not fiscalism, social statism, nor the reduction of our working hours

134

that have increased its rate; the real culprit is capitalistic dictatorship, whose mastermind and secret puppet master divides his activities between Wall Street and the Federal Reserve Bank. Just like those poor peoples in the Third World and the oppressed Muslims, we too, ladies and gentlemen, are being subjected to the effects of American imperialism'.

***

Those who direct their hysterical criticism at the USA render themselves inefficient by targeting America with their *reductio ad hitlerum* and contrasting the American attitude with their own naïve, irenic, pacifistic, judicial, moralistic and ultimately unrealistic notion of both political philosophy and the relations between different nations. This does not come as a surprise in the case of the Leftist adepts of OHAA, who, stupidly and mechanically, reiterate the nonsense professed by Western Marxism. It is, however, surprising coming from the (admittedly more extremist) followers of OHAA who belong to the 'New' Right. Their hateful demonisation of America, which is seen as an omnipotent Great Satan, completely contradicts their self-proclaimed philosophy that rejects anathema and binary thought and claims to favour the values of 'pagan' polytheism over those of 'precluding monotheistic systems'. This noteworthy contradiction cannot be accounted for solely through this thought current's intellectual deterioration, one that has seen it plummet from creative analysis to the level of invectives and dogmatic slogans (going as far as to implicitly call for terrorist strikes against the US). In actual fact, it is also due to a fascinated alignment with Islam.

***

In order to legitimise their OHAA, these boisterous preachers have openly chosen to disprove their own slogan of 'defending the European civilisation'. What they rather strive for is the latter's betrayal. By fully siding with the Left's multiracial notion of 'European identity' and thus completely disfiguring it (for they have labelled impossible and unrealistic the reversal of the migration tide), they lack the harsh (and cowardly) words to castigate the concept of a 'White Europe', meaning that of an ethnocentric and bio-culturally homogeneous continent. They indulge in Arabolatry, Africanolatry and Islamophilia, following the same ideological path as Ras L'Front and SCALP and resorting to foolish predictions regarding the 'empire' that a new, multi-ethnic Europe is said to embody. They do so without any consideration for demographic facts or historical experience, for the intellectuals that live on their own neo-Leftist planet never analyse, argue or ponder issues; they simply 'believe'.

***

These people have pulled off a perfect *reversal*, the feat of obliviating their own past and aligning themselves with the vulgate: they thus simultaneously espouse Third-Worldism, Islamism and OHAA, hating the dominative White Americans (the WASPs), who, in accordance with isochronal Marxist dogmatism, serve as the scapegoat for all the ailments that torment poor countries. In this process, however, they have so far failed to comprehend that American ideology, especially that of the NAI, is entirely multiracial and communitarian and therefore in harmony with their new convictions.

The extraordinary paradox that characterises these hysterical anti-Americanists (regardless of whether they belong to the traditional Left or the neo-Left, as the line that separates the two is growing ever thinner these days) is that they advocate the very same social philosophy and the exact same ideals as the neoconservative American administration that currently holds the reins of power, including multiracialism, the rejection of an ethnically homogeneous Europe, a desire to turn our continent into a pacifistic and counterproductive federation, a belief in the possible emergence of a democratic Islam, a Manichean worldview, the advocacy of violence against the Evil ones, etc.

***

In both its Left-oriented and Right-oriented form, OHAA thus plays a cunning role, namely that of leading Europe towards forgetting the identity of its *real* foes (meaning that of its invaders, colonisers and domestic collaborators), and it does so by designating America and those abominable Zionists as 'Europe's Absolute Enemies'. A mixture of spontaneous emotionality and intellectualism, OHAA does not, however, burden itself with anything specific or factual, for the latter is a source of major inconvenience to all those who are prone to devising their own delusions.

By decreeing America to be our sole enemy and the only threat to our continent, OHAA thus legitimises the notion of an Islamised and Third-Worldised Europe. Let us all unite against *Uncle Sam*! The ethnic kinship between White America and Europe is simply trampled underfoot. This kinship is so obvious that mentioning it becomes rude in the eyes of these truth defilers. They proceed to invent some fictitious 'solidarity' between Europe and the Muslim-Arab world (a world whose presence is already greatly felt on our continent, through demographic alteration and threats) against the fire-breathing American hydra. They also claim that Islamophobia reigns supreme when, in actual fact, it is Islamophilia and Arabophilia that have, during the past decades, dominated the sphere of political correctness and our country's entire political policy.

The paradigm is that of a multi-ethnic Europe rising up against America; this is of a confounding stupidity, since what the American administration strives to achieve is precisely to 'multiracialise' and Islamise Europe so as to weaken and dismantle it.

On the contrary, it is only a united Europe, deeply rooted in its ancestral, ethnic and cultural homogeneity and driven by its own will to power (and the effective means to implement the latter), that could manage to efficiently oppose its American *rival and adversary*.

A farcical and disfigured Europe that has allied itself with its worst enemies as a result of the gravest possible confusion between the *echtros* and the *polemos*, the *inimicus* and the *hostis*, meaning its enemy and adversary, is unacceptable. Among anti-American Leftists, who have all displayed great skill in exploiting this sentiment, this scheme is twisted, yet coherent. Their ultimate aim lies in the destruction of our European identity. On the other hand, their anti-Americanism is only a temporary political means, since they could still adopt the cosmopolitan American model and return to being pro-American at the first possible opportunity (should the Democrats reclaim power, for instance).

As for those Right-oriented intellectuals whose OHAA affliction constitutes a clinical case, they are drifting away uncontrollably, even more so than in the distant past when they cynically betrayed our European Identitarian values (this behaviour can, in fact, be partly explained by Stockholm Syndrome, which drives people to submit to their likely future masters). They have thus embraced a complete policy reversal. It is no longer cunning that accounts for their OHAA, but their confounding naivety. When the OHAA-stricken Left proceeds to ally itself with the invaders, in no way does it betray its own principles, but merely dresses them up in a highly clever fashion. By contrast, the Rightists that have been afflicted with OHAA truly play the role of useful idiots whose anti-American hatred truly requires psychiatric treatment.

It should also be noted that OHAA is far more unbridled, heinous, frenzied and frustrated among Rightists than among Leftists, who remain more skilful than their counterparts. In the eyes of those Rightists, *anything* remotely American (jeans, TV series, music rhythms, sodas, you name it) is automatically diabolical, in accordance with an anathemising and infantilising logic fraught with simplism, dualism and intolerance, thus mirroring an Islam that fascinates them, just like sparrows are fascinated by serpents. In several ways, the standpoints embraced by these Right-oriented intellectuals relate to profound ideological schizophrenia, a condition which they must be severely stricken with and which, to a great extent, accounts for their gradual loss of public support.

***

It goes without saying that OHAA and its invectives represent an intense factor which contributes to the reinforcement of American neo-imperialism. Nothing pleases the latter more than the sight of its European enemies succumbing to excess and extremism[6].

I am also open to the idea that those espousing OHAA not only among Leftists, but particularly within the extreme Right spectrum, are actually being manipulated (at the very least) by American secret services, whose ingeniousness is truly monumental. It would not come as a surprise to me if they had actually been infiltrated by the latter. For nothing could be more exhilarating for the CIA receiver located at the Place de la Concorde than witnessing these attention-seeking pen pushers, whose entire lives have been compromised by a vilified past, spew forth a torrent of insults and call for terrorist acts against America, while abstaining from any serious, composed and argument-based anti-American criticism and counteroffensive. Instead, they advocate an eco-pacifistic, ethno-pluralistic, socially utopian and Islamophilic model for our continent and never declare themselves in favour of a European superpower. As for Bové and the neo-Lefitsts, they strive for the very same goal. Extremist anti-American positions: this is precisely what the CIA's propaganda services long for. What they dread, on the other hand, are genuine *radical* standpoints.

***

Indeed, the evidence that supports the above-mentioned statements stems from the fact that OHAA lacks the ability to target the NAI with any sort of criticism on the economic and technological level (a topic that is covered in this book), although such critique is crucial for Europe's independence. The focus is always on the NAI's purely military aspect, as well as on insulting G. W. Bush for his mental poverty and warmongering frenzy, yet one hardly mentions, if at all, America's

---

6   TN: Faye suddenly resorts to the word 'enemies' instead of 'rivals', but this definitely due to his desire to emphasise the extremeness that characterises OHAA.

massive and secret endeavour to conquer the world through techno-economic means. Any criticism is restricted to bombardment issues and the implantation of McDonald's on European soil. The USA is only criticised when it lashes out at Third-World Muslim countries, but never for its desire to destroy Europe's economic power. In short, OHAA only acts as an objective means towards creating an Islamic and Third-World European continent and does not reflect any will to enable Europe's victorious emergence from its global rivalry with America.

B. The 'Uncle Sam' Myth

Anti-American passions are precisely what any consistent opposition to Americanism must be careful to avoid. Passion is always harmful to political judgement. Let us consider Islam, for instance: it is *the* doctrine of conquest, and yet it is perfectly able to resort to calculating behaviour and stone-cold hypocrisy when the balance of power is not in its favour (*Dar al-Sulh*).

Anti-Americanism is synonymous with overestimating America (in line with 19th century myths), thus unknowingly and unintentionally transforming the US into a promised land. When reading the countless diatribes expressed by French anti-American intellectuals, for example, one is not only struck by the latter's profound ignorance of what America is actually like (they are only familiar with New York and, to some extent, Los Angeles, neither of which mirror America's essence), but also by their upturned and almost morbid fascination for a deeply detested (and therefore somehow adored) American 'anti-model' (which is still basically a model). They bestow upon the latter a mischievous omnipotence that is completely fictional. Anti-American intellectuals invariably succumb to the 'Uncle Sam' founding myth, centred around his tutelary power that allegedly governs the world. The sole difference is that instead of depicting him as the Pope, one renders him the Anti-Pope, and instead of regarding him as the messiah, one considers him the Antichrist, which, in the end, amounts to the absolute same thing.

***

Just like Americanophobes, the Americanophiles belonging to the ruling French intellectual caste set America apart from all countries by putting it on a pedestal and adorning it with peacock feathers. Through their anti-American romanticism, which keeps them completely disconnected from reality, Americanophobic theoreticians acknowledge their Americanomania, just like obsessional Judeophobes are essentially Judeophiles. They proceed to criticise a mythical America, this omnipotent Satan against whom only the most desperate terrorist acts come into consideration, targeting it with invectives. These people cannot conceive of the world *without* America and thus render it a great service. For nothing destabilises American minds more than the display of *indifference* or the expression of cold and collected judgement towards the US. This is because the American mentality requires either love or hate and cannot bear the horror of a truthful assessment. These boisterous Americanophobes would cause their hated/cherished enemy far more grief if they placidly embraced various programmes contributing to Europe's rising power, thus following the Chinese example...

C. The Worshippers of 9/11

The 9/11 attacks triggered endless outbursts of joy in OHAA milieus, whose central argument was the following: in the name of the Greater Good, the USA had been bombarding the world for decades on end, but now, at long last, America itself has become the target of terroristic bombardment. The Americans were asking for it. Well done! They got what they deserved! This form of dialectics is rather poor and, as is always the case with OHAA, has more to do with passion than reason.

***

In his work entitled *Understanding the Bombardment of New York*, Lyons-based neo-Leftist 'academic' Jacques Marlaud turns himself into an indulgent commentator on the massive New York attacks. By implicitly approving of the latter's main pretexts (represented by Islamic terrorism), the author makes an unshakable argument in favour of American imperialism. This argumentation follows the same (yet less severe and pathological) line of reasoning adopted by Alain de Benoist in the aftermath of the military invasion against Iraq when he called for anti-American attacks, a topic that is covered elsewhere.

Even the most radical imams are cautious not to fall into such a trap, for everyone is well aware of the fact that, in civilian terms, to 'understand' someone is to absolve them. The *cowardliness* of such standpoints far outweighs their counter-productivity. What would these gentlemen say if their close ones lost their lives in an Islamic attack? In truth, never would these slipper-wearing imprecators, who, with a cat in their lap, hurl their anathemas at the world with utter impunity by means of a computer keyboard, have ever dared profess an ounce of such hatred against our Islamic and Third World conquerors. One has to vent their frustrations somehow, right?

There are, however, more extreme cases in the subservient 'useful idiot' category. I am obviously referring to those 'European nationalists' who have chosen to convert to Islam. A textbook case of such psycho-pathological affliction is embodied by a certain Tahir de la Nive, who preaches 'Euro-Islamism' and has close ties to the 'New' Right. He is the author of an utterly astounding book that explains to the world how Islam actually represents both Europe's and America's salvation, regardless of the fact that the latter are its worst enemies. This ethno-masochistic theory is quite commonplace in the above-mentioned milieus. In its effort to legitimise its disregard for all rules, the NAI is in dire need of such overzealous, lunatic opinions.

***

Only the weak would express their resentment in such a manner. Even if the US Air Force is indeed guilty of numerous unforgivable acts (and yet, it is far from being alone in this respect, since the Dresden war crime was actually perpetrated by Churchill's RAF), this cannot serve as an excuse for anyone to rejoice at the demise of thousands of innocent people, whether the latter are 'American' or not. The most comical, extraordinary and contradictory element, however, is that in France itself, hysterical anti-Americanists *simultaneously* espoused the following positions, neither of which is compatible with the other:

1) The 9/11 attacks were fomented, or at least authorised, by the CIA in cooperation with the Mossad so as to create a pretext for an offensive against the Muslim world, a world that threatens the existence of Israel.

2) We all rejoice at the sight of the terrorist attacks that have stricken the very core of our detested America.

These people had better make up their mind…

***

Adopting a position in which one feels joy at the thought of the people who met an untimely death in the World Trade Center or a standpoint where one calls for anti-American attacks betrays a lack of honour that is foreign to our traditions. Some French intellectuals have chosen to side with barbary, with the worst kind of comfortable, barbaric behaviour, just as they once did when they glorified Stalin and Aragon, our poet, dedicated entire verses to Stalinian crimes. Why have these overzealous individuals not come forward and volunteered to act as human targets (human 'shields', so to speak) in both Bosnia and Iraq? American pacifists do have such courage, at least. There is a detestable and ridiculous aspect to all those calls for murder and violence uttered by bearded living-room intellectuals who, having been exempt from military service, have never fired a weapon, been shot at, nor even heard a gun being discharged in their entire lives. They would never dare use the underground at one a.m., nor at four in the afternoon, for that matter; the only underground line that they would travel on in the summer is the first, which is only used to transport harmless American tourists to their destinations.

***

OHAA partisans are mostly recruited among the supporters of Europe's Islamisation, which is seen as 'a solution to our decadence' and an opportunity for us to 'rely upon Tradition'. With regard to this particular level of mental delirium, it is the Italian, neo-fascist intellectuals who admire both Evola and Guénon that are truly very gifted. It must be said that there is a certain Italian intelligentsia that manifests a bizarre penchant for a contrived line of thought which can viewed as a form of 'mental falsehood'. The latter can prove anything on the basis of nothing, covering its claims with the verbose and slimy coating of prosodic expression, which represents an equally severe flaw as the dogmatic and vindicating fury that characterises its friends among the ranks of the Parisian intelligentsia. Neo-fascist Claudio Mutti, a man who converted to Islam and whose words always leave us wondering whether his statements are to be understood as a *joke*, did not hesitate to write the following:

> During his triumphant visit to Libya, Benito Mussolini paid homage at the grave of one of the Holy Prophet's Companions [sic] and brandished the Sword of Islam. [...] Meanwhile, in Berlin, where the Palestinian flag was the only one to have the privilege to float alongside the Reich's, chancellor Adolf Hitler favoured people's conversion to Islam and declared: "the only ones who I consider to be trustworthy are the Muslims". (Taken from *Uncle Sam's Crusaders* by Tahir de la Nive.)

Lo and behold — even such stupidities can be expressed through erudite terms…

This utterly delirious opinion does not, of course, grant the current state of affairs (namely the dramatic Islamic chokehold smothering

Europe) any attention. It contents itself with intellectual masturbation around Hitler's and Mussolini's allegedly close friendship with the Muslims. 'Since Hitler fought against both America and the Jews, this implies that…', and other such deliria. Elementary, my dear Watson.

***

It is highly likely that a certain number of extreme Left and far Right milieus, ranging from isolated individuals and small groupings to structured associations, have actually fallen under the simultaneous influence of the American secret services and that of the Islamists. Indeed, the extremism displayed by OHAA serves both their interests: in the case of the former, the reason is that such extremism robs intelligent and efficient anti-Americanism of all credibility; as for Islamists, they approve of it because it allows them to divert people's attention away from Europe's Islamisation and to establish the fallacious notion of a 'Euro-Arab' or Euro-Islamic resistance front struggling against the USA. It is all too easy for manipulators or professional provocateurs to infiltrate diverse movements or magazines and 'arouse' the managerial staff's passions, since the latter are ever prone to naivety and romantic musings. As soon as one becomes aware of the pronounced candour and adultescence afflicting some intellectuals, such schemes no longer seem difficult to manage. In the cheapest possible fashion, the pseudo-Identitarian followers of OHAA embrace rebellious and dissident posturing, never incurring any risk whatsoever. Nothing is more contempt-worthy than revolutionary theatrics. Instead of shouting out one's anger at the *real* invaders, which is too dangerous and risky an endeavour, one directs their attention towards America (and in correlation, towards the 'Zionists'), or refocuses on abstract entities with intricate denominations, including 'utilitarianism', 'major corporations', 'global mercantilism', etc. Such is the behaviour adhered to by the paleo-Marxists of the MAUSS, whose texts require a French intellectualistic dictionary of jargon so as to be read.

OHAA thus functions as a means for people to *vent their frustrations*. Dissatisfied with the world they live in and frustrated by the lack of recognition they receive from a System that scorns them, second-rate intellectuals (who are all too frightened to tackle genuine threats and ever conditioned by the notion of a unique, anti-racist and pro-Third World line of thought) use anti-American hatred as a sort of risk-free emotional outlet.

How fortunate it is then that the (blatantly) imbecilic Bush has chosen to lash out at the Arab world! Low-rate intellectuals will thus find themselves in a better position to indulge in their favourite activity: the defence of the oppressed (the Third World, the Palestinians, and so on). Let us be clear in this regard: the French version of OHAA is accounted for by a fear of Arabs and Islam, as well as by the desire to adopt an attitude of fake rebellion. We must gain those people's favour, you see. For it is always preferable to side with the future (supposed) victors. Just like those young European girls who put on the Islamic veil in order to protect themselves against harassment in their own neighbourhood, proletarianised intellectuals and Trotskyite 'welfare workers' stomp their feet in indignation in the face of those who would persecute poor countries, protesting against the South's contemptible exploiters and tormentors. The old leitmotiv proposed by the Leftist vulgate never ceases to fascinate the Parisian Right.

***

Upon seeing anti-American protesters marching through the French streets with Arab flags in their hands, one can only wonder who the real invaders actually are. What is more humiliating for a Frenchman — to watch as masses of demonstrators, all of whom are, at heart, utterly indifferent to the French and European identity, flaunt their Islamic banners across our boulevards, or to witness a parade of American and British flags (which has never happened, mind you)?

Never would those boisterous anti-Americans, who claim to be 'Identitarian', dare answer such a question.

D. OHAA, the Third World's Ally

OHAA and its intellectual supporters are not as focused on resist-ing the American chokehold as on exploiting anti-Americanism to defend their cherished Third World. It is also obvious that, as part of the school disciplines that aim to create 'cultural awareness', French children are to familiarise themselves with African tales, Arabian mu-sic, the Thousand and One Nights, and the magnificent sonorities of Bwadambas and Tam-Tams, rather than with Disney nonsense such as Donald Duck, Mickey Mouse, Snow White, Sleeping Beauty and the Three Little Piggies (those impure animals). As understood by our suburban 'youths', America's sole positive aspect is not to be found in those repressive conservative milieus whose suit and tie-wearing members scream in outrage the moment a youth lights up a joint and which embody the heinously White, racist *establishment*; instead, it lies in Black people's sublime cultural attitude, with its hip-hop music, rap tunes and fascination for Islam, which are of course a sign of glori-ous rebellion.

I would obviously be happier if school children were introduced to the various native European tales and legends extending from the days of Antiquity. Should this never actually take place, it would, by any standards, be preferable to tell our children of the conquest of the American West, the adventures of Davy Crockett among the Indians, and the friendship of Tom Jeffords and Cochise, rather than to overwhelm them, deracinate them and burden them with guilt by introducing them to Third World popular cultures, especially those of Black Africa and the Arab world. Why? Because lurking behind the pseudo-imperative of 'familiarising our children with other cultures', one finds a tenacious desire to inferiorise European and White cultures to the benefit of the peoples that inhabit the South.

By exaggerating the Americanisation afflicting our European societies and granting it delirious proportions, OHAA allows people to forget, obliterate and turn a blind eye not only to our continent's rampant Third-Worldisation and Islamisation, but also to interbreeding. 'Goodness Gracious! A MacDonald's has just opened in the Beaucaire or Tarascon area! We must mobilise immediately! Our heritage is being disfigured!' What they all seem to be forgetting is that these two ancient communes, located in Occitania, are becoming increasingly similar to North African villages.

The insurmountable contradiction pervading OHAA lies in its claim that, while welcoming Europe's Arabisation and Islamisation in the face of our continent's Americanisation and its submission to the Jewish chokehold, it simultaneously denounces the latter as being the main causes behind the Arabisation, Islamisation and Third-Worldisation afflicting Europe! On the one hand, they assert that our Arabisation and Islamisation are favourable developments that protect us against those Zionistic and American monsters, but on the other, they state that our disastrous Arabisation and Islamisation is a tragedy orchestrated by those cunning Judeo-Americans. So which is it ?

***

Is it the USA or Europe that is responsible for our immigration issues? OHAA has a completely demobilising effect and absolves us from any responsibility: we are not accountable for anything and it is America that, globally speaking, is the real culprit. We are thus mere victims, meaning utterly powerless. As stated by Alain Laurent:

> Anti-Americanism is essentially a full-scale ideological passion that has now turned into pathological obsession. Whatever they do or fail to do, and regardless of whether they are isolationists or interventionists, it is the Americans who are always in the wrong, remaining ever guilty and monstrous. They have thus become a globalised scapegoat upon which one can heinously project any and all responsibility for one's own failures and frustrated resentment; America is the "Great Satan" and the target of ritualistic public execration. (*Les 4 Vérités* weekly, 22/03/2003.)

OHAA relies on Europe's mental Third-Worldisation: just as Africans are presented by these anti-American hysterics as the unfortunate and blameless victims of horrendous 'neo-colonialism' (which, as demon-strated by Bernard Lugan, is but a figment of people's imagination), so are Europeans depicted as the innocent victims of the diabolical 'Uncle Sam', the almighty and Machiavellian 'Yankee'.

Nowadays, this mental disorder prospers among an entire popula-tion of proletarian intellectuals who hold a fascination for Islam and its 'Tradition'. Unable to find their own European roots, they thus seek out the antidotes to Americanism elsewhere.

***

The radical opposition between the US and Europe is considered irreconcilable, global, absolute and final, while Islam and the entire Third World are unrealistically displayed as our continent's friends, when, in actual fact, this Muslim-Arab civilisation has, ever since the 8th century, never ceased to clash with ours. Our conflicts have always been sanguinary; its worldview, mentalities and way of life are utterly incompatible with ours, all the way to the most intimate details; and it has initiated its third major historical offensive against Europe by means of the current colonisation effort known as 'immigration'. The French intellectuals who preached of a Soviet-Stalinist paradise back in the 1950s immediately spring to mind. Reality is of no interest to them; the only thing that holds their attention is fanaticised ideology and an imprecatory line of thought based on slogans, insults, condem-nations and anathemas.

***

In my view, Europeans will, depending on the circumstances, be able to form temporary alliances with their adversary and rival, namely their American prodigal son. However, the distance and structural diver-gences that separate us from the Muslim-Arab world are too ancient and too profound for us to even ponder the slightest cordial agree-ment. Our balance of power and extremely distrustful relationship is bound to be permanent. Islam's ever stronger presence on European soil acts as the counterpoint to the American strategic and cultural chokehold, yet turns out to be far graver.

Due to their relative civilisational proximity and their common ethnic basis, the opposition between the USA and Europe could never, in fact, take on the shape of definitive estrangement. One would have to be narrowly dogmatic and lack any and all common sense to deny this fact. American and European economic and cultural interests are highly divergent as a result of the Atlantic barrier's geopolitical impact, as this ocean embodies, according to Mary Kaldor's analyses, a border rather than a point of contact. However, European and Muslim-Arab interests are even more divergent than that. In this regard, I have always been critical of any notion of Occident, preferring to counter it with that of Europe and, more recently, that of Euro-Siberia (i.e. the ethno-geographical union of Europe and Russia). The USA has been waging an economic and cultural war against us, which is all too logical from a historical perspective. All that is left for us to do is resist it and retaliate, an attitude that Europeans have often been capable of.

A word of clarification: any criticism targeting the USA, the NAI, globalism and ultra-liberalism can only be taken seriously if it originates from the bold milieus which display equal courage in braving the principal danger that threatens Europe, namely massive ethno-cultural submersion.

E. The Great Satan

OHAA feeds on the (incidentally very biblical and highly American) idea that the USA embraces a satanic sort of international behaviour; that, ever since Hiroshima, its war crimes have equalled Stalin's; that its 'democracy' is but a plutocratic sort of totalitarianism which, although *softer*, is comparable to Saddam Hussein's late regime; and that the mass subculture that the Americans have been flooding the world with mirrors George Orwell's descriptions in *1984*. On the basis of these alleged historical facts, one thus proceeds to 'satanise' America, even if it is equally possible to demonise any other country or civilisation.

***

In order to demonise the USA, OHAA makes use of the cheap argument surrounding the genocide of American Indians and Black slavery, as if the practice of genocide were specific to the American republic. What about the Spanish genocidal actions against Native Americans? Or the Armenian genocide? Or the 'blood belt' that has surrounded the Muslim expansion ever since the birth of Islam? Or the slavery which has been practiced in Africa and the Middle-East for a thousand years? I could go on and on. Genocidal acts are consubstantial with human history. By the way, the 'genocide' of American Indians (which has largely been blown out of proportions) was conducted by European immigrants as part of a certain conquest phase and beyond any specifically American ideology. In the process, one omits to mention that Indian tribes resorted to abominable acts of retaliation and that the allegedly '*great* Native American civilisation' was often akin to sheer barbarism. The discourse which turns American Indians into victims is reminiscent of the statements made in connection to Black slavery, during which one selectively avoids identifying those truly responsible.

Do all those complaints made by OHAA supporters regarding the 'genocide of American Indians' not embody yet another means of burdening Whites with guilt and equating them to natural-born torturers? In no way is OHAA's purpose, therefore, to defend a European power against American Imperialism; in accordance with a highly skilful Trotskyite ambition, its actual aim is to deify all so-called coloured peoples and depict them as the victims of all those who are of European descent. What I should also specify at this stage is that there are many 'liberal' intellectuals in the US who act as willing accomplices in this ethno-masochistic disinformation campaign.

***

Despite its repetitive bombardments and relentless militarism, the USA has not displayed an overly murderous attitude compared to other world powers during the past 3000 years. It is thus simple-minded, senseless and counterproductive for anyone to found their anti-Americanism on an exclusively moralistic accusation that might easily backfire against those who utter it, regardless of whether they are of European, Arabian, Chinese, Russian, African or any other origin. It is likewise wrong, counterproductive and absolutely unreasonable to root one's anti-Americanism in the alleged 'domestic totalitarian-ism' of American society. Such convictions are mere intellectualistic daydreams and pure anti-sociology. Americanolatrists such as Guy Sorman and Jean-François Revel truly soar and revel[7] in such blunders and excesses. The same applies to all those who accuse the USA of 'cultural debility', basing their claims on all those American TV se-ries and talk shows, as well as on the cultural industry that America exports, which, admittedly, tends to lack quality (even if this is not always the case). But is there anything that prevents Europeans from outdoing their American rival? Do the popcorn munchers that attend baseball games define America? Is their intellectual level inferior to that of those superstitious and hysterical masses that embrace certain well-known religions?

***

OHAA stigmatises the US with enormous, satanic flaws, meaning that it *deifies* America. Unequalled in their debility, corruption and destruc-tiveness, Americans are thus always the masters and it is we who are all pitiful victims that cannot be held accountable for anything. One thus wallows in the position of 'intelligent slaves'. It is very difficult for those afflicted with OHAA to admit that people are unfortunately more attached to their European civilisational roots overseas than in Europe itself. There is nothing pleasant about this confession, yet it remains the truth. What those anti-Americans fail to explain is why

---

7   TN: Pardon the pun.

our European 'high culture' and legacy enjoy more support in overseas universities than within our French national education system.

The fact of depicting the Americans as being 'barbaric' by means of numerous incontestable facts and examples does not relate to historical or sociological objectivity, but to political or ideological passion. Due to the specifics, one loses sight of the overall picture. OHAA acts as a machine that leaves Europe homeless.

Whenever American bombs result in the deaths of Iraqi civilians or Tsahal[8] kill Palestinians, it all reflects the eternal law of war. I only speak out against American bombardments when they are directed against Europe, as was the case in Serbia. Those who defend Iraq are reminiscent of those who defended the Vietcong back in the 1960s. Why do they meddle in such things? The supporters of OHAA are not even driven by moral motivations, because if that were the case, they would also campaign against the violence perpetrated by the Chinese in Tibet or the countless killings witnessed in the 'blood belt' that spreads from Nigeria to Indonesia, surrounding the Islamic domain.

***

The American world power is hardly impressed by this sort of anti-Americanism, which, quite to the contrary, only serves to reinforce its own moralising arguments. The calls for murder and terrorist attacks uttered by irresponsible intellectuals who are fascinated by Bin Laden are a genuine boon for American propaganda. The latter can thus present anti-Americanism as an attitude reserved for psychopaths and extremists (as was the case during the desecration of military cemeteries). It would not come as a surprise to anyone if the desecrators of Anglo-Saxon graves (in Étaples, for instance) and those who print hateful and infantile anti-American 'communiqués' were given discreet support and 'encouragement' or simply manipulated by

8   TN: The Israeli Defence Forces.

specialised American secret services (attention-seeking and frustrated people tend to be the ideal puppets).

Another source of OHAA, especially in the extreme Right spectrum, lies in the vital need of a whole nebula of overexcited and sectarian units to be noticed (without great risk) by a System that practices a policy of silence and implements a complete *blackout* on all such activities. The headlong rush that leads to delirious anti-American imprecations is but a select means to ensure that people 'talk about' them. But how does one come across as being 'tough' without actually incurring any risk? By embracing OHAA, of course.

***

American neoconservative ideologists, Islamists and those who have surrendered to OHAA all abide by the same line of thought, one that was previously followed by communists: *Manicheanism*, meaning the embracement of a black-or-white worldview. The NAI identifies the Axis of Evil as its absolute enemy (instead of the former 'Empire of Evil'), whereas Islamists consider the Great Satan to be their foe, as do all their intellectualistic European friends. We thus have the pure and victimised on one side and the scoundrels on the other.

There is, however, a *compensation* phenomenon within the anti-Americanism adopted by those intellectuals who have been harassed, demonised through accusations of 'Fascism' and driven mad by this unfair ostracism, a phenomenon whose essence is almost psycho-analytical in nature. They thus feel compelled to identify a 'Fascism' of their own, an absolute 'Evil' that lies at the source of all ailments, so as to divert against others the opprobrium that they themselves have been subjected to. They could have obviously targeted Islam (as a kind of 'green Fascism'), which would not be a difficult endeavour when one examines its history, current practices, ideology and 'sacred' texts.

Yes, but the catch is that such a position would not be fashionable at this time, since this conquering Islam is looked upon favourably by the System. To attack the Muslim religion would be synonymous with sinking deep into the quicksand of 'racism', a suspicion that weighs heavily upon the shoulders of the unfortunate folk belonging to the neo-Leftist Parisian intelligentsia, despite the latter's constant and desperate efforts and its declarations of love towards the Third World. What is the solution, then? New Fascism must be embodied by America, namely White America, with its insolent, militaristic and selfish WASPs, considered the source of all earthly ailments. Our intellectuals thus define themselves as avengers, Don Quixotes, and the protectors of 'oppressed peoples' against the imperialistic hydra. 35 years have passed since the May '68 events, and yet nothing has changed.

***

There is a common factor that brings OHAA, the NIA and Islamists together: a binary worldview, including an Absolute, immutable and inhuman enemy that exists outside the boundaries of history. This foe's identity may be changeable, but the logic remains intact and mono-theistic. In a faithful imitation of Soviet propaganda and Khomeinist understanding, one thus considers the USA to be a sort of demonic Superman, wallowing in the humiliation that one suffers at the hands of this satanic America and never, of course, proposing any power policy to counter the latter. Such anathema-ridden (or rather *fatwa*-esque) thinking seldom offers any arguments: it remains vague, emotional and general, resorting to simpleminded images and formulas ('Down with MacDonald's!', 'Long live the oppressed Indians!', 'Death to Jeans and Rock music!', etc.). This logic displays a preference for slogans over analyses and disregards the real symptoms and causes of American dominance, namely our brain drain, bureaucracy, the rejection of any research or defence effort, and so on.

Rather than demonise the USA from an emotional perspective, one had better champion reason and thus remedy the real cause be-hind American hegemonic insolence: our European weakness. When faced with a void, America only reacts the way any other power would:

it simply fills it. If I were a member of Bush's neoconservative team, I would rejoice at the shape that European anti-Americanism has now taken, for it is vindictive, moral, accusatory, intellectual, impassioned and extremist. What Washington dreads most is *non-Americanism* and specific manifestations of power and independence on the part of European countries.

***

Beyond this desert-like analytical aridity, one reencounters the old mental dispositions that typify the French intellectual petty bourgeoisie and which the extreme Left has embraced as its own: resentment and anathema. There is nothing worse than the inability to hierarchise and the need to paint everyone with the same brush. Depicting the American culture as a sheer abomination and the peak of abjection, as initially done by de Montherlant (and subsequently by other less gifted authors), is the perfect example of an argument which, as a result of its own excesses and hysteria, simply destroys itself. In order to actually combat American mass culture, it is preferable to target it with a critique that is cold, argument-based, hate-free and devoid of ridiculous superlative statements, just like Walter Benjamin or Christopher Lash did back in the day. Unfortunately, critical analysis has been replaced by almost theological condemnations.

The absolute demonisation of America, as practiced by *Le Monde Diplomatique* through Ignacio Ramonet's repetitive editorials, has an aspect to it that is so utterly simplistic, fluid, obvious, mechanical, pre-arranged, acknowledged, automatic and mandatory that it all becomes tedious and lacks credibility. It is nothing short of pseudo-anti-Americanism, since all these self-declared anti-Americanists actually share in the *official cosmopolitanism* embraced by the puritanical and mercantile American republic.

***

Declaring oneself to be America's adversary, just as I have, frustrates American leaders far more that stomping about and anathemising the

US by labelling it one's *absolute enemy*, which is normal. Every major power (or any power at all, psychologically speaking) is far warier of serious and determined competitors who display moderation in their statements than of boisterous histrions whose hatred is merely a reflection of their own impotence. Likewise, what such powers dread most are all those who advocate a European power without succumbing to visceral anti-Americanism, in a display of utter indifference...

CHAPTER VIII

Non-Americanism

A. The Hazardous Demonisation of the US

The notion of *non-Americanism* is far more credible than that of anti-Americanism, because being opposed to something is actually synonymous with being in favour of it. It also implies one's refusal to define themselves in accordance with their own identity, displaying a preference for a foe's photo-negative version. Anti-Americanism is an utterly negative attitude that assumes that America has no *moral* right to behave the way it does and thus represents *Evil*, which, between you and me, constitutes a typically American argumentation. Instead of resting upon the principle of *counterattack*, it is founded on a denunciation reflex, one that is always fraught with impotence and miserableness.

On the other hand, non-Americanism means saying to America: 'We are not judging you; from your point of view, you are absolutely right; only the balance of power and competition matters'. It is thus a matter of establishing a European power in a show of Machiavellianism; calmly, by acquiring the necessary means to do so and abstaining from any criticism towards the American policy and avoiding any sort of moralising and offensive verbalism. The 'multilateralism' that is ever so dear to Chirac should not be the focus of mere theory, but be implemented in practice. Having a temper tantrum against

American unilateralism is just whistling in the wind; likewise, as long as Europe allows its demographics to collapse, opens its borders to the Third World, spends more on 'social' benefits than on worthwhile investments, discourages its own entrepreneurs, makes no research or armament efforts, does not react to American diktats, etc., any desire to construct a Paris-Berlin-Moscow axis is just an attempt to build castles in the air. All major geopolitical intentions presuppose independence and power; and the latter cannot be claimed by targeting the Americans with invectives, but through political will and courage, those very qualities that European elites have never lacked as much as they do today.

***

Intellectual anti-Americanism does not act as a well thought-out strategic position, but as a frustration-based pruritus. It bears no relevance to a will to defend the European identity or turn Europe into a counterpower to US hegemony, but represents a jealous denunciation of this 'evil' America, a country which, from a moralising point of view, is guilty of being powerful, without there being any desire for Europe itself to attain such might. It is a purely resentful position permeated by unfathomable naivety, one that confuses morals with politics. This approach is all the more ridiculous considering how, in matters of adopting a social model, our French intelligentsia has proceeded to align itself with the theories preached by its American counterpart: ethnopluralism, communitarianism, multiracialism, ethnic discrimination and the current affirmative action, and so on. It has created a faithful copy of America's anti-Identitarian model for Europe to follow.

***

At the start of the Anglo-American attacks against Iraq, Alain de Benoist, the head of GRECE and the 'New' Right, sent everyone a communiqué in which he incited people to commit anti-American attacks all around the world, thus reiterating *jihadist* Islamic discourse word for word, as uttered by Al-Qaeda and Bin Laden themselves. Readers can find this delirious piece of heroism, or rather cowardliness, at the end of this chapter (Note 1).

This *fatwa*, one that is worthy of Parisian intellectuals and that Benoist himself could never implement, only represents 0.1 % of his passionate exhortation. It is highly revealing when it comes to the mental state that pervades OHAA, a mentality that is as Manichean as it is demonising and identical to the one espoused by Islam and American Protestant sects. Indeed, the author of this staggering communiqué specifies that the USA '*has been ostracised*'. This is the very same demonising and dehumanising attitude towards one's enemies which Carl Schmitt condemned in *The Concept of the Political*, an attitude that characterises all monotheistic delusions and is shared by Islamism, Communism and all sects, including the most overzealous neoconservative American Protestants. In the absence of any distinction between the American population and the US government, America, a maleficent entity and a nest of 'lecherous vipers', to use the Marxist political cant of the 1960s, has been labelled by this fringe of our intellectual proletariat as a 'satanic bloc' against which anything is fair game (meaning that these intellectuals have taken excommunication to greater extremes than Iranian Ayatollahs do). This constitutes a *reductio ad Hitlerum*, one that always comes from people that need to be forgiven for something and direct people's attention away from the skeletons which they themselves have in their cupboards.

What we have here is not merely a Manichaean worldview, but a *totalitarian*, inquisitorial, invective-ridden and short-winded viewpoint, one that is impervious to reasoning, doubt and analysis and steeled with sectarian certainties. Imprecation has thus replaced critique and insults superseded discussions, with idiocy holding this entire approach together.

Its perverse effect, however, is that of reinforcing American positions, legitimising US imperialism, ridiculing any and all efforts made by Europeans to define themselves as non-Americanistic, and preventing

the latter from serenely and earnestly imposing themselves as a counterweight to Washington's unilateralism.

***

These hateful anti-American declarations are naturally only met with
contempt by the Arabs and the general Muslim population, who detest brownnosing zealous publicists, especially when the latter declare
themselves to be 'pagans'! Just like the Germans in France back in 1941,
they look upon collaborative ardour with great suspicion. Coming
from ever-sated Westerners, such hysterical anti-Americanism (which
goes hand in hand with a boisterous sort of anti-Zionism, as well with
blissful Third-Worldism) seems both dubious and implausible to the
Muslim-Arabs.

***

The aggression against Iraq and the delirious *neocon* policy have reinforced hysterical anti-Americanism further by means of a pro-Arab
and pro-Islamic approach. 'Reactionary thinking' is as concise as it is
appealing to simpleminded people: As a result of one's anti-Americanism, one becomes profoundly pro-Arab and pro-Islamic whenever the
USA attacks a Muslim-Arab country. Such is the logic of imbeciles.

***

It is a sign of utter stupidity when one blames the USA for absolutely
everything and anything. In the arena of History, no one has ever been
100 % 'wrong'! And what does it mean to 'be wrong', anyhow? Only the
vanquished are wrong, as a result of their defective will.

Some claim that if it wasn't for America's unilateralism and
warmongering, its support of Israel and its complicity with corrupt
Muslim regimes, terrorism would not exist and Islam would be a religion of peace. The truth, however, is that, with or without this famous
American imperialism and the Israeli-Palestinian conflict, the Islamist
instinct towards world domination would still be manifested in the
very same fashion, especially with regard to Europe. Terrorists would

still come up with an ideal pretext, as repeatedly demonstrated through history. Even in the absence of American financial support, the various despotisms that reign over Muslim countries would remain intact, because this is the only form of governance that those peoples have known since the 7th century, as audaciously stated by Jean-François Revel in an interview with *Le Figaro* (08/09/2003).

What is on the other hand true is that the manner in which the American neoconservative administration has dealt with such threats since the 9/11 attacks has been absolutely disastrous and has objectively strengthened the very forces that the Americans claim to be fighting. The war in Iraq, regardless of whether it is legal or not, is bound to lead to global mobilisation and a more uncompromising attitude on the part of the Muslim-Arab masses and their *mujahideen*. Despite Chirac's pacifism, not even France will be spared. Meanwhile, the *mujahideen* can only rejoice at the warmongering displayed by Texan petro-politicians and thank Bush for his abysmal naivety (to say the least).

B. American Lessons

One of the most dangerous aspects of OHAA lies in the fact that it considers American qualities to be flaws, even when the latter are necessary for Europe's regeneration. Once the US has been demonised through a kind of meta-religious attitude, all that is American becomes equally flawed in essence, which is also true of America's entrepreneurial dynamism, the adequacy of its reflection and actions, etc. As far as such intellectualistic delirium is concerned, the specialist is A. de Benoist, a man who constantly denounces an Empire of Evil that he has never even set foot in, as confirmed by the following clichéd statement, expressed in pure intellectualist Newspeak in his private diary entitled *Dernière Année* (meaning *Ultimate Year*, L'âge d'Homme editions, 2001, p. 225) and reflecting a highly common opinion among the petty bourgeois intelligentsia:

In the USA, the process of shaping the "I" through thought-out existential practice — the so-called *Bildung* [sic] — is seen as absolutely pointless, and one only encounters disdain towards every intellectual itinerary that is not extended through practical action. On the other side of the Atlantic, thinking is synonymous with acting, and, from the American perspective, thoughts are only proven to be well-founded through the very efficacy of their implementation.

The underlying idea is this: Europeans must steer clear of any and all pragmatism and efficient thinking, as the latter are vulgar. Specific thoughts that generate action are contempt-worthy. Erroneous, yet 'sublime' thinking is preferable to that which leads to something specific and to actual results. What a disastrous lesson of powerlessness and mental bedazzlement for Europe to adhere to! In this regard, Benoist mirrors Sartre, albeit on a microscopic scale, of course. One can only stand confounded in the face of the persisting French inclination towards pipe-dreams and inactive divagation and before the pretentiousness of our stagnant thinkers, who tend to mistake both their vague speculations and their essentially simplistic and risk-free intellectual masturbations for 'reality'.

Europeans will only be able to resist American imperialism and reclaim their own position in the flow of History the day when our theoreticians, thinkers and analysts re-adopt a pragmatic approach and a philosophy of efficacy, both of which are encountered on the other side of the Atlantic, in American universities, foundations and think tanks. In other words, we are to think in specific terms and in harmony with our own experiences, instead of our mere opinions, systems, prejudice, dogmatic constructions and ethereal moralism. When the mediocre intellectuals who have espoused OHAA incite us to scorn experimental truth and palpable efficiency (which are horridly satanic, materialistic and American) and embrace vague verbosity, assisted economy and idle-handedness instead, they play right into the hands of the American power (a power that strives to mentally disarm Europe) and imitate Islam's retrogressive dogmatism, without however enjoying the latter's demographic vigour, nor its wilful desire for conquest.

***

What must Europe do to counter America, then? To begin with, it must imitate the USA on two levels: the first lies in the acquisition of power, the other in the embracement of geostrategic egoism. Thirdly, Europeans must consider America to be a *global competitor*, one with whom it is possible to enter into temporary arrangements. This is because the NAI's aggressive impudence only stems from European weakness, a weakness that it scorns. A powerful and united Europe would demand respect and the NAI would then collapse on its own. The mere verbal advocacy of 'a multipolar world' (Chirac) is to no avail when one is unable to embody a genuine 'alternative pole of power'. Historically speaking, *ideas have no value whatsoever unless they are supported by actions*, and ideologies can only survive thanks to the practical will that implements them; and this is no longer the case in Europe. There is no point in targeting America with verbosely expressed anathemas. Our hysterical anti-Americans are still expected to adopt a position in favour of establishing a specific European power and support the renewal of our continent's economic and demographic dynamism. Those (pseudo) ecologists-pacifists are only spitting in the wind.

On the other hand, a great Europe must be extremely wary of avoiding (like the plague!) imperialistic temptation and the idiotic dream of global domination, both of which are likely to lead the American military-mercantile republic to its doom. Power does not lie in converting other peoples to one's own values, but is founded on the creation of a vast space within which a civilisation can flourish. The messianic dream embraced by the American and French republics will only result in misfortune and act as a boomerang that backfires on them.

Respecting other peoples and keeping one's distance from them is perfectly feasible. This is why, unlike those Leftist or neo-Leftist alter-globalists who firmly believe in globalism, I do not think that the future belongs to some kind of interconnected global village from which all states and powers will have disappeared, having been replaced by various 'networks' and a patchwork of 'communities' and 'tribes', in accordance with Michel Maffesoli's intermittent belief. I, for one, am convinced that we shall, on the contrary, witness the emergence of major statal and civilisational blocs that will not only be in competition, but will necessarily clash with one another.

C. A Clash of Civilisations?

Our future world shall not consist of networks, but of blocs whose very essence shall be of an ethnic nature. We are heading towards a simplification of the domain of ideas that govern our world. Over-ornate intellectual analyses are always a source of disorder.

The dividing lines are easy to grasp. One can distinguish several of them during the 21st century, as if they were some kind of historical tectonic plates:

1) The septentrional civilisation of European origin, meaning Euro-Siberia, and the White portion of North America, along with its South American and Australian appendices. The fracture between the two sides will be blatant, yet not insurmountable.

2) The Asian zone that falls under the Chinese sphere of influence.

3) India, acting as an isolated vessel.

4) The Muslim world and its amazing primitive dynamism, whose core is Arabian, Indonesian and Pakistani.

5) The rest of the world, meaning those Third World masses dispersed across all continents and bound to offer their allegiance to the highest bidder.

Contrary to the analyses of ever-blind intellectuals (including Sartre, who, back in 1960, believed that Marxism could not be 'outdone'), it is *states* that shall embody the dominant aspect of the 21st century. This development will ensure Hobbes' posthumous triumph. Peoples will regroup around clashing giga-states, and no 'global state' shall ever see the light of day.

***

Taking heed of the anti-American wave pervading public opinions, Olivier Chalmel writes:

> One can wonder whether famous professor Samuel P. Huntington was not severely mistaken when announcing *The Clash of Civilizations* in 1996. Are we not, rather, witnessing a conflict between WASP America and the entire world's long-lasting civilisations? (*Terre et Peuple*, summer 2003, p. 15.)

This theory is an interesting, yet insufficient one. As explained in my book entitled *Avant-Guerre*, such a conflict may very well involve a clash with China, for instance. In the 21st century, the USA is as much of a warmonger as Islam is... One could, however, cast doubt on the bilateral conflict opposing 'White America' to the rest of the world. I personally rather believe that, in the long run, we shall be faced with a transcontinental clash between the 'White world' and the rest of our planet.

***

Chalmel develops a ('declinist') theory that is highly similar to what Emmanuel Todd has stated in his book entitled *After the Empire*. The new, puritanical leaders in Washington respond most violently to America's domestic and global decline, resorting to straightforward militarism. The author emphasises the following with regard to the American campaign in Iraq:

> America has demonstrated its highly relative power — its very real callousness and brutality — both in order to frighten its future adversarial

competitors and to convince itself of its own power. A major endeavour
has thus been accomplished, one of communication and self-intoxication.

The author goes on to define the NAI as the exacerbated and pathological extension of traditional American imperialism. The neoconservatives cannot acknowledge our world's newfound multipolar
aspect because

> ... they are convinced of the fact that they have been chosen by God,
> entrusted with the accomplishment of an eternal mission whose inspira-
> tion is divine and universal, and thus embody a timeless and unrivalled
> norm. We are witnessing an insane and violent neoconservative attempt to
> reclaim — or acquire — absolute global power. [...] This represents a head-
> long rush and the rejection of a future which, owing to its *unquestionably*
> different character, is a source of fear to them.

In other words, by proceeding to fabricate an imaginary future for
American hyperpower, the neoconservatives long to return to a past
when America was still powerful. And this is all taking place at a time
when the USA's decline is actually commencing. They reject the old
American position of *primus inter pares*, meaning that of *leadership*
and 'free world governance', so as to adopt a genuinely insane ambition, namely that of unshared *hegemony*, an ambition that is obviously
destined to fail.

∗∗∗

Chalmel also believes that the violence and arrogance characterising
the ultra-religious neoconservatives actually embody the first convul-
sions and initial symptoms that accompany the waning of the US as we
know it. His conviction is that '*the 21st century will not be an American
century, or at least not that of WASP America*'. The American economy's
growing dependence on the rest of the world heralds the end of the latter's submission to the US. This pronounced tendency will only be ac-
centuated. '*This dependency upon the world shall inevitably drive the US
towards implementing a predation policy*'. Hence America's 'hijacking'

of Iraqi oil and its rejection of the Kyoto ecological protocol, etc., in an effort to maintain a domestic consumption frenzy.

However, America's ethnic composition is undergoing rapid changes, especially through the growth of the Latino immigrant population. The decline of WASP America may well end up upsetting the USA's global policy. As a result of the new Hispanic arrivals, America is experiencing a communitarianisation process, as the White demographic backflow picks up pace. This growing Latino community does not share Protestant America's messianic worldview at all. Territorial partitions are thus not to be excluded. Whatever the case, 'the tensing of the "White overclass"' is said to be a response to the horrible dangers threatening traditional America. The wishes expressed by Paul Wolfowitz (the former US Deputy Secretary of Defence and a neoconservative imperialistic ideologist), S. Huntington, and Zbigniew Brzezinski regarding both their refusal to acknowledge any other 21st century power than the USA and the American implementation of total hegemony may well remain unfulfilled, as America displays absolute tolerance towards immigrant invasion. And this is how the author develops his analysis: once it has experienced a geopolitical offset, the USA may drop out of the game. Not only is its legitimation of bestowing happiness upon the world through liberal democracy not to be taken seriously, but it also fails to protect America against the emergence of rival powers, especially when considering the fact that American imperialism tends to arouse nationalistic and Identitarian reflexes on a virtually global scale.

The interesting side to the author's views lies in his extreme caution not to surrender to OHAA and the manner in which he actually advocates a consistent kind of non-Americanism. His view is that a European power (whose future existence he advocates, just as I do) will have much better relations with a *New America* that shall no longer be 'WASP' in nature, an America that will ultimately be either South-Americanised, or shattered. This theory is an appealing one, yet it does build castles in the air. Is a 'decreasingly White' America truly something desirable for us Europeans, who are faced with an even worse and more tragic demographic metamorphosis? If there is indeed an answer to this question, I, for one, do not know it.

***

There are numerous ideological groupings that exist in a sort of hermetically sealed mental bubble (as seen in the case of the Trotskyites, Atlanticists, sects, etc.) in which all free thought is impracticable, every deviance prohibited and any discussion banned, since analysis is no longer the result of autonomous individual reflection, but a *road map* devised by a certain doctrine or guru. The followers are thus under the latter's influence and interpret everything through a certain grid, one that is *always* binary and thus renders any and all debate impossible: the USA, major investors, the Market, etc. are all simply demonic in essence — period.

One thus proceeds by means of affirmations and not on the basis of demonstrations. Factual or historical experience is of no importance: 'Islam and the Muslim-Arab world are Europe's allies and do not pose any threat. The Palestinians are eternal victims. The Third World is the martyr of neo-colonialism. The Yankees are bastards', and so on. The opposing camp behaves similarly: 'The USA is the embodiment of innocence and the very pillar of our world's democratisation; a European world power is sheer utopia'; etc. Neither side sees the world for what it is. Demonising others is our French intellectuals' daily bread, especially in the case of those who claim to struggle against such behaviour. They *rage*, are *indignant* and *denounce* things in a most impassioned fashion, but do not ponder anything and rarely seek out the necessary information. Their observational capacity and ability to predict a likely future (meaning their common sense) are virtually inexistent, to such an extent that they draw counter-diagnostic conclusions worthy of mad doctors, just like the dominant vulgate, an expert at producing heaps of such nonsense: 'Immigration is an opportunity for France, the advent of Islam is an enrichment', and so on.

***

Regardless of whether we are faced with a family, a village, a tribe, a nation or a people, 'Others', meaning foreigners, can never be considered equal to those closest to us, nor enjoy the same rights. Europeans, who have been mentally deformed by the egalitarianism that stems from the Gospels, have become oblivious to the facts that all peoples abide by. Such egalitarian theories are nowadays formulated by ethnopluralists and the advocates of communitarianism, who all preach the 'right to difference', which is no longer a reference to the right to be personally different, but an 'Otherness' privilege that allows people to enjoy their difference while benefiting from all the advantages offered by our system. What we are facing here is thus a preference for foreigners.

In order to last, a nation (as understood in the etymological sense of the word) must preserve its ethno-cultural homogeneity, the unity of its customs and, of course, the central energy of a ruling state which, even in its federal shape (where is the issue with that?), can only tolerate differences within very specific limits and must be able to seize absolute power in the event of a crisis or deviation (which applies even in the case when it intelligently grants 'subsidiarity'). Never have great civilisations been polycentric. Unity of command is indispensable for the survival of long-lasting nations, as manifested by China and Japan for centuries on end. Can anyone imagine the existence of a ship, an army or a business that offers its deputy heads of department absolute 'autonomy'? They would all be doomed to sink. A lasting state can, historically speaking, only allow the presence of tiny minorities within its spectrum, and only insofar as the latter relinquish any and all excessive specificity (whether religious, cultural, linguistic or of any other kind) and smelt their traditions and mentalities into a common mould. In this regard, the neo-tribal philosophy advocated by sociologist Maffesoli is utterly utopian and antipolitical.

Indeed, the principles in accordance with which an organic state is formed demand that the 'central symphony' remains undisrupted by dissonances and that the unitary civilisational model only tolerates minor variations. This is because variety is only enriching provided that it occurs within a context of homogeneity, meaning that of global and fundamental ethnic and cultural kinship. In this respect, the presence of allogenous enclaves within a given nation have, ever since the Antiquity, always led to civil war.

A state must have the capacity to claim an *absolutist position* at any given moment, particularly in case of an emergency. There can be no lasting people in the absence of a powerful state that represents it, for the state is the very structure that holds a people together, acting as both its skeleton and its brain. If decisions were left in the hands of 'communities', tribes, and local forces that claim to exercise their own micro-despotisms, anarchy, disaggregation or regression towards backward civilisational forms would not take long to surface. However, this authoritarian state cannot obviously act as a bureaucratic mammoth, but must, instead, play the role of a lean and powerful central structure. It is the very keystone located at the top of the ogive, maintaining the latter's soundness. And this is precisely how the world of the 21st century is bound to be organised: it will be characterised by the polemical cohabitation of different states rather than the global state or 'village' predicted by McLuhan.

Predictions regarding possible 'networks' and 'transversal' logical reasoning do not correspond with human nature, nor even the laws of History. This is due to the fact that, as demonstrated by ethologists, human societies are *genetically* determined by the hierarchy and concentration of the decision-making authority at the centre of the apparatus.

Meanwhile, China, whose discreet power is experiencing an inexorable rise, awaits in ambush, akin to a groundswell … Both Napoleon and Alain Peyrefitte understood it well: '*The world shall tremble when China awakens*'. China, a colossus that had long been dormant, is of an entirely different calibre compared to the 'Muslim-Arab world' or Black Africa… *The Awakening of the Dragon* is one of the principal challenges facing America. China aims to become the foremost world power by approximately 2020.

Owing to the fact that the promethean spirit is entirely absent from their profound mentalities, never would the peoples of the Muslim-Arab world, let alone the various African cultures, be able to master techno-science. Their sole strength lies in their demographics and ability to seep into the northern soil.

Who could ever claim that the Faustian possibilities offered by our techno-science, especially within the scope of its three essential disciplines (namely nuclear physics, informatics and biology), will be unable to resolve numerous *global* issues, provided that the process is governed by a Nietzschean mentality, meaning one that ventures beyond contemporary morals? Demographic and migratory destiny could thus be reversed.

Notes

(1) What follows is the actual content of the incredible communiqué sent during the night of March the 20th by Alain de Benoist, who, in all likelihood, was in a state of utter delirium:

> On Thursday March the 20th 2003, at 03.32 A.M, the military-industrial complex led by George Bush (its current spokesman and a man renowned for being both sociopathic and feeble-minded) initiated a unilateral, cowardly and monstrous war against the Iraqi nation and people, a war that nothing but the American desire to dominate the world could ever justify.

> This criminal aggression heralds other such acts, thus marking the official end of international law and ostracising the current American government on a global scale.

The vocabulary that pervades this political cant is that of Soviet propaganda at the time of the Vietnam war, which was subsequently adopted by Khomeiny. What is noteworthy is de Benoist's claim that the aggression against Iraq constitutes the very first violation of 'international law'! By making such an assertion, what he does is overestimate Washington and reveal his lack of historical knowledge. Dreaming himself into the role of a French Ayatollah in the struggle against America, he then goes on to issue his own *fatwa*, a genuine call for terrorism and murder which he will never be prosecuted for, just as Mister Punch has never died as a result of his ridiculousness:

> As of this Thursday, March the 20th, at 03.32 A.M [again], all global acts of reprisal targeting both American interests and US military, political, diplomatic and administrational personnel are both legitimate and necessary, regardless of location, magnitude or scope and no matter the means and circumstances.
>
> Paris, March the 20th 2003,
Alain de Benoist

On the next day, having perhaps sobered up under the impact of the probably panicky injunctions expressed by his accomplices and lawyer, our heroic yet hardly audacious predicator-in-chief sends out the following rectification, which testifies to his panic-stricken state of mind. At this lowly level of cowardly denegation, ridiculousness may end up being fatal after all, even without the involvement of our political police. Brace yourselves:

> (Follow-up) Communiqué and clarification
>
> I have sent a small number of addressees [sic] a communiqué, in which I have strongly condemned the abominable American aggression against the Iraqi people. Certain reactions [sic] to the above-mentioned communiqué have brought to light a misunderstanding that I would now like to clarify.
>
> When I declared all global acts of reprisal targeting American interests to be legitimate and necessary, I was actually alluding — too hastily, perhaps — to all possible actions that could allow us to impair American hegemony and adversely affect its interests and those of its representatives, and, in short, respond to the aggressive pretentiousness of a hyperpower that has now deliberately displayed a preference for sheer force over legality [how noble of him to preach 'legality' after advocating terrorism, I must say].

It was obviously not a matter of condoning such terroristic actions, even if it may have seemed so, since the very principle of terrorism is always reprehensible, especially when it targets civilian populations [In other words, I have never actually written those words; it was a slip of the tongue on my part. Please forgive me, Mr. potential examining magistrate]. I therefore ask all those who have taken the initiative to relay my communiqué to pass on this clarification as well.

Paris, March the 21st 2003
Alain de Benoist

I thus relay both the author's vindictive communiqué and his pathetic clarification, leaving it up to my readers to make their own judgement and enabling them to become aware of the harmfulness and excess that pervade obsessive anti-Americanism. This constitutes a clumsy alignment with Islamism, whose followers rejoice at the spectacle, and acts as a blessing for American secret services, who, more than anything else, adore powerless and harmless provocateurs that lack genuine arguments. In actual fact, such arguments only serve the interests of 'anti-terroristic' imperialism by turning those provocateurs into useful idiots.

One can only be astounded at the sight of the adultescence that characterises the delirious standpoints embraced by a group of 'intellectuals' who, by now, should have long overcome the naiveties of youth. They are blatantly 'under someone's influence'. The only question is to find out whether the influential factor lies in their own doctrinal logic or in some external agent. I myself would be intuitively inclined to choose the second option.

CHAPTER IX

The USA and the Domestic Threats It Faces

There is no denying the Islamic implantation in America. Every year, between 50,000 and 80,000 Americans convert to Islam. Instead of slowing the process down, the 9/11 attacks have only served to increase its pace. 87 % of the 1,209 mosques found on American soil were built less than 30 years ago, and as much as 25 % have been constructed during the past ten years. More than half of the faithful encountered at the Islamic Cultural Center in New York are converts, the majority of whom are Black, Asian and Latino. Furthermore, 40 % of the 5 to 8 million American Muslims are converts. As a result of the increasing Muslim immigration originating from Asia and the Arab world, the number of Muslims in the US will have surpassed that of the Jews by 2005. Since the 11th of September 2001, the Koran has become a bestseller. American converts are becoming extremely puritanical and distancing themselves from the *American way of life*, which they consider both 'immoral' and 'decadent'.

As reported by the UPI agency, the Imam of the Dearborn Heights mosque in Michigan (who 'immigrated' from Iran 10 years ago) made the following statement in a sermon last March: '*We are spreading our faith's good word across all of America, just as you once sent your missionaries to sub-Saharan Africa*'. According to nationalists such as Patrick Buchanan and Pat Robertson, instead of conducting neo-colonial military campaigns in the Middle-East, the American government had better repress the rise of Islam in the US itself.

Mexican illegal immigration is picking up pace along the southern border. According to *The USA Daily News Report*, an unarmed private militia known as the Civil Homeland Defense (CHD) has been patrolling the US-Mexican border in California and Arizona since March 2003, in an effort to put a stop to the influx of illegal migrants. This motorised militia, consisting of 37 volunteers, apprehends all *intruders* and hands them over to the Border Patrol for subsequent deportation.

These immigrants are growing ever more numerous and violent, a fact that has led to several pitched battles with intruder groups comprising around one hundred Mexicans who have attempted to forcefully enter US territory. American police authorities have granted the militia their implicit consent. However, the illegal immigrants that are intercepted and repatriated always hurl insults at both militia members and the police force, before promising to return. The CHD, whose recruitment efforts have been making great headway, uses the following slogan: '*Supporting Border Patrol to help defend our borders from the invasion*'. American nationalists have labelled the Governor of Arizona, Mr. Napolitano, and Congressman Grijalva, both of whom are stout supporters of the war in Iraq and of Mexican origin, as '*traitors*', accusing them of acting as those illegals' accomplices and of preferring to '*send GIs to parade through Mesopotamia rather than defend White America's southern border against the threat of invasion*'. They believe that Mr. Vincente Fox, the Mexican President, is far more dangerous than Saddam Hussein ever was. This issue demands further attention, as its geopolitical weight is bound to increase.

***

Inexorably, the Spanish language is gaining ground in the US, resulting in an ever-increasing gnashing of teeth. Here are some facts reported by *The International Herald Tribune*. In Santa Maria, California, during a district meeting on the topic of school policies, a board member proceeded to slam the door angrily because the pupils' parents were asking their questions in Spanish. In San Diego, a school principal demanded that parents only speak to their children in English, even at home. In a certain Arizona school, a new rule has been introduced to compel pupils to speak exclusively in English while in the classroom, cafeteria and hallways.

However, an increasing number of Americans are choosing to learn Spanish, a language that gathers 50 % of all foreign language learners. In some schools located in California, Arizona and Massachusetts, lessons are virtually no longer conducted in English! Due to the Clinton decree, school administrations are under the obligation to provide people with bilingual brochures. In Las Vegas and Phoenix, the police officers who elect to learn Spanish receive a monthly bonus of 100 dollars. Moreover, Spanish is gradually becoming the main US business language. Additionally, Hispanic spending power is expected to experience a 315 % growth between 1990 and 2007. There is, however, a more worrying development for American anglophones: from a total of 35 million Hispanics, a mere 4 million speak English fluently; simply because they do not need to... The number of Spanish-speaking TV channels and advertisements keeps increasing. There are several pressure groups currently attempting to impose English as the sole official language in the US, just like French is in our country. They are all fighting a losing battle. Domenico Maceri, a language professor in California, predicts that by 2020, 'the USA will be as bilingual as Belgium'.

***

Concerning the 'Mexican invasion of the US', an invasion that has been denounced by American nationalists, but does not appear to trouble current American leaders, who are more preoccupied with conquering Mesopotamia and its oil reserves, *The Washington Times* published the following information on the 2nd of February 2003, as a follow-up to the figures released by the INS (Immigration and Naturalisation Service):

> During the past decade, the illegal alien population has, according to a report published yesterday by the INS, increased more than twofold, reaching a total of more than 7 million people, most of whom are Mexican. Every year, an estimated 350,000 illegals enter the US, primarily from countries whose residents arrive with a visa and then remain here. [...] This represents an increase of 75,000 people compared to the previous decade. Steven A. Camarota, the research manager at the Center for Immigration Studies, explains: "The basic fact is that America has lost all control of its borders. This does not arouse any confidence in these times of war, when terrorists are attempting to enter the country to blow us up". He adds that "the scale of illegal immigration can only be described as enormous".

In the very same newspaper, Republican conservative Paul Craig Roberts stated without mincing his words:

> At a time when President Bush is about to violate the Iraqi borders, ours are being crossed by people who are legally defined by our federal government as "favoured minorities". This designation means that, due to their skin colour, these new immigrants enjoy preferential treatment compared to White natives in various fields such as university admittance, federal job contracts, private sector employment and promotions, regardless of whether they are here legally or not. This unconstitutional policy of inverted discrimination targeting White natives has been gaining momentum for almost two decades now, and no administration has ever undertaken anything to contain the process.

Fortunately for Mr. Roberts, MRAP[9] and LICRA[10] have no counterpart in the USA.

***

---

9   TN: 'Mouvement contre le Racisme et pour l'Amitié entre les Peuples', meaning 'Movement Against Racism and For Friendship Between Peoples'.

10 TN: 'Ligue Internationale Contre le Racisme et l'Antisémitisme', or 'International League Against Racism and Anti-Semitism'.

Illegal immigration to the US is faring well and does not seem to trouble Bush and his neoconservatives, who are more intent on conquering the Near-East than on containing this invasion. According to the information published by Audrey Hudson in *The Washington Times* (01/02/ 2003):

> [T]he alien population on US soil has, according to an INS report, increased more than twofold during the past decade, thus reaching 7 million individuals, most of whom are Mexican.

Based on the overall population, this figure seems greater than that of the European Union.

***

The current American power is highly temporary in nature. The reason for this is that the USA is neither a genuine nation, nor a real empire, but a merely ephemeral economic and social structure. Unlike China, for instance, a country that rests upon an age-old ethnic and civilisational foundation, the USA has only been established on the basis of a materialism that is supported by a rather sketchy sort of Christian religiousness. The American nation is quite the opposite of a 'long-lasting people' (to use Raymond Ruyer's expression); instead, it is akin to a 'short-lasting' civilisation.

A parallel can be drawn between the Roman Empire and the American imperial republic. Owing to the very same causes, the former is now long defunct and the latter shall soon meet its own demise. As demonstrated by André Lama in *Gods and Emperors*, the Roman Empire was initially erected around a bloc of 'old Romans', before being diluted in ethnic chaos and unmanageable military adventurism as the centuries went by. The essential difference between the two imperialisms, however, is that the Roman Empire was attacked by its foes on all fronts, while the American imperium is rather prone to attacking others.

The notion of an empire is, in itself, untenable as long as it is not rooted in a minimal amount of homogeneity among all encompassed populations, which presupposes the rejection of ethnopluralism, meaning the dismissal of any and all excessive population intermixing.

No empire is viable if it does not rest upon ethnocentrism, a mutual understanding between kindred peoples that share the same civilisation and ethnic globality. A cosmopolitan type of empire, as nowadays embodied by the American republic and previously by a perishing post-Caracalla Rome, both of which attempted to impose their own worldview on extremely diverse peoples (I mean, American democracy and Islam?!), could never last. On its part, the Roman Empire conveyed, at least, a very enriching 'civilisational message', which is not the case of the US. The 21st century will not be an 'American century', as typically formulated by the neoconservatives, but rather a Chinese one…

CHAPTER X

In Favour of a European Response

A. 'Euro-America'

As already stated, the central difference between the NAI and traditional imperialism is that Washington has now taken heed of the fact that even a weakened Europe lacking political will (as is the case today) may turn out to be a threat. In the past (since the days of Jean Monnet, in fact), America had supported European unification, for better or for worse. Europe was considered to be an American extension, a submissive and likeable vassal that served as a 'buffer zone' against the USSR.

However, the moment Europe's unification process began to gather pace and the Euro currency was created, it was suddenly a wholly different matter. In *Le Figaro* (24/04/2003), Baudoin Bollaert points out that *'after initially supporting the construction of a European union, Washington opted for a complete change of direction'*. So as to resist the French and German position at the start of the war against Iraq, *'two Yankee-inspired "letters" have sufficed to spread discord among the 15 member-states, as well as between the "old" and "new" Europe'*. The NAI's main ambition lies in dividing and conquering the European Union, thus neutralising it. It is of course Great Britain that acts as America's principal accomplice in this endeavour, with Central European countries playing the part of American supporters and Spain and Italy

losing their nerve as usual. It was Tony Blair who, towards the end of
April 2003, rejected the 'multipolar world' advocated by France. He
expressed, instead, the following delirious wish: '*What we want is a
unipolar power encompassing a strategic partnership between Europe
and America*'. From Blair's perspective, Europe should, in other words,
dilute itself in the American ensemble and relinquish its own will and
interests. Under no circumstance must Europe embody an independent power pole, even in the shape of a submissive ally. What it should
do instead is inhabit the American abode, so to speak. Declaring unthinkable any rivalry or divergence of interests with the USA, Blair has
almost explicitly formulated what not even American theoreticians
have dared express openly: Europe must cease to exist and become a
'Euro-America'.

Washington is taking advantage of the fact that Europe is changing
from a union of 15 members to one of 25 (not to mention Turkey) in
order to dilute our continent and transform it into a simple united
economic zone that remains open to the outside world and lacks any
diplomacy and Defence policy (other than submitting to the American
will). It is meant to be a European Union that reflects the current
British situation in a most faithful fashion: Europe would thus not even
be a vassal state, but a protectorate. For the NAI is now following an
interesting *anticipation strategy* (resembling that of 'pre-emptive war'):
sensing the threat of a rising rival power, the Americans '*anticipate the
emergence of any competitor with the ability to contest their power*', says
Harald Müller (in *The Chaillot Notebooks*, number 58).

***

There are those who, just like Eddy Marsan, analyse the facts in a
Hegelian manner, believing that the importance of actions transcends
that of the agents who perform them and that the latter merely obey
some sort of historical reason which is beyond their own understanding, without ever becoming fully aware of it. The theory expressed
by Eddy Marsan in his *Letter* is that the American war against Iraq

has prompted and awakened a Paris-Berlin-Moscow axis. Although this constitutes a wonderful surprise, words must still be reflected in actions. Germany's official pacifism, for instance, prohibits the birth of any specific axis of power. The French-Russian military accords dated May and June 2003 are, by contrast, more interesting, albeit very limited. So as to respond to the American challenge, let us rather discuss a Paris-Moscow axis, one that embodies Finkielkraut's pet peeve. This Atlanticist thus proceeds to vilify it in his work entitled *The West Versus the West*.

***

Fortunately, the methods to which the Bush administration has resorted in order to impose the *Pax Americana* have destroyed every notion of the latter. The *Pax Americana* was founded upon the Roman concept of protective sovereignty and implied that US hegemony was a factor of peace and collective security. However, the whole world is under the impression that it is rather a factor that leads to unnecessary military conflicts and our planet's global destabilisation, which is a truly grave development in the eyes of the NAI, whose leaders are as callous as they are naïve. Indeed, for the first time in US history, the Americans now come across as being trouble-makers and a source of disorder; at a time when they define themselves as the White Knights that combat the 'Axis of Evil', they are, instead, seen as an incarnation of this very 'Evil'. This paradox and boomerang effect are a logical outcome. What Soviet and Communist propaganda once almost accomplished (especially during the Vietnam war), namely designating the USA as a 'fascist power', the Bush administration and its NAI are actually succeeding in as a result of their supreme stupidity.

After tarnishing its own image during the 'Vietnam years', America enabled its reputation to make a complete recovery, beginning in the 1980s. Anti-Americanism started to recede on a global scale. The world's 'progressive' intelligentsias began to bask in the warm waters of Americanism. The public opinion world war seemed to have been won. However, things were to turn awry, as the cowboy was too hasty in pulling out his gun. The Iraqi campaign, combined with the calamitous manner in which the response to the 9/11 attacks was handled, led to the collapse of America's world image. It is, in fact, not a matter of chance that, due to its awareness of this unpleasant development, the American administration is putting together a massive and desperate propaganda (or counter-propaganda) apparatus, mirroring the now defunct KGB. Anyone who longs to impose a reign of imperial order can only do so by skilfully arousing his potential subjects' sympathies. The Romans understood this back in the day. Should the pacifiers ever be hatefully perceived as foes, as is currently the case with the 'American imperial republic' (an expression coined by Raymond Aron), their dominance will no longer be guaranteed.

Only Colin Powell and Condoleezza Rice, the sole intelligent members of the Bush government, seemed to be conscious of this serious issue. And yet, no one chose to listen to them. Whatever the case, the neoconservative and Atlanticist dream of geostrategically integrating Europe into the Empire's 'close circle' in the shape of a 'Euro-America' has been terminated by the very clumsiness of those who had previously theorised it.

B. Economic Warfare

Those who protest most boisterously against the openly military form that American imperialism has adopted often forget that it does not represent a greater threat at all. The gravest issue from the European perspective lies in America's economic and technological supremacy. Just like in the military and strategic fields, the NAI has altered and harshened its domination methods, especially by freeing itself from the free-trade principles that govern international commercial law and that the Americans themselves had previously established. The new rule is now as follows: the world is to embrace an open (ultra-liberal) economy, while the US adopts a protected and controlled economic system.

In this regard, the NAI surpasses all previous forms of American imperialism in its use of the economic weapon. It is no longer merely a matter of dominating commercial fluxes or preserving America's industrial hegemony, but a question of destroying both Europe's autonomous cutting-edge industries (in the military field, as well as that of informatics, aerospace, etc.) and its techno-scientific innovation capacities. The ones who bear the sole responsibility for the current state of affairs are obviously the Europeans themselves, since they choose to neglect any and every effort in the research-development sphere and lack the courage to defend themselves against this new kind of American economic imperialism. Paralysed, they do not dare to use the weapon of their own will, nor that of aggressive cynicism, which lies at the source of the American success. The USA is actually compensating both for the frailty of its own speculative economy and for the frightening deficit burdening its commercial and financial balance by targeting its domestic economy with a kind of technological doping, one that attracts the world's brain power and its capital. It also wields the weapon of intelligent dirigisme, which transforms the state into a pillar of American techno-economic aggressiveness, despite the presence of a hypocritical sort of liberalism.

The Internet embodies the most striking example. This communications system, created in the USA and experiencing an annual growth of 25 % per annum, is almost entirely under American control. Marie Dewavrin, a specialist on the issue, writes:

> The Internet may well become the decisive driving force towards ensuring the political and strategic domination of all the nations which control it. [...] The Internet is now at the heart of the ever more intense rivalry between "ancient Europe" and the proponents of the "Pax Americana". (Le Figaro économie, 14/04/2003.)

David Nataf, author of *La guerre informatique*[11] has made the following remark: '*No one can contest the fact that the internet acts as an equality tool under the yoke of the dominant American culture*'.

Indeed, from the American perspective, the economic-technological offensive and the cultural one are necessarily related, an attitude that Europeans have never implemented on their own behalf. On the other side of the Atlantic, the fact of imposing linguistic and mental reflexes, as well as American points of reference, is considered a primary means towards achieving hegemony, and rightfully so. The internet is actually at the core of this strategy, thus equalling, if not surpassing, Hollywood, Disney amusement parks, musical styles and sodas. Not only is the entire planet expected to sing and entertain itself in the American manner, but also to *think the American way*.

In fact, the Department of Commerce considers the means of controlling the Internet to be virtual state secrets. The USA has grasped the fact that the Net is destined to become the new global circulatory system; and it is therefore necessary for America to appropriate its guardianship. There are several methods to achieve this: the English language has succeeded in imposing itself as the Web's hegemonic language; a major part of intra-European liaisons must be conducted through the USA, since 10 out of a total of 13 global 'root servers' are located overseas; the same is true of the so-called *backbones* or 'information highways' and of access providers, in addition to all address, protocol and domain name management. Techno-economically and culturally speaking, the solution does not lie in any anti-American invectives, but, once again, in Europe's enormous effort to counter this situation. The weapons industry is slowly becoming aware of this fact.

C. Anti-Third-Worldism: The NAI's Sole Positive Aspect?

There is a field in which the NAI does deserve to be praised: its reinforcement of Washington's traditional tendency to be wary of European

---

11   TN: *The Informatics War.*

Third-Worldism, and especially the French one; this is particularly true whenever the latter takes on delirious proportions, as advocated by Africanolatrist Jacques Chirac. Here is a recent example:

For several years now, our French President has had a specific fad: that of suspending all agricultural subventions in the North so as to rush to the aid of his beloved Africa and thus allow it to cheaply export its products towards developed countries. What does it matter that this behaviour is harmful to French agriculturalists? Such economic altruism is part of a Third-Worldist utopian ideology according to which it is only by means of international charity and subventions that one can 'save' Africa, despite the fact that Bernard Lugan has already demonstrated, to the great displeasure of the self-righteous, that Africa is not 'salvageable' due to its structural inability to integrate itself into a global civilisation that has neither been conceived by the black continent, nor for it.

On the 29th of April 2003, at the OECD, Robert Zoellick, the American negotiator for commercial matters, rejected the 'French commercial initiative for sub-Saharan Africa'. Zoellick's argument was of a highly skilful nature: '*Why limit this proposal to Africa? Such an attitude seems rather neo-colonial to me*'. In other words, by making Africa the (sole) beneficiary of a sort of 'affirmative action', the French create the impression of disdaining it. The sophism comprised in this statement is enormous and very much in line with American style and the USA's habit of resorting to 'candid lies'.

Whatever the case, one of the NAI's positive aspects may turn out to be its ability to cure us of our assistantship mania towards the Third World as a whole, and Africa in particular. Unlike Europeans, who are always burdened with their own feelings of guilt, American governments do not consider themselves to be Africa's nurses or its Ladies of Charity. The American mentality is inclined to believe that those incapable are responsible for their own incapacity and that the best means to help them actually lies in not aiding them at all, so as to force them to face themselves and their own responsibilities.

***

What difference does it make to Europeans if the Pentagon bombards Baghdad and Tel-Aviv pounds the Palestinians? It is all part of the age-old game of power policies. What does the destiny of Near-Eastern Muslim-Arabs have to do with Europe? Have the latter ever defended the European identity? On the contrary, what they are doing is encouraging our continent's colonisation through *jihad*.

The gullible apostles who preach a 'pro-Arab European policy' and the necessity to grant Palestinians massive aid are unable to comprehend the fact that this will not benefit us in any way, nor will it bestow any dividends upon us. This attitude relates to pure anti-politics, which is always rooted in charitable altruism.

D. Towards a 'Disorderly, Multipolar World'

Believing it possible for international relations to remain peaceful on a long-term basis is a sign of utopianism and of a blatant contempt for History itself; especially in the context of a 'full planet', a situation that we are all well aware of and in which plethoric peoples rub against each other. We are thus beginning to witness the paradox in which different civilisations are fighting each other against the common backdrop of a single global techno-economic infrastructure.

It was already impossible for China, India, the Muslim world etc. to play a highly active role during World War I and II, since they were still part of 'another world', namely a pre-industrial one. This is, however, no longer the case today: various civilisations are now rubbing shoulders, forming enormous blocs of different morals, beliefs, races and traditions, at a time when a certain material civilisational infrastructure (the fruit of Western techno-science) has been established and is now shared by all of mankind. This constitutes an explosive cocktail: the concomitant homogenisation of heterogeneity. Everyone shares the same playground, although their interests are becoming ever more divergent.

***

There are four possible developments in this regard:

1) A pacifistic multipolar world where all peoples and powers cooperate with one another within the UN's harmonious framework and in which migratory movements, the Islamic expansion and the ambitions to secure scarce resources are wisely managed through mutual agreement. In this world, any and all imperialism will have disappeared thanks to the enchantment of wisdom. Such a world embodies the Kantian utopianism embraced by the French, German and Belgian foreign policies. The hopes of ever establishing it total 0 %.

2) The development centred around the traditional form of American imperialism, one that was, until recently, advocated by Washington: it is founded upon 'the sharing of power' and involves a gentle sort of American hegemony that resorts to cunning rather than brute force. This Machiavellian solution (that of the fox rather than the lion), previously the most skilful and profitable option from the American perspective, has gradually been relinquished since the fall of the USSR and the 9/11 2001 attacks. All the better for us: this approach was the most dangerous one for Europe, since its numbing effect is unequalled in strength.

3) The NAI's prevalence, meaning that of a unipolar world subject to America's policing authority, with the US representing the sole source of international law. In the very short run (10 years), the chances of such a world coming to pass total 50 %. In the medium term, this rate decreases to 20 % and, beyond that, to 0 %.

4) The prospect of a disorderly, multipolar world seems most likely, not only because it is already taking shape, but also because it reflects all the historical observations made during the past centuries with regard to international relations.

The dream of a *Pax Romana* was more or less accomplished during a century and a half, stretching from the initial establishment of the Empire to the very first Barbarian invasions into the *limes*. Times have greatly changed, however: the idea of implementing a *Pax Americana* upon our current planet (a bubbling cauldron where, soon enough, 10 billion people will flock together) by maintaining some sort of 'order' through armed threats and technological superiority may be possible from a theoretical angle, but will turn out to be nonsense on a practical level. This is why, as I myself have outlined in my previous work entitled *Avant-Guerre*, we must brace ourselves for the imminent emergence of a period characterised by immense, chronic clashes which the NAI will certainly find itself unable to control; it will, instead, only manage to foment them.

Indeed, once the sheriff realises that he is unable to maintain order in this 'global village' as a result of his own lack of means and the fact that his callous methods have only served to increase the motivations driving the various thugs and rebels, his actions will trigger a chain of international crises, as well as a global rearmament policy. And it is only in this general atmosphere of disputes and tragedies that History will give birth to a new European civilisation.

E. Against Anti-American Moralism

Beyond the incredible stupidity pervading the unilateral war waged against Iraq by the Bush administration under the deceitful pretence of an international coalition (in the long run, this war's consequences are bound to be the opposite of its intended purpose, as admitted even in a report published by the US army's war college on January the 13th 2004), one should refrain from judging the USA from a 'moral' point of view, one that is founded upon the self-righteousness of preventing all violations against human rights and international law. And it is indeed very bizarre to witness many intellectuals who have previously praised jurist and political scientist Carl Schmitt, a theoretician who championed power as a source of right, display utter ignorance of his ideas and condemn the American 'aggression' in the name of utopian and universalistic arguments that can only be described as Kantian, thus aligning themselves, once again, with the Left's formulas, female pacifism, the dream of a spontaneously recognised globalist legality and the negation of all power relations and their historic legitimacy. The anti-Americanism that they succumb to is thus no longer European and Identitarian, but Leftist, a faithful copy of the American campuses that once opposed the war in Vietnam.

***

International legality is always defined in accordance with the will of the most powerful. The USA is absolutely right to change its standpoint and adopt this realistic philosophy. Ethically speaking, one cannot reproach the Americans anything either, since ethics are inapplicable in the geopolitical field. One could of course mock their neophyte ardour in matters of Machiavellianism, rejoicing at their clumsiness and the fact that they overestimate their own power in a bout of *hubris* which robs them of all awareness. The only essential thing is for the Europeans and Russians to claim, in turn, the position of the most powerful ones, so as to define *their own* international legality. It is high time we stopped looking at international politics and polemology from an egalitarian point of view and in accordance with morals that are becoming of convent nuns.

Unfortunately, the pacifistic position espoused by France and Germany with regard to the American military campaign bears no relevance to a 'grand European policy', nor does it reflect a desire to resist the US; it only relates to the necessity to avoid offending the Muslim-Arab world, whose populations are pouring down upon our continent. Europe has thus entered what geopolitician Louis Sorel has termed '*the era of emptiness*', meaning that of renouncing any claim to power. Believing Europe to be oblivious to its '*civilisational identity*' and to have renounced power in the name of moralistic utopianism, he writes:

> What power designates is the ability to act forcefully in order to impose one's will. Power is both material and measurable ("How many divisions"?); it is a dynamic that relates to vital momentum, lying at the very heart of politics [...]. In his *Power and Weakness*, neoconservative political scientist Robert Kagan develops the theory according to which Europe's ambition is to establish a "post-historical paradise" that lies beyond the notion of power. By attempting to actually give birth to Kant's "project for eternal peace", the Europeans seem to be condemning themselves to political inexistence in the strong sense of the word. (*The Audacity of Power*, Les Quatres Vérités Hebdo, 29/03/2003.)

Quoting Carl Schmitt (*'Should a people cease to be politically active, this would not lead to a decrease in politics, but to the world being one people short'*), he criticises the irenicism and naivety pervading the new world order advocated by Chirac's France. Founded upon ethereal ethics and powerless living-room diplomacy, the latter keeps itself in balance by leaning against the UN 'thingy' and using the globalist delusion of an 'international community' as a prop:

> It is in accordance with these eternal truths that the words uttered by Dominique de Villepin, the self-proclaimed spokesman for both Europe and mankind, are to be assessed. The fact that he concluded his UN speech with a reference to "the construction of a better world" testifies to his mental confusion. The realm of politics bears no connection to eschatology and such means-end discourse is thus, accordingly, tarnished with illegitimacy. [...] There can never be any common European destiny beyond space, time and power.

✳✳✳

The issue with the new American global policy is that it has, at long last, assimilated a sound and historically accurate philosophical principle, but has, for the past decade or so, been implementing the latter with grotesque clumsiness. Genuine Europeans should be rejoicing at this, under the condition, of course, that they finally manage to comprehend the fact that countering their American rival and competitor will remain impossible in the absence of military, economic, financial and cultural power and without demographic dynamism. Within both the national and international political arena, words have no value whatsoever as long as they lack the necessary ability and actions.

F. Atlanticism, or the Whore Syndrome

The American desire to eliminate Europe from the global power game is one of the NAI 's central characteristics. In the past, it was only a matter of *dominating* our continent, but now, all means have become acceptable, even those that are founded on commercial illegality, the disrespect of treaties, and the bribing of decision-makers so as to push Europe, America's main rival, completely out of the game. This applies to all fields, as the US strives to sabotage Europe's autonomous military industry and its spatial capacities, while undermining the EU's agricultural policy, imposing American GMOs, etc. The list is a very long one.

However, this strategy, one which no longer attempts to merely weaken Europe, but embodies an effort to *emasculate* our continent, is only made possible by the complicity of European politicians and that of the authorities in the Brussels Commission. The USA is playing its game and counting on the corrupt blindness and stupidity that typify the European atlanticist camp, including Alain Madelin and José Maria Aznar, not to mention proconsul Blair. But why speak of stupidity? Because European atlanticists are the only ones to have swallowed whole the fictitious claims regarding a Euro-American 'Atlantic solidarity'. And yet, a single argument would suffice to discredit the Atlanticism advocated by those Americanolatrists: not a single American administration, whether Democratic or Republican, has ever believed in such fables, which is truer now than ever before. The White House has always been convinced of the existence of a divergence (or a rupture, even) between American and European economic and geostrategic interests. The atlanticist ideology is but a means for the USA to mislead Europeans into believing that there could actually be a common transatlantic interest and thus conceal the presence of unequal treaties, rigged commercial partnerships and a global strategic dependence beneath the veneer of fictional equality.

Is it not, for instance, an enormous blunder for Europeans to have displayed such stupidity that they placed EU diplomacy into the hands of former NATO secretary general Javier Solana? Doing so is synonymous with placing it under Washington's tutelage. Faced with this callous and cynical domination, Europeans kneel in submission, overestimating America's power to retaliate and inflict punishment. Despite his rebellion, de Gaulle never had any reason to fear the USA at all, but American propaganda has managed to present anti-Americanism as a disease requiring treatment, especially when it happens to be French. Such is the view espoused by America's own agent of influence, Jean-François Revel. Europeans are thus expected to acknowledge their own weakness (for their own mental sake), as well as the fact that it would be suicidal for Europe to reclaim its former power, right?

The atlanticist camp is but a collaborationist party, just like the Islamolatrists. There is a certain kinship between Atlanticism and OHAA: instead of considering the US to *be a power like any other*, both camps see it as a sort of *metaphysical superpower*, one that represents all that is Good on Earth for some, while simultaneously embodying all that is Evil for others. No one looks upon America from outside the realms of passion, beyond any Absolute notions; they all thus fail to see it as a nation that could, at any given moment, lose its ally status and become an adversary, or the other way around.

Atlanticists have adopted the same behaviour towards the USA as a demimondaine — or a whore — would towards her 'protector', who views his 'protégée' as a luxurious prostitute, while she persuades herself that he is her actual spouse and that they represent a united and egalitarian couple.

CHAPTER XI

'Septentrion', or the End of the American Dream

A. America Is Not Immutable

One must not believe America to be *immutable*, as those obsessed with anti-Americanism do. On the contrary, this comet-like nation may well be experiencing a complete metamorphosis affecting its innermost nature. In this regard, the NAI could be considered the ultimate expression of Americanism, the final blossoming of the American rose. America's accelerating Hispanicisation will result in turmoil that one can scarcely imagine. The days of America's *Manifest Destiny*, a uniquely puritan characteristic and the very foundation of US imperialism, may well be numbered. The same goes for the American patriotic attitude surrounding the US flag (with its *Stars and Stripes*), a patriotism that is growing ever weaker and is in dire need of shocks — such as the one caused by the 9/11 attacks — in order to be resurrected. Can one truly be certain of the fact that a part of America's White public opinion will not end up experiencing an increasing feeling of solidarity towards Europe and Russia?

***

In the end, History is the one that allows events to unfold and evades any and all human predictions. No one could ever foresee what it has in store for us. In spite of the civilisational rupture between the USA and the Euro-Siberian continent, and regardless of the constant anti-European policies implemented by the various American administrations, there is an undeniable basic fact, an unavoidable *ethnic* reality that historical developments could drag into their unforeseeable currents.

This fact is the following one: even though European and North American populations comprise an ever-growing percentage of 'coloured' minorities, the common anthropological stem uniting Europe and North America (in addition to Argentina, Australia, etc.) is still that of the White race; this Europoid compost of Germanic, Latin, Slavic and other Caucasoid populations is endowed with a common atavistic mentality and predisposition.

This bio-anthropological kinship is obvious and thus creates an opposition between the *European ethno-civilisation* (including its global extensions) and all other ones. Hence the novel conception that I am now proposing, one that completes the notion of Euro-Siberia: *Septentrion*.

***

The war waged by the Bush clan is but an epiphenomenon that only those intellectuals who lack any vision of the future and all historical intuition focus on (through the small end of their spy glass). The act of confusing the North American ethno-biological *germen* with the corrupt administration and financial forces that govern the USA is a sign of utter ignorance regarding the long-term developments and underlying movements that guide different peoples. One thus stupidly neglects both our world's ethnic dimension and its profound cultural connivances, reasoning as if White Americans were complete strangers to us and we had closer bonds to the Iraqis or the Algerians than to Iowan farmers or Texan entrepreneurs.

'Francophony' is prone to maintaining the very same delusion: even if they do speak French, there are numerous African or Maghrebian peoples that do not form a single civilisational unit with ours at all, and this mental chasm can never be bridged. The simultaneously abstract and moralising fabrication of a complicity between Europe and the Third World (a fabrication that reflects its purely Evangelic origin, with Chirac acting as its self-declared herald) does not correspond in any way to Europe's interests and actually represents the greatest threat to our continent's identity. As for the view that Europe must rely on the Third World, and especially the Muslim world, in its struggle against the Great Yankee Satan (as is fashionable to believe in numerous delirious intellectual circles), it relates to sheer political oneirism.

∗∗∗

The American government will not endure in its current shape forever, and the neoconservatives will not remain in power indefinitely. Islam, on the other hand, will never change in any way, and neither will the Third World and the South, displaying a common will to occupy our lands both physically and demographically. Is the USA driven by such a will too?

I apologise most sincerely for subjecting Islamophiles, Third-Worldists, ethnopluralists and OHAA supporters to such a shock, but let us suppose that a cataclysm were to compel millions of Americans of European descent to *return to Europe*: as far as I am concerned, this would be infinitely preferable to the non-native immigratory fluxes that have been pouring down upon our unfortunate continent. I would even consider such a development to be a favourable one for the regeneration of our *germen*.

Since the beginning of the 20th century, the relentless anti-Europeanism displayed by American governments (for essentially geo-economic reasons) must not lead us to forget the presence of American populations whose members are of European origin, a presence that is still massive nowadays.

∗∗∗

Who knows if, in the course of the 21st century (a century that promises to be a terrible one, wreaking the greatest devastation upon our
planet since the fall of the Roman Empire), the world will not end
up undergoing a re-composition in accordance with an inexorable
North-South logic, as hinted by several current events? Such a development would topple several dogmas. When it comes down to it,
anti-Americanists abide by the *American dream* of inhabiting a unified
and pacified planet. Washington and the NAI would like this to occur
under their own leadership, while Islam envisions this outcome as part
of its global caliphate. These two utopias are kindred in essence, since
they both stem from the same monotheistic attitude.

We must do Islam justice by being realistic and placing warfare at
the centre of its worldview, for *jihad* is the temporary war that precedes
the great Islamic unification. Just like the US, however, Islamism has
failed to comprehend that war is an eternal strife and that no unification, whether liberal, Islamic or communist (or UN-based, for that
matter), could ever come to pass, since no victory can ever be final.
History cannot simply come to an end.

B. The Stupid Dream of a European-Islamic-Third-Worldist Alliance against the USA

As emphasised by the director of the Foundation for Strategic
Research, François Heisbourg (in the image of many others who preceded him), it is very likely that the Occident will experience a '*major
schism*' between Europe and the US. Indeed, back in the 1980s, I myself
wrote about this issue in several books, recusing the very notion of an
'Occident'.

However, one must be entirely blinded to write what Alain de
Benoist, an advocate of OHAA, did in his internet communiqué.
De Benoist is the author of a book entitled *Europe and the Third
World — United by the Same Struggle*:

> A clash of civilisations will definitely take place; unlike what many people believe, however, it is quite likely to involve a confrontation between Europe and the United States, instead of a conflict between "Islam" and the "Occident".

Talk about mistaking one's desires for reality…

First of all, it is clear that the clash between Islam and Europe (or perhaps even between Islam and the rest of the world) has already begun, as a result of the will displayed by this warmongering religious civilisation, which is as fanatical and expansionistic as it is 'de-civilising'. Some people's inability to realise this, or the fact that they pretend not to be aware of it, is either a matter of partisan deceit or one of intellectual idiocy. Furthermore, as demonstrated by A. Del Valle, there is an implicit and subtle US-Islamic collusion against Europe and Russia. Thirdly, the reveries to which anti-American hysterics surrender regarding an admittedly possible cold or hot 'war' opposing Europe to America (for none can predict the future) are utterly suicidal. For nothing would please Islam and the Third World forces that march under its banner more than a Euro-American confrontation, as this would weaken their common foe; and they do see us as one, whether we like it or not.

Nevertheless, I suspect that, owing to a mixture of masochism, hatred and cowardliness, the people who write the kind of nonsense quoted above harbour an inner desire for an Islamised, Third-Worldised and therefore disfigured Europe, one that would act as America's adversary. Such is the explicit position embraced by the peripheral movement within the 'New' Parisian Right, whose members have converted to Islam (including Tahir de la Nive, Bouchet, Mutti, etc.). In their eyes, hatred towards the USA takes complete priority over the defence of Europe and its identity. The sort of 'civilisational clash' they long for would have Europe ally itself to Islam (after being invaded by the Third World) and enter into a military conflict with the Great Satan.

As might be expected, my standpoint is diametrically different. For one should, on the contrary, hope that the Americans (or the American government in Washington, to be precise) will become aware of the inanity pervading their current policy and take heed of the fact that their interests do not lie in weakening Europe. One must hope for a reversal in the American position. This endeavour is a far more promising one than the rather unhealthy reveries regarding an unnatural alliance between Europe, Islam and the Third World. In future, Euro-Siberia and the US may well become adversaries and competitors, but they might still form an alliance against their common enemy. Such a development is obviously far from being in line with today's global geostrategic configuration, but I, personally, wish for it to come to pass. And I am not the only one to feel this way, as all the facts point to such a new global evolution.

C. Solidarity with 'White America'?

I am driven by a certain solidarity, an ethnic kinship, so to speak, with all Americans of European descent (and with all the subjects of the British commonwealth who belong to the same category). I do not harbour the same feelings towards the francophone populations located overseas. This has, of course, no bearing at all upon the necessary struggle against the *American policy* and, in particular, Washington's current political approach. Unlike certain members of our Identitarian milieus, I do not rejoice at the sight of the demographic diminishment afflicting the White (and especially WASP) populations in the USA, as I share the feelings expressed by Georges Suffert and Claude Chaunu in their premonitory book entitled *The White Plague*, which was published back in 1976. I, too, find a global solidarity with all populations of European origin to be more crucial during the 21st century than the geopolitical rivalries that divide Whites.

I know that my attitude is a sin in the eyes of the prevailing ideology. Forgive me not, Father. I am culturally closer to the Anglo-Saxon civilisation than to the Muslim-Arab one and the African conti-nent's 'early arts'. I would rather visit the Museum of Astronautics in Washington than explore the future 'primitive arts' museum that Third-Worldist Jacques Chirac intends to establish. I would also prefer to send my children to an American university than to have them study in an Islamic one. I would, of course, favour French universities, but taking into account what they have become...

Enough delirium: the claim that we are 'very distant' from our kindred American civilisation (I deliberately chose not to use the word 'sibling') does not stand up to scrutiny, even if it is indeed possible to detect major differences between our European values and those espoused by Americans. The fact is, however, that these differences are very minor in essence compared to the precipice that separates us from the Arab-Islamic and Asian spheres. Should anyone intend to write a thesis on the topic of European history (stretching from Mycenae to our era), I would advise them to base it on the information holdings available at American universities, rather than on any documents pro-vided by Islamic or Third World universities. There are, however, many thinkers and sophistic scholars who remain utterly deaf to the voice of common sense. Indeed, all these professional anti-American hysterics are but arrant hypocrites. Given the choice, they would rather live in Boston or San Francisco than inhabit Algiers or even Barbès.

***

The 21st century will be a *Spenglerian* one and will involve clashes between the different civilisations and races, as inherently understood by Samuel Huntington in his *Clash of Civilisations*. Even if this vision is a caricature (and yet, every caricature does reflect reality, simplify-ing it without actually betraying it), we shall witness a confrontation between Whites and all others, as part of a process that has already begun and that intensifies year by year, even if it does take on distorted and extremely diverse shapes. When I say 'Whites', I am obviously referring to all the peoples who have, ethnically speaking, inherited the European civilisational matrix.

Even if, from a historical perspective, the American approach has been one of rejecting Europe, and regardless of the fact that strategically, economically and geopolitically, the American government has embraced the *temporary* role of Europe's fearsome adversary, I am convinced that White America and White Europe are bound to draw closer to one another (they are both, after all, experiencing a decline on their own soil). Is there any genuine reason for the *current* situation to persist? Washington's NAI will perhaps be swept away by the new historical circumstance of a geo-ethnic confrontation; I prefer the latter expression to that of a 'civilisational clash'. The *current* geostrategic divide must not be allowed to conceal *tomorrow*'s ethnic reality, the reality of a world in which Whites will find themselves ever more threatened and in a minority position, and will thus be compelled to regroup. The great majority of our Western elites is of course completely blind to such predictions, however easy they are to formulate, since they only see short-term developments and are paralysed by their own cosmopolitan ideology.

Let us, at this stage, return to the initial issue: would it not be possible to combine the admittedly mythical notion of *Euro-Siberia*, which I have expanded on elsewhere, with the conception of *Septentrion*, a conception that is very vague, of course, but may still come true, even if we cannot yet predict what historical shape it might take?

Although we cannot imagine its exact form (unlike us, however, History has all the necessary imagination for this to happen), *Septentrion* can be defined as the regrouping of all peoples of albo-European descent located in the northern hemisphere, spanning from North America to Europe and the Russian Federation, in addition to two crucial septentrional extensions: Argentina and Australia.

I am well aware of the fact that such a *myth* may well turn out to be fallacious and inapplicable and that it would shock all those who abide by the prevailing ideological hegemony, as well as all anti-Americans, pro-Americans (since American domination would no longer be possible) and, of course, all universalists and globalists who identify with Christianity, Leftism, liberalism, Islam, and so on. Undoubtedly, this prediction regarding the possible (and desirable) birth of a *Septentrion* presupposes the disappearance of the USA as we know it, which will probably occur in the aftermath of a territorial partition and the relinquishment of a number of States.

***

A dream and a utopia, you say? Is there anyone who, at the beginning of the 20th century, would have predicted the Islamic rise to power, the outbreak of religious wars, the brutal collapse of Communism, Europe's rapid Third-Worldisation, etc.? Despite all the revelatory indications, the answer is: no one at all, which is particularly true of intellectuals. Spengler was alone to have detected some of those premonitory signs back in the 1920s. And in the 21st century, History will progress at an even faster pace.

White American mentality may yet change, and change it shall as a result of the tempests that are bound to rage (regardless of whether the latter are of an ethnic, economic, religious or any other nature). The current American administration is of little importance and its presence highly temporary. The same goes for 'capitalist globalisation', a liberal dream whose stupidity is equal to that of universal 'alter-globalist' Communism. Who's to say that mentalities will not pivot and current ideologies collapse under the impact of the rising storms? We must not perceive the world through the narrow, small end of our spy glass, but through its large end, which allows us to catch sight of all incoming asteroids.

***

Strangely enough, those who are most convinced of the veracity of such theories (while simultaneously fearing them, of course) are none other than the representatives and elites of the Third World (regardless of whether they are Muslims or not), who have initiated their attack against the White world. This is because these southern countries and the prolific populations that have been settling into Europe and America share a view of history that is considered abominable by our Western elites: the long-term infrastructure surrounding the destinies of different peoples reflects the ethnic and demographic power relations.

Never since Ptolemy has any multi-ethnic or even multiracial society been able to function on a long-term basis. How could one ever change this fact? Through some kind of ideological miracle, perhaps? Following the daydream of universal miscegenation and the delusion of European and American 'communitarianism' under the authority of a federating and integrating nation-state that was predestined to fail, we are now inevitably entering a time of ethnic consolidation, as if through a swing of the pendulum. There are none yet who can predict the exact manner in which this worldwide native European solidarity will take place, and none can be sure of whether it will occur on separate micro-levels or take on global proportions. One thing is certain, however: the idea is already *lurking* behind the corner, just like a vagabond. It begins by infiltrating people's minds in the shape of a roguish thought, before exploding like a bomb and imposing its presence as a vital sort of necessity once everyone is *urgently* called to order.

***

Allow me to reiterate, once again, that *Septentrion* is but a myth, one that does not mirror the current state of affairs, but espouses the future developments whose outlines can nowadays be discerned. Account taken of the ever-increasing pace at which our planet is being reshaped, I personally think that the US-European confrontational model, which can still be observed today, will come to an end as a result of evolutionary pressure. The *Septentrion vs Aliens* model seems more likely to me, although I could be wrong. And yet, I was not mistaken when, at the start of the 1980s, I predicted the fall of the USSR and the Islamic breaking wave.

I will now proceed to reassure some people, especially the anti-Americans amongst them: in no way is the notion of *Septentrion* incompatible with that of Euro-Siberia, since its centre can only be located on our own continent and motherland, acting as the physical, spiritual and geopolitical midpoint of what must be termed the White race. Furthermore, this *Septentrion* presupposes not only America's demise (for it will not subsist in its current form), but also the possible homecoming of some Americans of European descent into the sphere of a new ethnocentric and Euro-centric empire. *Septentrion* shall mark the end of the American dream and coincide with the return of the prodigal child to its European, parental bosom.

Conclusion

Let is now summarise the important points that we have touched upon in this book:

The adequate response to the New American Imperialism could never stem from hollow moralising discourse, but must be rooted in a wilful reacquisition of power conducted by the Europeans themselves. Current American leaders are without qualms: their morality and democratic messianism are but a façade ridden with holes, one that can hardly conceal their desire for global economic predation. Historically speaking, such an attitude is nothing new. In contrast to the delusions embraced by obsessive and hysterical anti-Americans, the USA does not embody any sort of novelty in the saga of successive imperialisms that the world has known since the days of the Pharaohs.

The greatest service that one could render America lies in demonising it, which is actually synonymous with the fact of worshipping it. Current anti-Americanism has produced a mythical notion of what America is by fashioning it into a global historical exception. The NAI is, however, doomed in advance, since it is founded upon a principle claiming that American domination is virtually eternal in essence, when, in actual fact, all hegemony is of an ephemeral nature. Likewise, the fact of presenting the American society as a social reign of terror, lowliness, oppression, poverty, uncultured behaviour and decadence does not relate to any observable reality, but rather to the kind of ideological exaggeration that laid the clumsy communistic propaganda to waste.

***

What hardly any observer or commentator focusing on the NAI's adventurism has ever pointed out is that, ultimately, all decisive events take place in the ethnic and demographic arena. Every people and historical power is but the embodiment of a specific, biological and cultural strength and form that characterises its own population. Everything, from geopolitics to economics, is basically determined by this factor.

This is why the American threat against Europe, although admittedly real, is infinitely less important and critical than our demographic decline and rapid submersion at the hands of southern masses and Islam. It is we ourselves who are exclusively responsible for both these developments, which American imperialism takes advantage of, even though it did not actually cause either of them. This imperialism is not the source but the result of our domestic decline. The reason for our waning lies within us and must not be sought anywhere else. What the NAI thus does is fill not only a power vacuum, but particularly a void of will.

In no way is the Muslim-Arab world, for instance, in any danger with regard to the NAI or the Likud's policy, even if the American army does undertake military campaigns across Mesopotamia as part of a ridiculous *remake* of 19th century colonialism. Why? Because its demographic strength, fertility, culture and religion all act in its favour. Throughout history, the sole long-term victory ever achieved by various peoples has been that of their *germen* and will, thus reflecting two realities: a material one and a spiritual one, which are organically connected to one another.

What purpose would it serve for anyone to hold a long artful geostrategic discourse on the power relations between the USA and Europe, including Germany, Russia and France, if one remains oblivious to the fact that what is essential — indeed, absolutely vital — is for us to avoid depopulation and the destruction of our ethno-biological substratum at a time when both these processes have already been initiated? As witnessed in the past, a Europe that is perfectly healthy demographically speaking and preserved against the kind of dramatic ethnic colonisation we are currently experiencing would not find it difficult at all to free itself from adverse imperialism or resolve an economic crisis. However, it is infinitely difficult for one to convince the elites to heed such reasonable remarks, especially at a time when the prevailing ideology prohibits everyone from discussing ethnic and demographic problems, which represent the central issue.

***

In the long run, both cultural Americanisation and our strategic / economic submission to the USA are but fleeting and benign ailments which can be rapidly cured and whose source is not to be found overseas, but right here, among the 'Euro-mericans'. Our domestic invasion, decadence and sub-replacement fertility will turn out to be mortal maladies unless they are very quickly treated. And let no one claim, as all those sophists do, that the USA has conspired to trigger European depopulation, family reunification and the construction of mosques, or that suburban 'youths' are the agents, victims and products of cultural Americanism, when it is their ethno-religious Islamisation that is actually on the increase and their Americanisation on the decrease.

***

Europe must therefore struggle on two fronts, which are more or less interconnected, even if not entirely: on the one hand, it must fight against a specific domestic invader, as well as against the collaborators, who are as pro-immigration as they are Islamophilic and include the above-mentioned pseudo-Identitarians, while simultaneously opposing American imperialism on the other. The main question at hand concerns the manner in which these threats are hierarchised, a question that I believe I have already answered when rejecting the nonsense preached by all those devotees, idiots and blindmen.

Those who rely on their love of the Third World and their Islamophilia in their struggle against American imperialism are following a descending suicidal path; the mistake made by the Atlanticists, who are under the fallacious impression that the American 'power' will protect a mythical 'Occident' against the *jihadi* onslaught, is a very similar one. As for the politicians who claim to believe that American and European interests are one and the same and that Europe and America are actually two halves of a single superpower (which is the case of Blair, Madelin, Aznar, etc.), their lies are those of a vassal and a courtesan.

It is unfortunately obvious that the standpoint in which I identify the invading Third-World, Islam and the European collaborative faction as our *principal foe* and the NAI as our *main adversary* presupposes the ability to liberate oneself from the prejudice which prevents people from contemplating the fact that one could actually struggle on two fronts, in accordance with two different confrontational methods.

As in the case of all americanolatric Atlanticists and those overexcited and hysterical anti-Americanists, this pathological state, afflicting the most impoverished minds, compels people to define themselves according to *others*. One is never *pro*-European, but *anti*-American and *anti*-Zionistic and therefore *pro*-Palestinian, Islamophilic, a Third-Worldist, and so on. All these terms can of course be systematically reversed: *pro*-American, etc. In fact, the European civilisation and its peoples do not interest these gentlemen in any way, whatever faction they may belong to. Obsessive anti-Americanists, for instance, are never troubled by the economic war that the USA is waging against us; what worries them instead is the fate of the 'unfortunate Iraqi people', whose destiny is, with all due respect, as unimportant to me as that of the now extinct Indian tribes.

***

What is noticeable is that the most fervent Americanophiles and the most hateful anti-Americanists share the central trait of *not being familiar* with the USA. For what is America if not an ephemeral empire that lacks the necessary features to subsist in the course of history and become a 'long-lasting' people (Raymond Ruyer). The USA is governed by a strictly mercantile, and therefore short-lasting, power logic. Messianic justifications (embodied by a simplified form of Protestantism) will make no difference in this regard. This nation, or 'enterprise-nation', rather, resembles the ephemeral Spanish empire, which was equally founded on gold; the difference, however, is that America is rootless.

***

What are the USA's strengths and weaknesses? The former ones are well-known: economic dynamism, a willingness to work and make efforts, pragmatism, entrepreneurial will, institutional stability, and a social and moral kind of conservatism that allows it to export its viral decadence to Europe without being afflicted by it, in addition to cementing the American society through the veneration of 'law and order'. What is also worth mentioning is America's appreciation of efficacy and its philosophy of achieving results, paired with the rejection of useless ideas and dogmatic speculation; its faith in techno-science and the necessity to make enormous investments; its neo-Keynesian and semi-protectionist economic system, which involves an inseparable association between statal planning and enterprise, since American 'liberalism' is merely an exportation product targeting the competitors that are meant to be disarmed; its massive financial investments into the field of research and development; the exceptional quality that typifies its universities, which absorb European and Asian elites; optimism and elitism; a clear conscience in all its endeavours; its sense of conquest and will to domination; its espousal of patriotism as a supreme value; and so on. These characteristics obviously horrify our European intellectuals, as well as the Leftists that inhabit the east coast and the Hollywoodian milieu, although they all abide by the iron logic that governs this type of society. This strength can be summarised as being a *primal* state of mind (which is not meant pejoratively in any way) rooted in self-contentment and ethno-centrism, through which

America itself becomes the supreme value and all inclinations towards 'repentance', masochism and self-criticism are always overcome, unlike what is happening in Europe.

***

Nevertheless, America's weaknesses outweigh its strengths. Its speculative, casino-like economy is fragile, burdened with considerable external deficits and financed through inconstant international savings; it is experiencing a rapid and profound ethnic modification which benefits Latino-Americans, who lack the Fausto-Promethean culture that stems from Northern Europe; the NAI has triggered a generalised, global wave of anti-Americanism; its volatile public opinion is prone to demoralisation at the slightest defeat and remains reluctant to make any sacrifice whatsoever; its global imperialism is both adventurous and costly; its militarism is devoid of military qualities; it strives for the oneiric goal of world domination without actually possessing the means to achieve this ambition; and so on. In short, what the Americans are doing is entering into a bridge contract that they will be unable to uphold.

Let us now highlight further sources of weakness that are even more crucial than the previous ones, since they relate to America's domestic situation: the absence of a genuine and profound 'national culture', which has, instead, been replaced by a *way of life* and an *entertainment culture* that prevent the US from defining its own identity (by attempting to Americanise the world, America is actually losing its identity); and the slow implosion and disaggregation afflicting the ancient North-American 'civilisational unity', a process that no amount of dollars, no global currency and no *Stars and Stripes* patriotism could ever durably cement.

What all of this means is that the global American 'empire' rests upon a specific bedrock, namely the USA itself, whose domestic homogeneity is ridden with cracks. It is quite possible that by 2030, southern American states (whose population will comprise a Latino majority) will have embraced secession. As for me, I predict that they actually will.

And unlike Europe, which is being invaded by the Third World and Islam, America is not endowed with age-old territorial enrooting and thus lacks any means to engage in fierce resistance. 'Their home is not their own', which means that they would perhaps not have sufficient mental strength to conduct a *Reconquista* should they find themselves on the edge of a precipice. America's fundamental structural weakness lies in the fact that its patriotism is factitious. It belongs to the mercantile and emotional-speculative sphere and bears no relevance to a long-term memory, because Americans do not have any *tangible homeland* of their own. In the short term, this rootlessness is indeed a strength, but becomes a handicap in the long run, since no person would readily defend and die for a *material homeland*, which the USA undoubtedly is.

***

Americans are useful idiots, in the sense that they exacerbate global tensions while striving to appease them, hasten crises while trying to avoid them, cause civilisational clashes while attempting to bring an end to History in a manner that advantages them, and fuel the Islamic fire while seeking to extinguish it. As a result of their cowboy-like diplomacy, they are akin to bulls in a china shop. This is partly due to the fact that the major political decision-makers in the American government are never selected among genuine elites.

Faced with American militarism and the resulting impression of America's invincibility, hysterically anti-American Europeans are struck with powerlessness and thus consider Islamic terrorism to be the sole means of countering and injuring the Giant; such is the unique response that the weak can have when confronted with someone stronger. They thus carry out a psychological and pathological transfer towards Islam, which, from their perspective, represents the only way for one to impede America's imperialistic omnipotence.

Psychological schemes, simplistic reflexes and pre-defined reactions thus take hold of their minds, soothing their resentments and frustrations: 'The USA is a materialistic and technological giga-power that abuses and humiliates us; let thus then ally ourselves to Islam, its spirituality, its 'anti-modern' civilisational counter-plan and its simplistic resistance tools, including justified terrorism, the vengeful weapon wielded by the poor and exploited'. These are the thoughts that lurk in the unconscious of all those who espouse OHAA.

This consolatory reasoning, which follows the Marxist logic of resentment, enables a simultaneous unification of traditionalists, Trotskyites, neo-Leftists and many others, as part of an unexpected convergence of impotent individuals in the framework of a *desperado*-like response. Let us call Islam to our aid in our struggle against Robocop and Mac World and place ourselves under the Prophet's protective scimitar. Allah's sabre will prevail over those bombers!

Their choice stems from a masochistic *self-renouncement* process, as well as from an alarming mixture of blindness and ignorance; the belief that harbouring rapidly growing Islamised masses on our soil is somehow preferable to an American presence (indeed, certain individuals go as far as to switch between idiocy and treason and *wish for* Europe's Islamisation, whether implicitly or explicitly) will not reduce the American chokehold on our continent by a single inch, but actually add another domination effort to it, namely that of Third World colonists, a development which can only please Washington.

***

This USA is undoubtedly an ephemeral, yet formidable entity, a highly original and historically unprecedented structure which one must be careful not to despise. Its very existence is exclusively and simultaneously rooted in a sort of extension, projection and rejection of Europe. In the eyes of future historians, North America shall thus remain a kind of *biopolitical monster*.

America is neither a people nor a nation, nor even an empire, but a sort of chimera which has taken on the attributes of an imperial republic and extends across a new territory that has been seized and taken from its original occupants. Of course, in no way is this the case with China, Europe, India and the like. In the USA, the mercantile aspect has absorbed the sovereign and military functions as part of a successful fusion, which has never been entirely true of other major world powers. The US is the only country in the world whose political leaders are simultaneously involved in the military industry, business matters and electoral manoeuvres and whose elections are entirely determined by industrial sponsors. It is a country with a single function, a plutocratic entity in the purest possible form (no pejorative connotations intended).

The 21st century shall be an age of civilisational clashes, or rather a century marked by ethno-civilisational conflicts that may transcend any strictly continental and geostrategic logic. Alongside, or perhaps beyond, the very notion of an ethnocentric Euro-Siberia (a European-Russian merger that I am personally wishing for), I find myself wondering whether, in harmony with our current era and the century that now lies ahead, the massive and global reunification of all peoples of European descent will not end up being a conceivable accomplishment. In the world that is about to emerge, will ethnography not be destined to replace geopolitics? This concept is what I have christened 'Septentrion'.

Islam may already be showing us the way. Despite claiming to be 'universal', this religion is also a civilisation. Objectively, implicitly yet palpably, it presents and sees itself as the banner of both coloured peoples and the South in the face of the White populations of Northern origin, which is true even in the case of Black Americans. Yes, I am schematising, caricaturising and simplifying, indeed, indeed; but is this trait completely inaccurate?

I therefore predict that, in the course of the 21st century, the great divide shall not oppose the USA to the rest of the world, but rather

Septentrion to the entire planet. This opposition will take place in a climate of continual clashes between major ethnic and civilisational blocs (or Empires, perhaps?) and involve economic, cultural and military competition between them.

ANNEXES (PART I)

Various Informative Elements

The Chinese Challenge

China is positioning its pawns against the USA. On August 19th 2003, WorldnetDaily conducted an (internet) investigation into Chinese espionage on American soil, an espionage that is said to implicate more than 3,000 businesses located in the US. This is the main source of worry for FBI director Robert Mueller. The spies are believed to comprise students, tourists, permanent residents and businessmen. Allegedly, this situation concerns Canada as well, account taken of its own Chinese immigrant rate. In one of its inquiries (20/08/2003), *The Asian Pacific Post* confirmed the fact that Chinese espionage has been focusing on the USA since 1998, with military and technological targets harnessing special attention. Overwhelmed by its struggle against 'terrorism', the CIA seems to lack the necessary means to devote itself to the problem...

***

With regard to China, some economists have furthermore highlighted the following facts, which are completely astonishing: it is widely known that a number of southern developing countries use their savings to finance the developed countries located in the North, which may appear to be unfair and abnormal, but is actually entirely logical. Indeed, the (wealthy) investors of poor countries prefer to invest their funds in developed economies rather than their own national economy, simply because the resulting investment returns thus enjoy a much greater degree of safety. For instance, the IMF has revealed that in 2002, the USA absorbed 75.5 % of all global savings, which totalled 528 billion dollars! When I say global 'savings', I am not referring to hedge funds, but to those that had been locked-in for more than a year.

It so happens that China has been showing great interest in the USA. The overall value of the American treasury bonds which it purchases on a yearly basis exceeds the total sum of foreign investments made on its own soil! China thus acts as America's creditor. This global financial influx into the USA enables the latter to finance its enormous commercial deficit. It is obviously a rather risky situation from America's perspective, as it finds itself in a delicate state of capitalistic dependence. And yet, if global capital flows are centred around the USA more than on emerging countries (despite the fact that the latter's development potential is truly significant), the reason is that the American economy is unrivalled in its ability to lead this capital to fruition, thanks to its productivity, efficacy and organisation. Why are there so few international investors in African and Arabian countries? Simply because they do not feel that they can rely on such countries and are reluctant to risk losing their capital or having it stagnate, which is an understandable position. Capital profitability is the golden rule of competitive economics, which is founded upon a kind of economic 'Darwinism' in which the less competent fail to attract investors, i.e. loaners. No Arabian billionaire Sheikh would enjoy placing his fortune into the hands of a 'sibling country', out of sheer love for his brethren; he would definitely prefer, instead, to invest his money in Great Britain or the USA.

Let us, however, return to the topic of China. Economist Pierre Robin explains (in *Le Figaro économie*, 11/09/2003):

> What American businesses strive for is not so much to increase their own exportations as to delocalise their production by investing in foreign countries, especially in China, which will, in return, export its products to

the USA (among others). When one calculates the global amount stemming from these movements, it is the Chinese that actually finance both
American consumers and the US federal budget. This also applies to the
American military sphere: the US military budget, totalling 379 billion dollars in 2003, is, in fact, entirely covered through foreign credit.

The presence of such American indebtment, particularly to the
Chinese superpower candidate, proves that the USA is somehow a
'credit-based empire'. It also demonstrates that Washington could
never allow itself to espouse a warmongering or even authoritarian
policy towards China, a country that has the fearsome means of exerting pressure through the suspension of all investment loans.

***

The notion that global US economic prevalence is coming to an end
(especially due to China's influence) has been developed by economist
William R. Hawkins (TradeAlert.org, 18/04/2003), in a study entitled
China Surges Economically While America Falters. His view is that
the USA will find itself unable to maintain its current military capacity as a result of insufficient funding. He explains that the American
economy lives off the credit granted by the rest of the world, especially Asian countries, which are delighted with their creditor status.
China is gradually becoming the world's foremost manufacturer of
products ranging from textiles to the engineering industry and is going to unfurl itself across western markets. Hawkins has adopted the
nowadays quite renowned theories advocated by professor Robert S.
Ross (Boston college) regarding the efficiency of China's new 'socialist
market economy' model. Ross states:

> Unlike Japan, China possesses the necessary natural resources to support
> its own economic development and strategic autonomy. [...] By following
> the rules of the market, Chinese businesses will gradually increase their
> capacity to exploit the continental Chinese workforce, whose members are
> beyond count, cheap and hardworking.

China is thus destined to become the 'world's factory' and the principal global exporter, which, according to Hawkins, will enable it to supplant and control US economy, with America no longer being *the world's most powerful nation*.

Domestic Disorder

Should George Bush be defeated in the 2004 elections, will the NAI and the current neoconservative dominion vanish? Such is the main issue not only for the current American administration, but also for the entire American political and mediatic spectrum, in addition to the world's chancelleries. There are, first of all, some members of the Democratic establishment who believe that if Bush is indeed re-elected,

> ... he will unleash an entirely uncontrollable policy that shall undoubtedly jeopardise the very stability of the American regime. One of these sources has implicitly confirmed Bill Vann's analysis by stating that European governments had an absolute obligation to "follow" the American policy and "contain" it without resorting to provocation, in an attempt to avoid any and all severe extensions. By doing so, however, what they suggest is but a desperate and double-edged tactic reflecting the current impasse; for being prudent in one's treatment of the Bush government is synonymous with reinforcing its chances of being re-elected. (*De Defensa*, 15/09/2003.)

In the event that Bush is not re-elected and a Democrat seizes control of the White House, it is not at all certain that we will indeed witness a shift in America's currently authoritarian, aggressive and warmongering policy, as pointed out by several well-informed commentators. Why? Simply because new American leaders will find themselves unable to accomplish such a shift, as the crease resulting from the NAI cannot be 'ironed'.

The first reason is that *'America is drifting away from us, falling ever more prisoner to its colossal plans to counter the terrorist threat'* (De Defensa), as well as to its catastrophically belligerent manner of dealing with the latter. Matthew Riemer, who works as an analyst at the PINR institute, wonders whether, '*upon its arrival, a new Democrat administration would continue to implement the Bush doctrine out of necessity*'. The answer is yes. In other words, America's neo-imperialist logic cannot be brought to an end, nor could the related logic of restraining the domestic public opinion and constructing an 'authoritarian state'.

So why is it that this evolution cannot be terminated in the event of a Republican defeat at the White House? Why is it impossible for America to relinquish the current neoconservative policy? Simply because, according to a number of American observers, both the Pentagon and the military-industrial complex have already seized power, whereas the presidential function, which is subject to 'democratic' election, abides by the presence of masters who stand above it and possess genuine sovereignty. We must forget about Tocqueville.

***

Real American power was once founded upon a cultural basis (that of mental influence) rather than a military one in the classical sense. It now seems, however, that the NAI has initiated a decline in America's global appeal. The number of foreign visitors, including tourists and students, has been plummeting since 2001, disheartened by the administrative hassles. Anti-American hostility is surfacing on a global scale, and we are witnessing an incredible mixture of neo-isolationism and interventionism implemented by the current American administration.

Above all else, however, what is crumbling is America's cultural prestige and its sway over global mass culture, which once represented the true pillars of US power and influence and peaked during the 1980s. All that was trendy was American back then, but this is no longer the case. In July 2003, British cultural magazine *Prospect* published a study conducted by Mark Cousins, in which he anticipates the onset of an opposite tendency: the very *style* of Hollywoodian cinema, American music and television is experiencing a decline in popularity among the global public. They are hated and considered 'corny', in an accusatory attitude that denies any right of appeal. It seems that American productions are no longer seen as creative, but repetitive. In Mark Cousins' view, 'America is fatigued' and its ridiculous new imperialism is but a desperate attempt to compensate for the world's 'disenchantment' with the USA, one that only manages to tragically reinforce the latter. Could it be that the neoconservatives have actually succeeded in putting the American myth to death?

If this is indeed the case (and the decline and depletion of the global American cultural model has been initiated), it would be a very grave development from America's perspective, since the USA has turned this sector into one of its main assets of influence. Paradoxically, although US foreign policy was previously supported in its undertakings by the impact of American productions and America's cultural appeal (in addition to that of the American way of life), the negative effect of US neo-imperialism and America's unilateral foreign policy upon the world's public opinions may well lead to the rejection of this 'way of life' and result in a diminishment of US cultural productions, which, in return, is certain to considerably weaken the American foreign policy itself.

***

According to an analysis published in *De Defensa & Eurostratégies* (19/09/2003), America's new imperialism and foreign policy have led it to perceive the world differently from the way it actually is, by causing it to regard the latter in a *virtual* manner, thus falling from the heights of realism into the depths of sheer delusion. First of all, this irresponsible espousal of virtual perception conjures up the image of '*a tremendous power on the point of increasing the state's indebtment, this bizarre phenomenon of "wealthy poverty"*'. Furthermore, it acts as a factor towards the dreadful creation of global disorder and destabilisation:

> America's capacity for disorder is of an unrivalled magnitude. [...] We have not seen anything yet. The apotheosis shall come from the banks of

the Potomac river, for it is there, at the very heart and core of it all, that ultimate disorder shall be born, a disorder that shall finalise our system's destabilisation. It goes without saying that we require neither a Bin Laden nor a Saddam for this to happen. G. W., Rummy and friends are perfectly up to the task themselves.

The global disorder that the NAI may well trigger and which could lead to a worldwide flare-up will not spare America either, as it may find itself shaken by a historically unequalled domestic crisis, one that has the potential to put an end to more than 200 years of constitutional stability. It is widely known that troubling rifts are emerging in the American states located along the Mexican border. Year by year, these states are being increasingly invaded by 'Latino' immigrants and have seen the emergence of a secessionist movement with the ambition of establishing an independent state known as *Republica del Nord*, in an amputation procedure that would reduce the size of the American territory by a rate of 15 %.

There are also speculations regarding the possible rebellion of certain states against the American central authority. For instance, there are *'ten north-eastern states'* that *'have decided to embrace a common environmental policy that abides by the norms of the Kyoto Protocol and contradicts Washington's own policy'*, thereby contesting the American anti-ecological refusal to submit to its anti-pollutive international obligations. *'This is one of those signs that demand our attention'.*

***

One also encounters some highly bizarre institutions at the core of the current American government. According to an investigation conducted by *The Times* on the 10th of September 2003 and which confirmed the information revealed by British secret services, it is the OSP (Office of Special Planning), a 'discreet' para-governmental organism lacking any official status of its own, that was responsible for implementing the plan against Saddam Hussein's 'weapons of mass destruction'. This agency, controlled by Wolfowitz, Douglas Feith and

Donald Rumsfeld, lies at the heart of America's neoconservative and neo-imperialist apparatus.

Wolfowitz and Feith, respectively the Pentagon's second and third in command, were responsible for the creation of the OSP, whose director is Abraham Schulsky. In addition, the OSP comprises numerous other neoconservatives who have no competence whatsoever in matters of intelligence or military affairs [which accounts for what is stated above, namely that the American policy, entrusted to incompetent individuals and influenced by amateurs, has become utterly erratic]. It comes as no surprise that Schulsky is the protégé of Richard Perle, the "Prince of Darkness" who resigned from his position of president of the Defense Policy Board just before the war started. The OSP has recruited Elliot Abrams, a man who supported the Guatemalan genocide back in the 1980s and acts as the National Security Council's director for the Middle-East. These neoconservatives are closely connected to the Zionist lobby, even if their reports were in complete contradiction to the Mossad's, whose services did not believe for an instant that Iraq could ever be a threat to either the US or Israel.

The OSP fully supports Ariel Sharon's uncompromising policy against the Palestinians. It is not surprising that, due to their vengeful state of mind, Perle, Feith and Wolfowitz now want to target Iran, Syria, Lebanon and Saudi Arabia using the same flood of falsified "secret service reports" that was resorted to prior to initiating the war against Iraq, accusing these Arab countries not only of financing, protecting and organising terrorism, but also of sending terrorists into occupied Iraq. All the fake "secret service reports" sent to the White House are provided and concocted by the OSP's personnel and networks.

European intelligence agencies have interpreted the termination of the "road map" created by the White House in a desire to reconcile the Israelis with the Palestinians as a deliberate move orchestrated by a number of Israeli militaries — in particular Ariel Sharon and his Defence minister Shaul Mofaz — with both the OSP's and Wolfowitz's complicity and in harmony with the latter's recommendations.

***

We are witnessing the revolt of senior officials against the ruling American administration, which is now being accused of having lost its mind. Thomas E. White, who resigned from his Secretary of Army post at the Pentagon, co-authored a book entitled *Reconstructing Eden*, published in early September 2003. The book, which has caused quite an uproar, openly states what an ever-growing number of political and military officials have been thinking and whispering; and the fact that one of the Pentagon's own pundits acknowledges such things is truly food for thought.

He explains that the Iraqi campaign was devised in a state of utter unpreparedness; that America's current failure to occupy and reconstruct the country was not only easily foreseeable, but had even been predicted by high-ranking officials; and that the pursuit of such an American policy in the Middle-East (as the USA finds itself trapped in a dead-end without being able to retreat) is certain to lead to various disasters. He mentions the '*accelerating disintegration of Washington's Americanistic system under the auspices of G. W. Bush and the policy inspired by the neoconservatives*'. The 'plans' elaborated by the Pentagon's 'experts' in connection to post-war Iraq are utterly imbecilic. This brutal hostility, displayed by a man who, four months before the release of his merciless criticism, was one of the Pentagon's leaders, testifies to the magnitude of the crisis afflicting the American government.

White had, in fact, been callously compelled to hand in his notice when, at a time when he still held his function, he began to voice such ultra-critical opinions. In his work, he castigates the utopianism of wanting to establish a pro-American country in the space of a few months and accuses his peers of being incompetent and disregarding (as well as despising) the facts on the ground, in addition to lacking any specific plan towards Iraq's reconstruction. The 'Bush doctrine' 's sole effect is the spreading of chaos, in a manner mimicking the outbreak of a contagion.

This event proves that the confrontation taking place at the heart of the Pentagon between the latter's chief, US Defense Secretary Donald

Rumsfeld, and numerous civil and military executives (including general Shinseki, the former Chief of Staff who stated that post-war Iraq was both '*unmanageable and disastrous*', believing that it would take half a million men to stand the slightest chance of controlling the country) is growing ever more intense. Since White himself was at the very core of the neoconservative team and not its Democratic challenger, his revolt should be viewed as a first indication of systemic disintegration. Another example of dissident behaviour is that of US Air Force Lieutenant-Colonel Karen Kwiatkowski, who left the team heading by Feith, one of the Pentagon's most uncompromising neo-conservatives, before pouring out her discontentment in adverse pamphleteering articles, in which she highlighted her former associates' cynicism, irresponsibility and villainy.

***

On the Pravda.ru website, US army captain Roniel Aledo has expressed the conviction that Russia will not allow the US to establish a global strategic superiority and that it has already begun to 're-fortify' its high-end military apparatuses (in '*Toward a Multipolar World again*'). This belief is supported by the fact that the Russian military manoeuvres which took place in the Indian ocean in spring 2003 simulated strikes against American targets, particularly naval and spatial ones. In a display of exaggerated optimism, Aledo has also expressed the belief that France, Germany, Belgium and Luxemburg will succeed in founding a 'mini-NATO', one that is entirely independent from the US. In his view, the 'unipolarity' advocated by Washington is but a dream.

***

On the 19th of May 2003, *The International Herald Tribune* claimed that, in order to continue demonstrating its power without incurring any risks, the USA will still need to attack (pardon me, I meant 'liberate', of course) further small nations. It published an inquiry that attempted to prove that Cuba could turn out to be the next target, so that Fidel Castro may be overthrown and a pro-American regime established. The advantage of such a development lies in limiting the exodus of illegal Cuban immigrants towards Florida (Author's Note: Mr. Mitterand's widow will definitely not be happy about this). If one is to believe the assertions published by the above-mentioned newspaper, the most passionate partisan supporting the Cuban invasion is none other than G. W. Bush's brother Jeb, the acting governor of the state of Florida.

***

On the WorldNetDaily website (19/05/2003), Patrick Buchanan remarked that the most prominent nations belonging to the 'Axis of Evil' (Iran, Iraq, Libya, and North Korea) had nothing to do with Al-Qaeda, Bin Laden or the 9/11 terrorist attacks, and that it was Saudi Arabia that actually financed terrorism and had '*truly vanquished America, since the latter is in need of its oil supplies and will not utter a single word against it*'. He considers the NAI to have failed and to represent '*a prelude to enormous future humiliations for the "Empire"*'. He adds that it is necessary for the US to '*go home*', in harmony with a neo-isolationist logic.

On the 8th of September 2003, Howard Dean, a Democratic candidate, made the following declaration:

> Our President has created a far more dangerous situation in Iraq than ever before. He has turned this country into the main terrorist front.

On the same day, we were treated to the following proclamation, made by Bob Graham, a Democratic senator in Florida: '*Our President attaches more importance to the reconstruction of Iraq and Afghanistan than to the resolution of America's own problems*'. This remark is an interesting one, as it demonstrates the fact that the Iraqi campaign and the current neoconservative policy are not necessarily perceived as signs of 'egotistical imperialism', nor are they always resisted in the name of pacifistic principles; instead, they are sometimes seen as the inappropriate manifestations of a costly sort of international altruism.

***

In *the Independent* (27/07/2003), Patrick Cockburn deemed America's invasion policy and its 'democratic' remodelling of Iraq to be '*utter nonsense*'. In his eyes, the USA has acted without having planned ahead, an attitude that borders on dangerous folly. America's global policy has become a worldwide '*crisis factor*', exacerbating our world's issues instead of resolving them. He also believes that Washington has been reinforcing both Al-Qaeda and Islamic terrorism. Cockburn has, in fact, co-authored a book entitled *Saddam Hussein: An American Obsession*, which was published in Great Britain.

***

According to the WorldNetDaily website (20/05/2003), the Muslims have decided to 'take care of' the USA. There is already a Virginia-based Islamic lobby and party in the US (the Muslim American Society) that intends to present its own candidates in all future elections, a fact which encourages Muslim immigration. The same is true of Minnesota and Michigan, both of which encompass highly important Islamic centres. There are already 8 million Muslims in the USA, which totals 153 elected representatives nationwide. This contradicts the 'Islamophobia' accusations targeting the Bush administration, an administration that has never opposed the Muslims.

***

According to historian Ramdan Redjala, it was in 1964 that the Americans initiated their support of Algerian Islamist association Al Qiyam. This organisation, financed by the Gulf monarchies, is considered the forefather of the Islamic Salvation Front (ISF) and the precursor of current terrorism (in *La Nouvelle Revue d'Histoire*, September-October 2003). America was actually one of the stoutest supporters of Algerian independence. The latter was one of several points that Kennedy touched upon in his 1960 presidential campaign programme.

***

In *Le Figaro* ('*America's mistake*', 07/08/2003), Islamologist Olivier Roy, member of the National Scientific Research Centre and a professor of political sciences in Paris and Princeton, demonstrated the fact that the US 'anti-terrorist' response to the 9/11 attacks only managed to increase global Islamic terrorist potential through its Afghan and Iraqi campaigns. He states that '*America's tactical choice contradicts its strategic intention*'. He is convinced that it would have been far more effective for American secret services to implement a policy of prevention and active struggle against the above-mentioned plague. Driven by the NAI's simplistic ideology, however, Washington decided, instead, to 'flex its muscles' for the whole world to see, with the neoconservatives relying completely on the rather primal patriotic fibre that characterises simple-minded American voters.

***

Islam is well intent on establishing itself on American soil not only through its mosques and immigration, but also through audio-visual means. Hypocritically, its purpose is to initially present itself as very accessible in nature (in accordance with the *Dar-al-Sulh* phase). Bridges TV is a television channel that is currently being developed in the US, one that is destined to indulge in *soft* Islamic proselytism. Headed by Muzzamil Hassan, the channel has close ties to the Council of American-Islamic Relations.

***

The desire to take full control of science is part of Washington's new statal highhandedness. The notion according to which the NAI engages in a totalitarian manipulation of America's civil society and resorts to statal deception in order to justify its own objectives is a very shocking one for common Americans, who have all been brought up to consider their country a model of transparency and free thought. And yet, one still encounters an entire current of sensibility in the USA, a current which believes that the American federal government manipulates and controls everything, dissimulates all that is inconvenient and strives to achieve secret aims, displaying a cynicism that evades all institutional control.

Charles Levendosky authored an article that was published in *The New York Times* (20/08/2003) and caused quite an uproar on the topic. The article, entitled *The White House Distorts Science for Political Ends*, is highly critical of the 'American system' and reveals several interesting, if not worrying, facts. The general gist is that, in order to justify its own policy, the American administration is exploiting and diverting the results of scientific research away from its actual conclusions, which applies to all possible domains. Levendosky proceeds to analyse a certain Democratic parliamentary report (the Waxman Report), otherwise entitled *Politics and Science in the Bush Administration* (August 2003). The first fact that the report points out is the existence of prestigious governmental agencies that focus on promoting research and safeguarding public health. These agencies, which have hitherto remained both independent and serious, include the National Institute of Health, the Food and Drug Administration, the Centers for Disease Control and Prevention, the Environmental Protection Agency, and several others.

At the beginning of 2003, *Science* magazine sounded the alert when it declared: '*The Bush Administration is invading this sector, which had thus far been preserved, and resorting to various manipulations in it*'. What is truly going on, then? More than 20 scientists are reported to have been discretely asked to steer their conclusions in a certain 'political' direction. A good example is that of the Centers for Disease Control and Prevention: as a result of the pressure exerted upon them by the Protestant fundamentalists belonging to the ruling neoconservative clique, they proceeded to delete all information concerning the use of condoms and the latter's efficacy with regard to combatting STDs and AIDS from their internet website, simply because these fundamentalists are convinced that abstinence is the only legitimate means of combatting AIDS. At the express request of the American administration, which abides by Bush's refusal to ratify the Kyoto Protocol and grants American industrials the 'right to pollute', what has also been suppressed are the warnings issued by the Environmental Protection Agency regarding the climatic dangers that stem from greenhouse gas emissions.

The American administration is also said to be pressuring scientists towards falsifying the results of their research into the harmfulness of GMOs, water quality, the dangers of industrial foods, and overfishing. According to the Waxman report, the Bush administration is active along three axes:

1) That of manipulating the various committees of scientific governmental advisors;

2) That of prevaricating or censoring any scientific information that contradicts America's official policy;

3) That of interfering into ongoing research programmes so as to steer the latter in the 'right direction'.

This attitude is rather similar to the practices that were once implemented in communist countries. In this regard, the American government is breaching a certain law, namely the Federal Advisory Committee Act, which guarantees the absolute independence of all scientific governmental advisors. Here is a scandalous example of this: three federal experts who had stood at the head of the Advisory Committee on Childhood Lead Poisoning Prevention were thanked for their services and replaced by 'scientists' with ties to the lead industry, one of whom made sure that the hitherto maximal doses of lead absorption into children's brains could be increased sevenfold with utter impunity!

What we are faced with here is a fundamental trait that characterises the new authoritarianism embraced by the American government: no longer serving the interests of the 'nation', the latter only serves those of the industrials that finance neoconservative politicians. Unlike the ancient autocratic European regimes, in no way does the American 'reason of state' mirror the incentive of governmental arbitrariness, but, similarly to what is witnessed in a banana republic, a subservience to private interests whose roots reach deep into the governmental core.

The conclusions presented by the Environmental Protection Agency in its reports on the atmospheric warming that results from industrial pollution have been softened through the exertion of pressure upon the experts, who were all asked to kindly resort to lies. It gets worse, however: this governmental agency has simply been refused the right to test the air quality in America, since this could inconvenience Bush's industrial policy. In Levendosky's eyes,

> ... whenever a scientific analysis differs from the American administration's point of view, it is simply discarded into the waste bin, along with any concerns for public well-being.

One is thus struck by the fact that the counterpart to the NAI's cross-border arbitrariness is actually found in the US itself, where anything that opposes the neoconservative policy is simply stifled.

Geopolitical Elements

In an article published by his own institute's magazine on the 9th of May 2003, Ivan Enland, an American geopolitician and the head of the Center of Peace & Liberty at the Independent Institute of Oakland (California), states that the Iraqi campaign, which was partly intended to intimidate Iran, will, on the contrary, drive the latter to secretly develop weapons of mass destruction and increase the pace of its secret nuclear programme so as to protect itself from a possible American 'folly'. From the author's perspective, the NAI will have a 'proliferation effect' upon the world's weapons of mass destruction, which is the opposite of the intended purpose.

***

What follows is a declaration made by Poul Nielson, the Danish European commissioner for Development, upon his return from

Baghdad, in the aftermath of the British-American 'victory': '*The Americans have appropriated the Iraqi oil! I think that the USA is gradually becoming a member of the OPEC*'. Echoing his statement, *The New York Times* wrote (28/03/2003): '*The USA may well end up pumping Iraqi oil revenues in order to finance its costly military operation*'; which is exactly what it has been doing and precisely why it has excluded the UN from all post-war oil management. This time around, France has chosen to toe the line and did not dare to resort to its veto.

***

According to Alain Bauer and Xavier Raufer (in *Scorched Earth Policy*, *Le Figaro*, 30/04/2003), America has opted for a headlong rush comparable to a '*slash and burn*' tactic, which may initially guarantee a harvest, but, in the long term, will transform savannahs and forests into deserts:

> America's foreign security operations, whether in the Balkans, Central Asia or the Middle-East, are increasingly becoming a global and geopolitical slash and burn tactic. [...] The American policy seems to be in grave contradiction with the very objectives that it has assigned itself: the War on Terror, the war on crime, and the anti-drug war.

From the authors' point of view, the actual methods used by the Americans only serve to reinforce these three plagues. In the Balkans, for instance, the CIA has proceeded to ally itself to both Albanian and Kosovar criminal factions.

***

According to Martin Wollacott, a British specialist on foreign policy issues, '*America has been weakened by its victory in Iraq*' (*The Age*, 05/05/2003). The Iraqi campaign has led to a Pyrrhic victory, one that poses more problems than it actually resolves. This is, first of all, due to the fact that America has failed to form a genuine coalition, antagonising not only its own allies, but also global public opinion. The next reason lies in the fact that, by pretending to be able to manage Iraq and the Middle-East in a proconsular fashion, the USA has accepted a burden that is impossible to bear. Thirdly, all of this has isolated the US from the rest of the world (and from the UN as well), as they all watch America sink into this quagmire, without ever attempting to help it.

For Wollacott, Buchanan and numerous others, the aggressiveness displayed by the neoconservatives is a catastrophe afflicting the US more than the 'rest of the world'. Wollacott notes:

> Ultimately, America has weakened itself because it has failed to develop what historian and foreign policy expert Walter Russel Mead calls "a coherent and applicable strategy to maintain American hegemony in times of peace".

***

Despite the presence of 5,000 soldiers deployed by NATO and 11,500 American ones, Afghanistan has fallen into the depths of anarchy. Various warlords have established themselves there, as have the Taliban. Islamists Gullbudin Heykmatyar and Mullah Omar (Bin Laden's assistant) have rekindled the holy war. Politically speaking, the Americans have already lost this war.

***

In an article entitled *The USA Privatises Iraq*, published by *Libération* on June the 26th 2003, European MP Sami Naïr (MRC) expresses the view that, due to business and oil-related motivations, the USA has been implementing a *'cynical colonisation in Iraq'*. He quotes the words of Thomas Friedman, the foreign affairs commentator at *The New York Times*: *'We now have a 51st state comprising 23 million people. For we have just adopted a new baby called Baghdad'*. In addition, Naïr mentions the comments made by Max Boot (of the highly popular USA Today), who, in an article entitled *American Imperialism? No Need to Run Away from Label*, declares without flinching that any armed opposition in Iraq is doomed to fail because

… more than 125,000 American troops occupy Mesopotamia. They are supported through the resources of the world's richest economy. In a race for the control of Iraq, America can outmatch and crush anyone who opposes it.

***

Here is yet another sign of the NAI's impudence, the like of which none have ever seen: the insistence on exempting all American nationals from facing legal action before the International Court of Justice (ICJ). It is as if US Army members were to be exempt or exempted from answering for potential 'war crimes'. Is such an expectation not an admission of the fact that American militaries do commit such crimes? Washington has even threatened EU candidate countries with sanctions should they sign the ICJ protocols.

***

American historian William S. Lind believes that American neo-imperialism represents a hegemonic flare-up akin to Charles Quint's during the 16th century, whose rise ended in defeat against France and led to the vanquishing of Philip II 's Invincible Armada at the hands of admiral Drake (*StageRight.com, USA*, 24/02/2003). His analysis states:

> The real question is not that of knowing whether the American dynamic towards global hegemony will be successful; for it will not. The question is for us to find out why this objective has become a priority.

***

Donald Rumsfeld, Bush's Secretary of Defence, embodies the NAI's central figure. In spite of his cheekily vulgar humour, Rumsfeld is the true theoretician behind the new doctrine. As the leader of the neo-conservatives already in 1998, he sent Bill Clinton a letter asking him to attack Iraq. His 2003 plan had already been devised at that time. It is actually Rumsfeld that represents the real partisan of a *global coup* and the genuine advocate of excessive American militarism. Dan Schorr, an editorialist at the National Public Radio, had this to say about him:

He displays great skill in hiding his own ideology behind a few jokes, and
yet belongs to those who believe that America must carve its own empire.
He is one of those supporters of pre-emptive war who wish to remain unrivalled on our planet.

Mentioning him in his memoirs, Henry Kissinger writes: *'Of all the
despots that I've dealt with, none was more ruthless than Rumsfeld'.*

Not only is Donal Rumsfeld the very symbol of American in-
consequence, but also that of the imbrication between the personal
business interests of American leaders and imperialism. In 2000, he
had already taken charge of Zürich-based ABB company, enabling it to
sign a 200-million-dollar contract to supply *North Korea* with nuclear
reactors! Two years later, in 2002, he declared that same country to
be a 'terrorist state', a condemnation that was especially due to North
Korea's refusal to freeze its nuclear programme, which had actually
been purchased from Rumsfeld himself (*The Guardian*, 09/05/2003).
Let us also bear in mind that in 1983, Rumsfeld had been sent to
Baghdad by Secretary of State George Schultz in order to renew the
political talks with Iraq. Upon his return, he praised Saddam Hussein,
declaring that he had become his 'friend'. His secret mission had, however, been aimed at obtaining a contract that would allow the Bechtel
oil company (whose long-term manager was none other than Schultz
himself!) to construct a pipeline between Iraq and Jordan.

***

In the unrefined jargon used by neoconservative imperialists, the
expression *'the USA and its allies'* is ultimately used as a synonym for
'America and its vassals'. Following the 'seizure' of Baghdad, George W.
Bush made the following proclamation on board the Abraham Lincoln
aircraft carrier:

> In the battle of Iraq, the United States and our allies have prevailed. [...] In
> this battle, we have fought for the cause of liberty and for the peace of the
> world.

Such political cant is as Orwellian as it is post-Soviet.

***

The USA has often pushed the countries it intended to attack towards committing an 'initial act of aggression' (Pearl Harbor), as part of an ancient tactic inspired by the Greeks and Romans. It is a known fact that, a mere few days before the invasion of Kuwait, April Glaspie, the American ambassador to Iraq in 1991, told Saddam Hussein that the USA was not interested in becoming involved in a quarrel that it considered to be 'Arab business' (Herbert Schiller, *Manipulating Hearts and Minds, Boulder*, Colorado, 1992).

***

In a response against the now famous comments made by G. W. Bush's Defence Secretary, Donald Rumsfeld, according to which France, Germany and Belgium now represented the 'old Europe' due to their opposition to the military campaign in Iraq, Graham F. Fuller wrote an article entitled *Old Europe or Old America*, which was published in *The International Herald Tribune* and caused a sensation overseas. In it, he develops the idea that the imperialistic, unilateralist and ruthless policy implemented by the neoconservatives mirrors a nostalgic longing for long bygone days, a longing that is not suited to the 21st century at all. Fuller is a former CIA official (the vice-president of the National Intelligence Council, to be precise) and the author of *The Future of Political Islam*.

In a study titled *South Gate: Mexico Comes to California*, which appeared in *The American Conservative* on May the 19th 2003, Roger D. McGrath describes California's 'Mexicanisation' through the example of South Gate, while highlighting the resulting degradation of public order and Third-Worldisation:

> While we are engaged overseas in remodelling other countries in our own image, many of our cities are being remodelled in the image of Mexican villages. Nowhere is this more obvious than in California.

***

Also in *The American Conservative*, James Bovard expresses the
conviction that the USA is gradually becoming a *'semi-police state'*
where, ever since 9/11, *'a spate of federal dispositions has reduced the
freedom of Americans without improving their security'*. He proceeds
to strongly criticise the Patriot Act (the new American law regarding
domestic security), whose inspiration has come from John Ashcroft,
the American Minister for Justice, and which limits public liberties
while simultaneously increasing the level of surveillance targeting individuals, especially by means of electronic and informatic espionage
and the denunciation of suspicious events and people. In his view, this
constitutes a return to McCarthyism, only in a worse form:

> Criticising the domestic policy of the Bush administration is assimilated
> with aiding both America's enemies and the terrorists.

Several authors, including professor Edward S. Herman of the Wharton
School University of Columbia (in *Manufacturing Consent*), expand on
the idea that the USA has become a semi-dictatorial entity governed
by a Big-Brother, which they refer to as 'Orwellian'. America is thus
said to be engaging in such global propaganda and disinformation that
it far surpasses the late USSR in terms of subtleness and efficacy.

***

Being more aware of the necessity of informational war than the
Europeans, the American government has just created two new organisms, namely the Under-Secretariat of State for Public Diplomacy
and Public Affairs, which acts as a sort of global ministry with
regard to propaganda and disinformation, and the Office of Global
Communications, which aspires to achieve the very same goals in
connection to the White House. The former's most notable function
is to *'provide the moral foundations for global American leadership'*.
According to professor Libicky of the National Defense University (as
quoted by InfoGuerre.com), the above-mentioned organisms have the

competence to conduct economic war operations, as well as any efforts relating to espionage, psychological intoxication, informatic piracy, and internet-based attacks. As can be seen, American neo-imperialism has adopted a philosophy and methodology highly akin to those of the KGB.

***

As far as American economist Alan Tonelson is concerned, a man who has authored numerous articles on the topic in the economic press overseas, the American commercial deficit (which totalled 435.2 billion dollars in 2002, increasing by 21.5 % annually) will soon become unbearable and usher the country on '*a road to financial ruin*', which may result in a crisis of the Argentinian type, only this time on a Pan-American scale. His theory is that America lacks the necessary means to implement its military imperialism and that the latter is thus highly temporary in nature.

***

UMP representative Pierre Lellouche, who was once an RPR deputy, issued the following warning (RFI, March the 25th 2003): '*Beware of an imminent American weakening in the aftermath of the war in Iraq!*'

He also expressed his regret at the absence of French support. In his view, but also that of the entire Atlanticist camp, an American weakening and retreat would be very damaging to France. I, on the other hand, fail to see how that could ever be possible. On what level does the USA protect us from potential dangers? Why should Europeans require an American 'shield'? Anyone who sees the Americans as our protectors is utterly delirious. This was not even the case at the time of the Cold war. Let us suppose that an ethnic war (the primary danger from our perspective) were to break out in France, a war that would obviously garner the support of all those Muslim-Arab countries that have been exporting their colonising human surplus to our lands: it is very unlikely that the US would assist any potential French or European resistance. On the contrary, what the Americans would do is behave as they did in Kosovo and side with our enemies. I am referring to the American administration, of course, not the Americans themselves. The US government would take on a mediating role and become a reorganiser, so to speak, rejoicing at the Islamisation afflicting Europe.

***

The hypocritical argument of a transatlantic solidary and unity continues to be promulgated everywhere. In *The Herald* (19/04/2003), Henry Kissinger expresses the belief that the birth of a Paris-Berlin-Moscow axis opposing the US during the Iraqi campaign is a potentially graver development than the bipolar tension of the Cold War. He feels that *'revitalising Euro-American relations is an imperative if one is to avoid a return to the power policy of the 19th century'*. He also warns against the emergence of a 'Gaullist vision of Europe', one that would have Germany and Russia follow suit. Furthermore, he obviously expresses his contentment at the pro-American 'follow-my-leader' attitude displayed by Great Britain and Spain. Kissinger dreads the prospect of a Europe divided between pro-American and anti-American countries, remaining averse to multilateralism and the '*UN's instrumentalisation in an effort to isolate America*'.

Acting as both the NAI's advocate and that of the neoconservatives, Kissinger states:

> Our European adversaries in this recent controversy [...] must refrain from presenting the USA as being Rambo and an obstacle to the pursuit of European interests; they must, instead, view America as a partner with common objectives.

Espousing Blair's viewpoint, he asserts that the contradiction between 'American unilateralism' and 'multilateralism' constitutes a hollow debate and that the US and Europe must form one whole, a single power basically, as if they were a couple united through conventional matrimony. All under American governance, of course... What Kissinger is doing is mocking everyone. His hypocrisy is absolute, since a diplomat and geopolitician of his calibre is perfectly aware of the fact that:

1) European interests are in complete divergence to those of the US, as demonstrated by the relentless policy of weakening, submission and economic sabotage implemented by America against Europe; for it is, in fact, the Americans that are the actual aggressors, not the diffident Europeans.

2) One cannot imagine how, following the end of the Cold War, the USA could ever assume the role of Europe's 'protector'. What threat does our continent require protection against?

It is therefore clear that the notion of alleged global unity between European and American geostrategic interests — a notion supported by Blair, all Atlanticists and (obviously) all American hegemonists and justified through supposedly shared moral values — is but a tool of 'mental disarmament'. Such arguments regarding the purported existence of a Euro-American unity of interests and power, which serve as one of the NAI's pillars, will not stand up to scrutiny and collapse in the face of the facts, and in the face of American behaviour itself, which is fundamentally anti-European. Only a minority of British supporters, honoured to act as the Pentagon's auxiliaries, still believe such nonsense. As a result of their anti-European approach, the American government and its new imperialism may end up being discredited by their own aggressiveness, even in previously Atlanticist milieus; and there will be nothing that Kissinger's sermons can do about it.

***

In *Asia Times Online* (12/05/2003), Henry C. K. Liu explains that the USA has moved '*from the Cold War to a Holy War*'.

***

'Do as I say, not as I do': in spite of all the pressure that America has been exerting upon us in an effort to accomplish the destruction of

Europe's single agricultural policy, what the US has been practicing, whether on this level or another, can only be described as pure protectionism, with Europeans lacking the courage to protest against it. In April 2003, the American Congress passed an 'agricultural law' that raises the subventions granted to American farmers by 80 million dollars in the space of a decade. Unlike their soft European counterparts, American leaders (whose economic policy is only 'liberal' by name) have decided to further reinforce the protection of their national industry and defence technologies using the 2004 *Defense Authorisation Bill*, which restricts the access of foreign companies to the American military market, an access that was extremely difficult to begin with.

***

Just like Europe, the USA now faces an extremely dangerous mass immigration. This, however, does not seem to trouble the NAI's neo-conservatives, whose 'patriotism' is limited to international imperialism and a concern to fuel both the American oil industry and the US military-industrial complex.

The survey conducted in September 2003 by the American Census Bureau yielded the following figures: in the 1990s, the number of Hispanic immigrants in the US rose from 7 to 14 million. The total count of immigrants that have been granted official residency (meaning that they were not born in the USA) has increased from 19.6 million to 31 million. During that same period, the rate of South-East Asian immigrants grew by 141 % and that of sub-Saharan Africans by as much as 174 %. If one only counts the development that has taken place since G. W. Bush became President, there are 2.5 million legal and illegal immigrants that have settled in the USA, despite all the measures that have been taken since 9/11 to bring immigration under control.

In relation to this, American nationalist and anti-imperialistic conservative Patrick Buchanan has used the term '*suicide pill of mass immigration*'. He has stated the following on Americancause.org:

> In America today, we have a nation within a nation, one that is growing inexorably and is composed of people who have come to us from continents and countries that have never been completely assimilated into western civilisation. Most of those who arrive here are illiterate, do not speak any English and have a very low level of income.

In Buchanan's eyes, the current immigration process is weakening America, whose real level of life began to diminish in 2002, especially since those immigrants consume social services and benefits without bringing anything in return in terms of work force and wealth creation. The Left is obviously pleased with this situation, while the Republicans in power remain idle-handed.

> In the meantime, thousands of industrial jobs are disappearing. We delocalise and export our industrial positions abroad, whereas foreign countries export their poor to the US. The latter are then sustained at the expense of the American taxpayer. This is what they call "free exchange".

Furthermore, Buchanan complains of the fact that American taxpayers finance immigrant schooling, even when it comes to the children of illegals. A solid analysis by any means, but what would Buchanan say if he analysed the situation in Europe, and particularly that of France? He then adds insult to injury:

> In 1960, 97 % of the American population was composed of inhabitants who had been born in the US, and school results improved year by year. However, since the number of Third World schoolchildren keeps growing, school results are plummeting, and our education lobby is getting worried about it, constantly demanding "more money and more means". It simultaneously demands, in a completely inconsequential manner, more open borders, which will cause the school level to drop a little further.

Deploring the fact that the Right is not remedying the situation by containing the immigrant inflow, Buchanan quotes John Stuart Mill's words: *'The Tories are the stupid Party'*. No further comment is necessary.

ANNEXES (PART II)

A Few Comments on the Topic of Neo-Militarism

On September the 16th 2003, *The Los Angeles Times* published a surprising declaration made by General Ricardo Sanchez, the head of American military operations in Iraq. In it, he begins by acknowledging the huge on-location combat difficulties and their impact on American troop morale (thus admitting that US troops are as fragile as they are inexperienced in combat). He then goes on to issue the following tragicomic warning, one that unveils the NAI's entire essence, with its simultaneously derisory and para-religious aspect:

> We are beginning to realise that this battlefield is critical for America itself. I am absolutely convinced that it is imperative for us to prevail here; for if we do not win, it is our American cities that will become the next combat zone. We cannot allow ourselves to let that happen.

Iraq's occupation and pacification are therefore presented as embodying the central confrontation between the civilised world and the barbarity of Evil. According to Belgian geopolitical website dedefensa.org:

> [T]his notion is, in fact, widespread among US military forces, whose members are constantly subjected to such conditioning and are thus convinced that they fight in the name of God [AN: And yet, Muslims are equally convinced that they fight in 'God's name']. One must not look upon this as an act of manipulation, but at worst, one of self-manipulation. Just like George Bush himself, each GI is convinced that God is on his side — regardless of

244

whether He actually is or not — and that the current conflict is the ultimate battle, meaning that of Armageddon.

What we are dealing with here is therefore a delusional reconstruction of reality, a purely virtual approach characterised by a grandiloquent dimension; this speaks volumes about the rather infantile and pathetic aspect pervading the NAI's 'imperial will and ideology':

> Yes, indeed, Iraq is where the ultimate overseas war is being waged. Should this war ever be lost, it would lead to the ultimate struggle for America's survival.

America proceeds to considerably exaggerate the stakes (now that it has trapped itself in the quagmire of this utterly pointless 'battle') so as to mobilise the simple minds of an ever-fragile American public opinion and raise GI morale.

However, one must not give in to the impression that this vision is cynical in essence, for it comprises a certain rate of childish sincerity. As revealed by Patrick Buchanan, the belief that if Americans '*do not fight against the terrorists in Iraq*', then they will '*have to fight them in American cities*' is a common one in Washington.

This represents a staggering psychological evolution from a 'triumphant America' stage (with the ridiculous Top Gun ceremony conducted by George W. Bush on board the USS Abraham Lincoln when, dressed in US Air Force attire, he declared the 'mission' to be 'accomplished') to a phase where America is in mortal danger: 'We must either claim victory in Iraq, or face America's total defeat'. One is thus truly under the impression of witnessing a tragicomic event in which the leaders of the 'Empire' are literally losing their footing.

***

In *the American Conservative* (15/09/2003), Patrick Buchanan expands on the naivety that characterises those neoconservative leaders who found themselves outwitted by cunning Bin Laden and Al-Qaeda.

In his view, by first invading Afghanistan then Iraq, Bush has done precisely what the Islamists required in order to resume their *jihad*.

> Our enemies know us better than we know ourselves. We react exactly as they have anticipated and do precisely what they want us to. Filled with hurt pride and outraged patriotism, we hasten into the trap and swallow the bait that they threw us on September 11th. The terrorists who hurled those planes against the Pentagon and the WTC were not hoping to overthrow the American government or force the US to surrender. They are fanatical, but not insane. They wanted to injure, bleed and provoke America by striking it with a whip. By sending an American army to occupy Baghdad, we have become toys in the hands of Al-Qaeda. We are thus exactly where they want us to be. Where they have us at their mercy. We are where they can kill us, in their own garden.

By giving in to provocation and intervening in Afghanistan and Iraq, the NAI has done what Al-Qaeda and the terrorists wanted it to: it has widened the field of battle and terrorism, spread the *Dar-Al-Harb*, the Domain of War, and lured the naïve 'Judeo-Crusaders' into the minefield, so as to convince the Muslim masses that an 'aggression' against Islam and its sacred lands was justified. The simple-minded American administration cannot contend with Islam's age-old strategy. The defeat that America suffered on 9/11 has thus turned out to be twofold.

✱✱✱

Within the new ideological atmosphere surrounding the NAI and its neoconservatives, one encounters certain traits of the McCarthyism that typified the 1950s, when all alleged communists were hunted. On a periodical basis, America allows the demons of intolerance to resurface. Here are a few examples.

David Frum, a *National Review* editorialist who contributes to the drafting of Bush's speeches, is among those who have openly declared themselves to be the enemies of the 'Axis of Evil'. Frum is, in fact, the man who coined the very expression ('*Axis of Evil*'). He displays hostility towards all conservatives and Rightists who do not follow Bush, labelling them '*anti-patriotic conservatives*' and urging the Republican Party to '*turn its back on these heretics*'. On its part, the Antiwar.com website has qualified Frum as a '*political commissioner*'. David Keene, who stands at the head of the American Conservative Union (ACU), has participated in a polemical debate in which he stood up for intellectual Robert Novak, a man who Frum accused of being '*anti-Semitic*' because he chose to criticise the Iraqi campaign. A very intense polemic ensued within the American Right, which the above-mentioned website described as follows:

> Due to their pretentious claims of being the moral and ideological guardians of the Faith, Frum and his friends have irritated the rest of the Right to such an extent that they have managed to achieve within the conservative movement what the American military has accomplished in Iraq: to trigger a generalised rebellion against the forces of occupation.

What we are thus witnessing may well be an attempt on the part of the ruling neoconservative apparatus to take control of the American intelligentsia and media on both an ideological and a propagandist level. According to anti-Bush Rightists, the destabilising attacks targeting Patrick Buchanan and Bob Novak, who are both opposed to the Iraqi operation for America's sake, are actually motivated by the fact that the two have been accused of refusing to aid Israel, a country which they are said to detest… As can clearly be seen, current American political debates revolve around the entity of Israel.

Indeed, the focus of numerous debates that shake the American conservative intelligentsia and involve a confrontation between the adversaries and partisans of the NAI and its neoconservatives is actually on the Israeli issue and the topic of antisemitism. What is certain is that the *neocons* have formed a kind of historical alliance between practicing Protestants and Jews; and yet, one must not submit to the belief that those who oppose 'Bush's wars' are actually anti-Jewish. There are, in fact, many Jews amongst them, including Elie R. Bernstein and Catherine Lewine, who espouse the view that, far from 'helping' the Jewish state, the American elephant's intervention in the Middle-East only serves to fuel the Muslim-Arab anthill that lies at the gates of Israel and will cause an upsurge of terrorist acts, which is already happening, of course. With regard to this issue, the same ideological division can be observed not only among American Jews, but also among Israelis.

***

American neo-militarism can be summarised using the following formula proposed by William Pfaff: '*straddling the world*'.

William Pfaff, a regular chronicler at *the International Herald Tribune*, is among the most pertinent critics denouncing both the NAI and its militarism. What follows is a synthesis of his analyses regarding the current bout of American militarism, which, according to him, greatly contributes to the development of the very terrorism that it allegedly longs to eradicate.

The American Secretary of Defence, Donald Rumsfeld, has reversed a tendency that the US had abided by since the American defeat in Vietnam: instead of reducing the number of American military bases located abroad, as was once the case, the Americans now find it necessary to increase their count. This novel doctrine, which is supposed to guarantee America's security, will only result in a growing number of American targets (through terrorist attacks, the taking of hostages, etc.) and further provocative acts, not to mention the astronomical costs that go hand in hand with such a mass presence.

This absurd policy, first of all, completely contradicts any and every global 'power projection' strategy, since the presence of new military bases is synonymous with troop immobility, in addition to the fact that the American army is in dire need of high-quality manpower and recruits and that the 'boys' are becoming ever more homesick and live in dread of all those bullets flying overhead. On the other hand, the desire to reinforce global American interests and US influence through sheer militarism and strategic occupation will, of course, only have an opposite effect.

However, the NAI is thus emphasising the existence of new geo-political ambitions that stem from the disintegration of the USSR: the purpose is now for America to establish military bases in the 'New Europe', meaning a previously sovietised Europe that now acts as America's vassal, especially Poland, Bulgaria and Romania, using its contingents located in Germany. Under the guise of controlling the so-called 'arc of instability', the Pentagon is also contemplating the establishment of such bases in formerly soviet Central Asia; but its real aim lies in encircling Russia and supervising (unavailingly, in point of fact) the local oil and gas routes and deposits. It is also a matter of sustaining the military bases situated in Iraq, thus maintaining the American presence in this country *ad infinitum*, as is the case in Japan. Furthermore, these military bases are said to be 'reception points' that would allow American forces to be moved urgently from the American territory in the event of a crisis. For instance, five military bases are expected to remain in Iraq, a country that the Americans hope will become a new client state. Talk about daydreams!

Pfaff obviously believes that these intrusive projects are a danger-ous folly. What neoconservative militarists are oblivious to is the fact that the 9/11 attacks, just like the birth of Al-Qaeda (an essentially Saudi network), was primarily due to the presence of American bases in Saudi Arabia, in the aftermath of the first Gulf War. The bases have since been evacuated, as part of a terrorism-evasion reflex. By hop-ing to move those bases to Iraq, the Americans are making a strategic withdrawal. What they have failed to grasp is that any permanent American presence in Middle-Eastern Arab countries can only be per-ceived as an act of provocation and aggression that Islamists secretly long for and that will justify the intensification of both Islamic *jihad* and terrorism. Indeed, how can anyone be stupid enough to pretend that they could vanquish terrorism on a military level by establish-ing GI bases in the Muslim world? Pfaff speaks of a globally 'fanciful' foreign policy. Ever since the 9/11 events, not only have the military interventions in Afghanistan and the Philippines (often aimed at impressing an American public opinion that is as infantile as its leaders) failed to eradicate Islamic terrorist networks, but have actually managed to reinforce the latter.

In Pfaff's opinion, the American Protestant ideology regarding America's 'Manifest Destiny' (which God Himself allegedly bestowed upon the US) has now turned into a desire for global hegemony which not only makes use of traditional strategies of influence, intimidation and twisted manoeuvres, but resorts to a straightforward militarism that is as rash as it is exalted.

> The neoconservative enthusiasm for new American bases around the world, under the pretext of universal goodwill, indicates that they all agree with the idea that America must straddle the world — just in case…

This image says it all. The NAI is under the impression that it could control the planet by scattering military bases across its surface. '*Are air bases in Central Asia or East Africa truly necessary for terrorist networks to be dismantled*'? It is an undeniable fact that the USA, the unrivalled specialist in aerial bombardment, has always believed the latter to be an effective means of crushing those that resist it, when, in actual fact, it only serves to increase enemy recruitment. The Israelis, too, follow the same line of inconsequential reasoning in their struggle against Palestinian terrorism, using heavy, mediatised and visible military means.

In Pfaff's eyes, this military expansionism

> … is a remedy with no bearing upon terrorist evil and, generally speaking, one that is completely inefficient when it comes to resolving any political problem.

Incidentally, it must be said that the massive terrorist attacks conducted on 9/11 had actually been organised by networks composed of Westernised Islamic fanatics who had settled into the USA and Europe (and had been integrated into them), and not concocted in the sandy expanses and deserts of backward countries inhabited by uncultivated tribes whose culture is primitive. Another fact worth highlighting is that the most subversive and dangerous form of Islamic preaching takes in Western mosques and that the *mujahideen* are funded by Saudi banks. What Pfaff thus implies is that the war against Islamism and its terrorist aspects can only be won on American and European soil (where unchecked immigrants abound), and not by means of bombarding pseudo-training camps or civilian populations comprised of poor wretches dressed in rags.

> The most efficient strategy against terrorism and Al-Qaeda networks is that of the secret police and not that of bombs and military bases... [...] Not a single attempt has been made by the current administration and the Pentagon to prove to the American public that the military adventurism we all know of and the establishment of military bases on foreign soil are utterly inefficacious in a "war on terror" [...]; which means that the large-scale attacks that the US has fallen prey to have every chance of reoccurring.

Not only is the NAI unable to protect itself against such acts of aggression, but it actually provokes and exacerbates them.

In his writings, William Pfaff leaves open the question whether this militarism is truly dedicated to the 'war on terror' (in which case it would be a sign of sheer stupidity) or whether it conceals some other, cynically hidden objectives, such as an imperialistic policy of global domination. Even if the latter option were true, this would be an equal sign of stupidity, since the militarism and warmongering described above are both far more damaging than effective for any dominating world power.

I have a theory in this regard. Overall, the American warmongering that lasted from World War I to the Vietnam conflict was motivated either by a struggle against objective threats (which originated mainly from states that enjoyed genuine military power) or by a desire for geostrategic domination in the name of the United States itself. It would seem that all of this changed after the collapse of the USSR and the gradual advent of neoconservatism.

The following suggestion has already been included elsewhere in this book, but it is always wise to highlight important theories. Washington's 'neo-militarism' (or 'neo-warmongering', perhaps) is no longer motivated by pressing, statal and targetable issues, but by *vague* and hazardous ones. Even the Pentagon itself no longer believes that the 'war on terror' could be conducted by invading Iraq, bombarding Central Asia and establishing military air bases on a global scale. It seems to be the case that, in the absence of genuine enemies and real military threats (following the fall of soviet Communism), the Americans — or their leaders, at least — are seeking to invent foes to struggle against.

Why? *To fuel the military-industrial machinery*, which is in constant need of new orders and funds politicians who often act as its agents or shareholders. The ruling American elite thus ignores American interests, regardless of all its 'patriotic' or 'biblical' professions of faith. Unlike Napoleonian or Bismarckian militarism, not to mention that of Louis the 14th, current American militarism may well be founded upon patriotic and nationalistic sentiments (i.e. 'Stars and Stripes'), but does not actually *experience* any such feelings.

Furthermore, it is often the case (Perle, Cheney, Wolfowitz and co.) that American militarism is not meant to guarantee America's economic hegemony by attacking its rivals (including Japan, Germany and many others), but merely serves as a means of increasing the personal wealth of warmongering leaders whose interests lie, for instance, in ensuring that all military orders received by Boeing, a company in which they themselves are shareholders, rise by 10 % a year, as can be seen today.

The only genuine and efficient 'war on terror' (considering that this is the pretext used by neo-imperialists) lies in waging a shadow war through obscure, ungrateful yet merciless police work that takes place at the very bottom, as part of efforts that cannot, of course, have any immediate electoral or financial impact. Let us also mention, at this stage, the fight against Muslim immigration in Western countries...

It is, therefore, not always a question of stupidity or blindness, nor one of ideological delirium (as witnessed in the case of our naïve European leaders), but a matter of short-term, calculating behaviour on the part of American leaders, who are focused on their own personal gain and on using their own country's foreign policy to their own advantage by establishing an unbridled sort of warmongering.

In no way are these leaders against Islam, nor even against China, a country which shall, in the very near future, become the primary contender for the position of the world's main superpower. They will, furthermore, never manage to maintain the already fragile American hegemony. By using the above-mentioned expression ('*All find agreement in the idea that America should straddle the world*'), William Pfaff may well have hinted at the typical ending of every rodeo, with the cowboy finding himself in the dirt, his arse above his head.

***

Hollywood has been doing the army's bidding for ages. Just like in national socialist Germany and the USSR, American cinema has long been at the service of statal imperialism and ideology. Lately, however, the phenomenon has been increasing pace. This is what Jean-Michel Valentin has demonstrated in his book entitled *Hollywood, the Pentagon and Washington — The Main Protagonists in a Strategy* (Autrement editions, 2003). He writes: '*The modalities of the cooperation between the security apparatus and the major studios are numerous, intricate and ever-increasing*'. Arnold Schwarzenegger's candidature for the post of governor in California confirms this tendency, as does Reagan's election (Reagan himself is a former actor). The army provides many films with the necessary logistics, script-writers and advisors, with the Pentagon using its 'black budget' to finance these cinematic releases. Countless super-productions thus relay the official US ideology in a most straightforward fashion and, influenced by the Pentagon, act as

plain and simple instruments of American national and global propaganda. Hollywood has been 'enlisted' and constantly uses its highly
spectacular humanitarian-military or disaster-themed films to develop
the idea that America is under threat so as to maintain a certain level
of patriotic mobilisation among the American population.

There is yet another highly interesting phenomenon related to all
of this, namely the Pentagon's domestic power in comparison with the
US civil administration and the elected American government. The
White House and the DoD (Department of Defence) constitute two
separate and distinct entities. The former is temporary and subject to
elections, whereas the latter is a long-lasting power with the ability to
dictate its will. Such a situation is unthinkable on our continent. In the
USA, the 'military-industrial' and 'military-cultural' complexes have
the capacity to impose themselves (as part of an alliance between the
mercantile and military functions) against the will of the government
located in Washington, using Hollywood as a means to achieve this.

Strangely enough, the American army (which, in the USA, is
connected to the world of business) dictates its every wish upon the
government, just like in Third World countries. To be more specific,
if one adds together the influence and independence enjoyed by numerous intelligence agencies and the police (the CIA, FBI, NSA, DIA,
and so on), it quickly becomes apparent that the federal state is both
heterogeneous and divided, always falling prey to internal conflict.
This is what accounts for the foreign policy's instability, even if it does
not impact American 'patriotic' cohesion in any way.

***

The gravest danger lies in the new nuclear doctrine embraced by the
Pentagon. In May 2003, following the 'brilliant American victory' in
Iraq, the Bush administration launched a novel idea. This idea had, for
decades on end, been expressed in various private circles by Donald
Rumsfeld, the overzealous and predatory politician who acts both
as America's Secretary of Defence and as a theoretician of absolute

militarism. In several serious milieus, the above-mentioned idea was deemed to be utterly insane, in addition to being decidedly typical of neoconservative *hubris*.

The concept revolves around the manufacturing of small-scale nuclear bombs known as 'mini-nukes', whose destructive power is (relatively) limited and totals 5 kilotons, meaning one third of the bomb that was dropped on Hiroshima. These 'mini-nukes' are meant to destroy underground bunkers that resist traditional explosives. According to *The Independent* (22/05/2003), secret research has been conducted into such weapons over the past ten years. Washington is said to be attempting to convince the American Congress to vote in favour of funding this development. According to some people, if the project were granted a level of independence becoming of a 'state within a state' (which the Pentagon has already attained, not to mention the opacity that characterises military budgets), any and all parliamentary authorisation would become entirely superfluous.

What is totally new (and extremely serious) about this programme is that it breaks the sanctification deadlock on nuclear weapons (even those of average intensity), which have hitherto been used solely as a deterrent against other nuclear arms or as part of second-strike reprisals. Nuclear arms are thus trivialised, becoming the 'battlefield's theatrical weaponry'. A certain group of Democratic senators has warned against the fact that such a decision '*would lower the utilisation threshold of nuclear weapons*'. Another warning was issued by senator Edward Kennedy in early May 2003: '*If we produce it, we will use it, and it will be a one-way street to nuclear war*'. Using words in the same vein, Illinois senator Richard Durbin made a cautionary declaration: *In the eyes of all countries, this project will signify that America is prepared to relaunch the nuclear arms race on a global scale*'.

One is obviously left in total disbelief at the sight of the neoconservative and neo-imperialistic aptitude (the 'Bush doctrine') to always bring about the very opposite international effect to the one intended, while resorting to incredibly clumsy provocations and initiatives: this approach has enhanced the Islamist terrorist breeding ground and fostered the emergence of an Islamic republic in Iraq, and is now inciting dozens of countries to arm themselves with weapons of mass destruction (particularly nuclear ones) by setting an example for others to follow and driving them to protect themselves against a possible American 'folly'. Not only is Bush unrivalled in his services to Islamism, but he is also the best sales representative in the field of nuclear proliferation.

In a display of typical simplism, Donald Rumsfeld gave the following response: '*It is only a matter of studying such weapons, no more, no less*'. Why would anyone choose to 'study' something that is not being considered for manufacture and use? Rumsfeld solemnly swore that the production of such weapons would require '*the Congress' special authorisation*'. Based on the Iraqi campaign, of course, we all know what neoconservative promises are worth. In addition, the use of these medium-potency nuclear bombs would soon become entirely commonplace and would definitely not be restricted to ultra-special circumstances. Such bombs would practically be equated with traditional ballistic weapons. Indeed, according to the Pentagon's masterminds, their purpose is not solely restricted to the destruction of underground bunkers (as 'earth penetrators'), but encompasses further usage on the battlefield, as is the case with conventional artillery and bombs (the so-called 'weapons for battlefield use'), with all the resulting radioactive repercussions upon our planet's atmosphere!

During the Cold War, France did develop some tactical anti-force nuclear arms (the Pluton and Hades Theatre Missile Defence systems), but unlike the current situation, in which the US army plays its battle-field games with small powers, these were only meant to stop a potential Soviet mass offensive that would have crushed Europe. According to the National Resource Defense Council, the Pentagon's suppliers have already completed the development of a deep penetration bomb, the B 61 Mod 11. All that is left is for them to equip it with a nuclear warhead. And it gets even better: it is rumoured that they no longer intend to

limit themselves to 5 kilotons, venturing all the way to 300 kilotons instead. In a most placid fashion, the NRDC acknowledges the fact that these weapons would result in fatal above-surface radiation even when exploding underneath the ground. And hold on to your hats, now: the NRDC is even considering the use of one-megaton bombs, which would explode at a 300-meter altitude above a given battlefield, wreaking 70 times more damage than the Hiroshima bomb!

The very fact that such options are not only being considered, but even being leaked to the public highlights just how irresponsible American leaders have become, intoxicated by their own militarism. Considering how inept American ground troops are at waging battle, this militarism is all the more callous and immoderate. The Democratic opposition has objected to the project, which, they say, robs the USA of yet another portion of its international credibility. These Democrats also feel that the Pentagon holds sway over the US foreign affairs ministry.[12]

To Washington's great displeasure, it did not take long for Russia, a country that is attempting to restore its military power, to react:

1) In the spring of 2003, its naval air forces conducted various military manoeuvres simulating nuclear strikes against both American and British forces;

2) Ivanov, the Russian Defence minister, gave a detailed presentation of Russia's new military doctrine, a doctrine that extends the cases where nuclear weapons are to be employed. Never in the entire Cold War did the Soviets behave in this manner.

This example demonstrates that the new American policy has become uncontrollable due to its excessiveness and thoughtlessness. It is now capable of triggering an atomic war and actually reduces our planet's security compared to the former 'balance of terror' between the East and the West. It seems that, in every conceivable domain, American

---

12 TN: The US Department of State.

leaders have taken it upon themselves to destabilise the world, which also applies to the economic level. The 'New World Order' sought by Bush Senior has now been transformed into global chaos by Bush Junior. Bravo.

***

The Euro-American antagonisms that pervade the Defence sphere are becoming increasingly self-evident. Will a European awakening result in efforts and decisions, rather than empty Americanophobic ideological declarations that are never followed by actions?

In the summer of 2003, the first ever 'Summer University of Defence' event was held in Arcachon. It was an excellent initiative which enabled all French industrials specialising in this sector to gather. The press barely covered the event, as this highly crucial subject does not, unfortunately, hold much interest from the public's perspective.

What follows is a summary of the topics that were covered in the debates. The latter were marked by a truly salutary realisation of the threats that the USA burdens the European Defence with and that must urgently be attended to, as well as by the overall rejection of any and all Atlanticism of the British kind. First of all, the debates exploded the myth surrounding the existence of a 'European fortress'. On the other hand, it is an undeniable fact that an American one does indeed exist. The USA has had several European countries grant it a total of 5 billion dollars to finance its Joint Strike Fighter combat plane, whose manufacture is meant to sink all rival European projects, especially the French and British-Swedish ones. However, no one can be blamed for this but the Europeans themselves, since they willingly agreed to collaborate with the Americans on making this fool's bargain.

The US refuses to import European materials, while simultaneously compelling Europe to purchase American ones without allowing Europeans to technologically control the materials in question, thus plunging our continent into unambiguous techno-military dependency. Militarily speaking, the Americans have a triple interest and a threefold objective with regard to Europe:

1) To sabotage our continent's ability to produce high-tech military material, in an effort to establish an American monopoly in this domain;

2) To take advantage of European brain-power and funds without, however, allowing any transfers of American technology;

3) To incite European countries to send their own ground troops (our soldiers are mere cannon fodder for the Americans) and increase the size of their infantry forces in matters of foreign intervention (all under American commandment, of course) so as minimise the number of casualties among the 'boys'. This is especially true now, within the framework of all current and future US military adventures. In other words, America awards itself all noble tasks (the use of high-end technology and military commandment), while Europe is left with all the menial work. These are the terms that the Poles and Spaniards, with their limited means and constant eagerness to create an impression of international importance, agreed to during the Iraqi campaign.

Fortunately, the participants in the Acarchon debates were mostly very sceptical about any possible techno-military cooperation with the USA, since the American partner is not perceived as being reliable. As far as the establishment of a European armament agency is concerned, an agency that is supposed to harmonise our continent's military industries and all intra-European material purchases, we must be careful not to allow it 'to turn into an American Trojan horse on our own soil'. Furthermore, none of the participants truly believed that the American market could, in time, open itself up to European Defence companies, unless the latter were first bought off by their American counterparts, which is already happening to the unfortunate British, America's consenting and mistreated vassals. For profoundly geostrategic and economic reasons, Euro-American rivalry is well-anchored and will remain so for a long time to come; which is not so much the fault of the Europeans, who, sadly, *do* lack pugnacity, but is rather due to America's devouring ambitions and Washington's duplicity.

In yet another piece of good news, the speakers unanimously adopted a measure advocated by a certain industrialist — that of applying the law of reciprocity to our relations with the USA:

> What we need is a reprisal policy in response to American protectionism. We must protect our European markets in the same fashion that American ones are, no more, no less.

He also proposed subjecting all EU states to the obligation of implementing a European purchase preference in the armament field.

Such measures will indeed have to be extended to include all non-military sectors as well. Unfortunately, the policy applied by Brussels goes in any other direction but that, since, unlike the Americans, who preach free exchange for others without practicing it themselves, it has chosen to shatter the common customs barriers rather than to abide by the doctrine of *self-centred economy* (with liberalism applied within a large, protected space). Ultimately, however, the notion of European preference is indeed making headway in the techno-military field...

There is a further idea that was embraced unanimously: unlike what prejudicial expectations would have us believe, Europe has not, technologically speaking, been lagging behind the USA:

> European research facilities are of an excellent quality, but in the absence of political will, our expenditure towards research and development is, compared to the US, outclassed by a ratio of 1 to 5, perhaps even a 1-to-10 ratio in certain segments. This attitude will eventually have fatal results, within as little as 5 to 15 years.

Indeed, American companies do enjoy massive research funding, and, unlike what we are witnessing in Europe, the government does not sacrifice its military budget, knowing all too well that the latter not only contributes to power growth, but also has an enormous technological impact on all cutting-edge civil industries. If Europe does not make an effort towards readjusting its research expenditures soon, especially in the military domain, it will rob itself of its own strategic independence.

A good example of this is epitomised by one of Europe's rare strong-willed and courageous decisions: the funding of the Galileo satellite-positioning programme, rivalling the American GPS system that currently holds global monopoly. Washington has obviously done everything within its power to sink Galileo, or, at least, to Americanise it through purchase. Its endeavour has, thus far, only led to failure, particularly thanks to French obstinacy. Let us hope that Europe will manage to stand firm in this regard, for

> ... the Americans are currently developing a modernised version of their satellite-driven guiding device in order to prevent some people from using it. How would Europeans be able to guide their own smart bombs one day if Washington decided against it?

Taking into account our world's growing dependence upon satellite guiding and positioning, America might additionally be able to paralyse a number of European military and public sectors.

As is apparent, an awakening has truly been taking place among our French industrialists, engineers and researchers. This, however, does not suffice. We must acquire the necessary funds and make an effort to finance our endeavours, especially when considering the fact that our European researchers and engineers, who are oftentimes superior to American ones, are being increasingly enticed by the seductive conditions and enormous budgets available to them overseas. All that is necessary is for Europeans to simply invert their financial priorities (a plan that requires the successful implementation of an immense mental revolution and a massive moral liberation), which is a burning issue that the above-mentioned Summer University obviously failed to tackle. There are some troubling questions to be asked here: is it preferable to inject finances into research and development within the field of high-technology, or to spend an entire fortune on social assistantship, the fictional employment of 'young people', the annulment of debts and the utterly wasteful and unnecessary direct aid granted to various Third World potentates, etc.? Europe's future will depend on what the urgent answer turns out to be. Our continent shall either be reduced to an impoverished economic zone that submits to the American will, or rise to become a genuine world power.

***

The ideologists behind Atlanticism lack any and all common sense and detest the mere idea of a 'European power'.

Despite the seemingly coherent approach embraced by these intellectuals, their reasoning leads to ever-increasing sophism and analytical mistakes; this is simply due to the fact that their minds are ruled by an underlying passion and moral dogma, as is the case with those hysterical anti-Americans.

Let us consider the example of André Glucksmann, who authored the book entitled *The West Against the West* (Plon editions). He is right when remarking that the Occident is growing ever more divided and is now split into two halves: Europe (or at least a part of it) against America and its accomplices. He has, in fact, adopted the observation made by William Pfaff in his *International Herald Tribune* chronicles. Europeans are said to be failing in their assessment of the 'war on terror' and succumbing to a '*secret longing for inaction*'. Owing to their own idealism and fearfulness, they are considered to be sinking into pacifism, just like pre-Hitlerian democracies once did. What we are thought to be dealing with is an alleged conflict between 'nihilism and civilisation', as Europeans refuse to concede the fact that terrorism is striving to destroy the Occident. By contrast, Americans are considered to be fully aware of this, which supposedly makes their warmongering understandable.

This tragedy is here to stay. War is upon us and has never left our horizons. [...] To achieve peace: such is the watchword of all civic and intellectual cowardliness.

In short, the basic expectation is for Europe to ally itself to the Bush doctrine.

Displaying a greater philosophical inclination, Glucksmann is making an attempt at polemology. And yet, his binary analysis is utterly flawed. Although he justly castigates pacifism, he basically fails to comprehend that rejecting American warmongering is not necessarily synonymous with pacifism or weakness. Not everyone who criticises the Bush doctrine is necessarily a pro-Palestinian Arabophile or a pacifistic Trotskyite. Completely blinded by his 'Euro-American solidarity', Glucksmann cannot see that the warmongering that pervades US neo-imperialism is just as nihilistic and pernicious as terroristic Islamism, the very same Islamism that it claims to struggle against while, in fact, reinforcing it. He cannot fathom the fact that those naïve neoconservatives, blinded by their oil greed and what they believe to be a profitable military occupation (in both Iraq and Afghanistan), have actually fallen straight into a trap set by the Islamists, as the American Gulliver was lured into a Middle-Eastern dead-end using a baiting tactic whose aim was to expand *jihadist* pretexts and fighting fronts.

Glucksmann has not grasped this age-old ploy, one that is already encountered in the Koran itself and consists in provoking the adversary, thus forcing him to react and come across as the actual aggressor in order to legitimise one's own offensive. He cannot admit that Bush is the useful idiot serving the interests of all *mujahideen* and that his warmongering provides all Western Islamophiles with further arguments in support of the notion that 'it is the West that is attacking and invading Islam', which, in turn, allows Islam's secret mass invasion to pass unnoticed. The Bush doctrine has thus given the Islamic infiltration into our lands a huge helping hand.

Displaying an enormous flaw that has long typified Parisian intellectuals, Glucksmann's reasoning is not based on *facts* as much as on

ideas, abstract concepts and feelings. He 'philosophises', a verb that has
now lost most of its meaning. In his lyricism on 'civilisation', not for an
instant does he mention the ruthless economic, cultural and technological war that the USA has been waging against Europe, including its
own European vassals.

What must also be pointed out at this stage is that since 1991, French
intellectuals have only offered us mediocre political debates, regardless
of whether they are pro- or anti-American. In both the US and Great
Britain, the confrontation between the opponents and the supporters
of neo-imperialism has been far more prolific. This is because it has
not been soiled by ideological prejudice, which remains ever so similar
to theological prejudgement.

***

Speaking of ideological prejudice, this is precisely what we encounter
in Stephen Launay's work entitled *A War Within a War — An Essay on
Western Disputes*. His conception is founded upon the very same premise as Glucksmann's, namely the Euro-American divide. Americans espouse the principle of '*justified warfare*', while Europeans succumb to
the utopianism of '*perpetual peace*'. These ideas mirror Kagan's and are
partially correct. However, being a profound intellectual with a greater
fascination for vague philosophical explanations than for pragmatic
and palpable reasons, the author fails to understand that European
pacifism is rooted in economic causes, namely the refusal to invest into
a genuine military-industrial complex. Just like Glucksmann, Launay
does not advocate the founding of a 'European power'. One can only
agree with him regarding his refusal to acknowledge the existence of
an Evil USA, yet one still feels that he drives the reader in the opposite
direction, one that is equally stupid: that of viewing America as the
embodiment of Good.

Launay approves of '*American idealism*', which he believes to be
fighting for human rights even on a militaristic level, distancing itself
from '*the hypocritical invocation of international legality*', a legality

which, similarly to pacifism, only leads to the consolidation of tyrannical sovereignty. And this where his thoughts and analysis drift away from specific facts and sink deep into pure morals, as is always the case with those 'philosophers' who choose to interfere in politics or geopolitics and prefer ethical 'pondering' to accurate and comprehensible answers.

Let us now return, in this regard, to Glucksmann's above-mentioned book and the topic of hyper-moralistic temptation, which diverts political analysis away from its intended purpose. Indeed, our 'philosopher' reproaches everyone who opposes the Bush doctrine for turning towards Russia, which is more or less demonised for being an autocratic power that contrasts with virtuous America. This is the very same America described by Tocqueville, whom the French credit with just about any conceivable words, just as they do with Nietzsche. Whatever the case, a Paris-Berlin-Moscow axis is thus perceived as being reprehensible. The author criticises the '*tenacious Russian preference*' embraced by a chauvinistic and frustrated France, which '*succumbs to a Tsar-like image in an effort to resist the cowboy figure*'. Next in line, we have the following utterly ridiculous formula:

> Down with the cowboy and his adventurism! [pro-Putin anti-Americanists are heard to cry] Long live the despot and his war in the Caucasus! Atlanticism is done for, the future shall be Eurasian.

This anti-Russian abhorrence and love for America is typical of such people, who, similarly to Glucksmann himself, were all Stalinists or Maoists in their days of youth, including Bernard-Henri Lévy.

In other words, it is for moral reasons (i.e. to save our very souls) that we are expected to turn to America (the embodiment of Good) and reject any and every odious power alliance with the Russian autocracy, in utter contempt of our own interests. Why? Because Putin, who has been the scourge of all Atlanticists since he began to 'de-Americanise' Russia's economy and acknowledged his intention to guide his country towards regaining its independence, has been putting some order into the ranks of those oligarchic mobsters with friendly ties to American neoconservatives, the very same oligarchs that Richard Perle is always so eager to defend.

In his book, Glucksmann lowers his mask, revealing that he is not *pro-European*. What he is, above all else, is *pro-American*. He is basically the mirror reflection of hysterical anti-Americans. It is a Euro-Russian alliance that he fears most. No more realpolitik for these people. Philippe Tesson, Guy Sorman, Alain Madelin and Jean-François Revel are all on the same wavelength. This attitude of voluntary servitude completely disregards all objective considerations relating to the harmfulness of a Euro-American alliance, the increasing American attempts to sabotage our European economy, the lack of American respect for signed treaties, the ancient geostrategic reality of a Euro-American rivalry in which the US is always the aggressor, the threat of an erratic American foreign policy that is already playing the Islamic card against both Russia and Europe, and, in short, all past and current affairs.

The Atlanticists are trapped in a dream, just like those Islamophilic and hysterical anti-Americanists. They have proceeded to replace the observation of facts and the perception of their own European interests with dogma and prejudice, as a result of their reveries regarding an America that they are not even familiar with and which they never subject to analysis, idealising it in the same fashion that others demonise it. Seldom do they speak English, furthermore, and are only able to understand translated texts, meaning almost nothing at all. For some of them, the *American dream* has replaced Marxist reveries.

And yet, no one is asking them to *hate* America, a hatred which reflects an equally foolish mental state and has been taken to absurd levels by the extremists belonging to today's' 'New' Right, who are ever in league with the Ayatollahs. All that we ask of them is that they respond in a European manner, without showing any love towards an

America which still scorns them, just as all powers despise collabora-tors. The Atlanticists are simply being cuckolded by *their American mistress.*

***

The strategic blunders that characterise the NAI and its warmonger-ing have been perfectly described by American analysts. One of the best explanations regarding the NAI's counterproductive stupidity was published in *The New York Times* on August the 20th 2003 and written by Maureen Dowd. In her article, entitled *Magnet for Evil*, she obviously alluded to the so-called Axis of Evil which Bush is bent on destroying. Her theory is that by attacking and then occupying Iraq, the USA has somehow created a new battlefield located at the heart of the Middle-East, towards which all fanatical Islamic *jihadists* now converge so as to 'get even' with the Americans. This development only serves to confirm France's warnings.

Several analyses of this ilk have been published in the American press, which, in a customary fashion since the Vietnam war, always begins by expressing its approval of the White House's adventurism, before hurling its horrified and affrighted criticism at the latter once failure has set in. I will now summarise the key points of the criticisms that were formulated in a dozen major American media outlets during the summer and autumn of 2003.

***

The Bush team has finally managed to create the very monster that it was supposed to keep at bay, a monster which had not existed until then, but is now as real as they come: Iraq. There was initially no con-nection whatsoever between Iraq and Al-Qaeda's Islamic terrorism, regardless of the lies that were used to mobilise the American public opinion in support of the Iraqi war; this connection is now, however, very real indeed. Islamist warriors are now converging on Iraq from all corners of the world — Bush the idiot has done them a truly huge favour.

Maureen Dowd states:

> Since America began its occupation, Iraq has become the mecca for every angry, hate-crazed Arab extremist who wants to liberate the Middle East from the "despoiling" grasp of the infidels. [...] In yet another spun-up government document on Iraq, the White House listed 100 ways that things were going great in the 100 days we've been on the scene. The report burbled with gimcrackery about the "10 signs of better infrastructure" — days before an oil pipeline and then a water pipeline was blown up — and about soccer balls and science textbooks. "Most of Iraq is calm, and progress on the road to democracy and freedom not experienced in decades continues," it said. "Only in isolated areas are there still attacks." [...] Even the Bush people, who tend to look at excruciatingly difficult problems and say no prob[lem], were shaken by yesterday's carnage, which delivered a terrible truth: just because we got Uday and Qusay, Iraqi militants are not going to stop blowing up Westerners. Even if we get Saddam, the resistance will no doubt keep at it, hoping the dictator will enjoy the carnage from paradise.

On the 19th of August 2003, *The Financial Times* published an enquiry which revealed that more than 3,000 Saudi nationals had enlisted and gone to fight in Iraq against the coalitional forces, which clearly confirms Arabia's fundamental hostility to an America that has naively viewed Saudi Arabia as its ally. The following idea surfaced: the 9/11 attacks had actually been motivated by the fact that Islamists could not tolerate the presence of US (Judeo-Crusader) troops on sacred Arabian soil. And despite this, the Bush administration's thoughtless politicians decided to invade Iraq, another sacred Islamic territory, so as to eliminate terrorists! It is rather similar to having a doctor inoculate someone against an infection in their right arm, when the latter has actually ravaged the left. In the eyes of all these commentators, George Bush is guilty of being objectively allied to Islamic terrorism. None will ever ask themselves whether Bush has been manipulated, which is a simple feat considering his weak intellectual capacities, nor will they wonder whether America has long been intrinsically incapable of implementing an intelligent foreign policy and should not have remained isolationistic.

Just like the highly pro-governmental *Washington Post*, the American media have finally taken heed of the fact that America had '*not only triggered terrorism*' in Iraq, '*but especially the emergence of a guerrilla in due form*'.

The best analysis of all has come from Maureen Dowd and the unfluctuating position espoused by *The International Herald Tribune*. What follows is the basic position that they both adopted, a position that is largely shared by 'fashionable' and systematically adversarial magazine *The Village Voice*, based in New York City: it is ultimately the dreadful Bin Laden that has come out victorious against the imbecilic Bush, despite the latter's whole array of advisors who have all graduated from the most prestigious universities on the East Coast and in California. Bin Laden's provocative act was crowned with success. The Muslim world's zealots are now pouring into Iraq, the Middle-East and Afghanistan, thirsting to fight those naïve Americans who have fallen into the trap of military occupation. The formerly secular Baathists, who once supported Saddam (a tyrant that Bush has turned into a hero), have now joined forces with the Islamists. The American 'anti-terror' strategy has managed to plunge Mesopotamia and Central Asia into utter chaos and reinforce both Islamism and terrorism on a global scale. The American dream of imposing 'democracy' is crumbling, as the US neo-imperialistic strategy drowns in quicksand and sinks into a quagmire, just as the French have predicted...

One can only be amazed at the lucidity displayed by these American commentators, who work for the most prominent media overseas. And yet, one is simultaneously surprised at their changeability and pusillanimity, for the very same people who have now proceeded to castigate the neoconservatives' militaristic adventurism once supported the latter and, for nationalistic reasons, targeted the French and German opposition to the Iraqi war with various insults. In actual fact, the American intelligentsia, save for a few exceptions, is truly inconsistent in its standpoints and does not abide by any clear doctrine.

Therein lies the foremost disadvantage of Anglo-Saxon pragmatism, which has otherwise numerous advantages (including the fact of never succumbing to immutable dogmatism, as is the case in France): it is tarnished by an incredible ability to suddenly backpedal in accordance with the circumstances, meaning to change sides.

There is, however, another part of the American media which, infuriated by the fact that American militarism is, as ever, sinking into a quagmire (just as the French diplomacy had warned the US and foreseen), is accusing France of actually '*wishing for an American defeat in Iraq and Afghanistan*'. It is one of the leitmotivs encountered in Rupert Murdoch's Francophobic press publications.

Within the American nationalistic media, whose tendency is as isolationistic as it is supremacist (thus belonging, by French standards, to the Extreme Right), an entirely different tune can be heard: their view is that we are witnessing a strange paradox. At a time when the Occident is being objectively invaded by Islam, American neo-imperialism seems to be compensating for this phenomenon in a most pitiful manner, by targeting Middle-Eastern Arab countries with a desperate kind of neo-colonialism and resorting to a military adventurism that seems obsolete in our time and age. This, historically speaking, is a paradox, one that is akin to a swansong. At a time when mosques are springing up like mushrooms all over Europe and the US, the Western 'coalition' led by the Americans has occupied the Middle-East, which constitutes a blatant mistake in terms of strategy and warfare. It is on our own soil that we had better clean up the mess, not elsewhere…

***

American power is not of a military nature; instead, it is technological, financial and especially cultural in essence. The Iraqi war has already proven that in order to vanquish a small country, the USA needs to mobilise more than half of its armed forces and actual strike force. All around the world, governments have now realised that the Americans could never take on a middle power. In terms of military cost effectiveness, the American army is likely to be among the worst. During the Iraqi campaign, it required the support of British troops and had to bribe Iraqi generals so as to have them desert their positions without combat. It is furthermore obvious that it lacks the ability to pacify the country.

On the other hand, the American imperium has succeeded in imposing itself globally thanks to the Americanisation of mentalities, using a constant and skilful policy of cultural and linguistic penetration: films, the showbiz sphere, music, television, and so on — this is how the *lingua Americana* has claimed worldwide dominion. The result is that even if the world's public opinions have become anti-American and are now demonstrating and burning American flags in response to the primal aggressiveness displayed by the current neoconservative administration, young people still choose to listen to American music, watch nothing but American films and dream of obtaining American diplomas and jobs overseas. Therein lies the real *spearhead*, America's greatest weapon. Be anti-American if you so desire, as long as you *think American*. Having said this, this situation may, as stated elsewhere, undergo a drastic reversal and American productions could suddenly find themselves boycotted by the world's public opinions.

***

American military technology is not as powerful as one might think. In spite of the enormous funds allocated by the US Congress for the purpose of research and development, it seems to be the case that the military-industrial complex's 'per-dollar' productivity is rather low. With their far smaller investments (even in the spatial domain), Europe, China, and Russia can outmatch the USA. Such are the findings that resulted from a study conducted by American magazine *Defense News* (22/09/2003). The study has indicated that the Pentagon, for instance, is highly interested in the new *Scalp* cruise missile, which has been developed by France and Great Britain and is more effective than rivalling American missiles. Additionally, Airbus in-flight fuelling performances are said to be superior to Boeing's; the same is true of both transport and combat helicopters, as well as the Dassault military plane. Unhindered by their much lower development costs, Russian manufacturers are also believed to be superior to their American competitors. Despite the unwritten rule that prohibits America from buying European military material, there are rumours that Pentagon leaders are nonetheless tempted to make such a purchase.

The industrial concentration transactions taking place in the American armament industry have led to the birth of two giants, namely Boeing and Lockheed Martin, and are a source of worry to the Pentagon. This is not only due to the fact that this military-industrial complex has thus acquired a power that overshadows the American military: having been granted a monopolising position thanks to all the orders placed by the American government (a position which ex-empts it from any and all emulation in the face of potential rivals and the international market), this military-industrial complex is no longer compelled to exert itself and is reported to be offering overpriced and mediocre products. This has recently been confirmed by the scandal surrounding the Boeing company, which allowed itself to overcharge the Pentagon during a material purchase.

***

The weakness of American militarism lies in its own army. This is especially true of its ground troops, whose combat skills are atrocious and whose morale collapses whenever difficulties arise. No material or technological superiority could ever compensate for this.

This is the notion advocated by two American periodicals: *The Daily Trojan* (25/09/2003) and *The Christian Science Monitor* (07/07/2003). The military occupation of Iraq, they say, has brought the American army's psychological weakness to light. A report aired by the ABC channel on July the 16th displayed an American soldier demanding the resignation of American Defence Secretary Donald Rumsfeld. The American military has already recruited a large number of near-mercenaries, Latino immigrants who are not American citizens but hope to be granted citizenship by joining the army. Through the rapid demoralisation that has stricken American troops, however, the Iraqi campaign has proven that US soldiers have not chosen their line of work on account of a desire to wage war, but as a means of obtaining a certain employment security. As witnessed during the Vietnam war, the American public opinion cannot bear the loss of human life, a feeling that is now incomparably stronger.

The contradiction between those extremist militaristic leaders (who have never actually belonged to the military, nor felt any shots flying overhead) and an American army which, in spite of its enormous means, finds itself demotivated and terrorised on the battlefield, is astonishing. There is yet another remarkable paradox that affects American society as a whole: the immense gap that separates the glorification of military force (which pervades this society and its media through the justification of 'legitimated violence') from the actual behaviour of American soldiers, a behaviour which, as acknowledged by various members of the American military mentioned elsewhere in this book, is truly low-rate in comparison with European troops.

The Internet has been flooded by the pacifistic protests of American soldiers who long to return to their country and seen several anti-war websites sprout up (in *The Independent*, 20/09/2003). One of those people's leitmotivs is that their wages are too low compared to the risks that they take. In fact, the Pentagon has chosen to reduce military risk premia by a rate of 47 % and decrease the financial benefits of 'family separation'. This is where it all becomes apparent: the NAI has very weak foundations; its militarism lacks the presence of skilful militaries. Not to mention the rumours regarding the diseases that have been spread through the use of impoverished uranium and anti-anthrax vaccines. In *the Daily Trojan*, Craig Stern has stated that '*many American soldiers have lost faith in the entire American army*', especially since they have been told that they would soon be returning home, but their repatriation keeps being postponed. The Pentagon has not succeeded in preventing American soldiers and NCOs from expressing their dismay on American TV channels and internet websites, which speaks volumes about the 'imperial system' 's efficacy. Mirroring the typical symptoms of the current American mentality, Tim Predmore, member of the allegedly elite 101st airborne division, confided in the *Peoria Journal Star* (22/09/2003):

> I thought I was serving a just cause — the defence of the American constitution. They lied to me. I cannot justify my military service any longer. I have been victimised by a bunch of liars. As soon as my contract ends, I will resign from this army, as will many of my comrades. We have all faced death, without reason or justification.

According to the American reporters stationed in Iraq, it is the American Army itself that represents the current administration's worst enemy. Recruitment issues are thus bound to surface in future. How could any country claim to be a superpower with a global military vocation when its population rejects its military conditions and the resulting constraints, and its army is willing to march in parades, but is reluctant to fight and suffer any loss of human life? The option of enlisting foreign mercenaries may well turn out to be necessary, as it once did in the waning Roman Empire… In America's case, however, it will definitely take many.

ANNEXES (PART III)

Notes On the 'Imperial Dream'

'To Finish in a Burlesque of an Empire'

As constantly repeated by Patrick Buchanan, empires often perish as a result of excessive military interventionism. The desire to maintain order on increasingly vaster territories (which was once the case with the Roman, British and French Empires) is synonymous with undertaking a task that is beyond anyone's power. By gradually entering the Middle-Eastern quagmire, the USA is making the same mistake as during the Vietnam war. It might be victorious in the (very) short term, but will eventually face defeat.

In one of his famous chronicles in *The International Herald Tribune* (dated as early as March the 8th 2002), William Pfaff had already highlighted the birth of what I have termed the 'New American Imperialism' (NAI), an imperialism founded upon hubris, the overestimation of its own abilities, immoderation, and, in short, a mental state of insanity. Pfaff had also noted the emergence of a neoconservative ideology whose militarism is of a biblical nature. Commentating on the public broadcasting of Wolfowitz's American plan for global domination (Wolfowitz was, back then, Rumsfeld's deputy at the American Defence ministry and referred to the 21st century as a *'new American century'*), the author was the very first to predict that this emerging doctrine — at a time when Bush Senior was President and the first Gulf War still raged — would lead to disaster, destabilise the world and weaken America, which mistakenly believed itself to be a 'global imperium' that could somehow resurrect the Roman Empire, granting it a more 'moral' dimension. In the chronicle's title, Pfaff had used a lapidary expression that is now renowned among all those who specialise in American foreign policy: *'To Finish in a Burlesque of an Empire'.* In other words, the NAI's ambitions will only lead to a failed empire that will collapse in a most ridiculous fashion under the weight of its own infantile objectives.

***

The NAI itself is, after all, 'American'. It is therefore in the USA that one can find its chief formulators, detractors, and founders. In France, a provincial country where 'intellectuals' are unable to read in English, German or Italian and where the translations of foreign texts are infinitely rare, there is a tendency to expand upon the resurfacing of American imperialism without having any in-depth knowledge of the latter's founding texts. One thus declares himself to be an 'anti-American' or an 'Atlanticist' without any understanding of the ongoing ideological debate in the US (a debate which one subsequently simplifies and mutilates out of necessity), believing that Americans actually constitute a 'bloc'. Here are some excerpts from this debate, reflecting American standpoints that can truly shed some light on the issue.

***

The disproportionate attitude and infantile dream of absolute power that has taken hold of American minds did so long before the 9/11 events, which only served as an accelerator, a catalyst. What accounts for this 'bout of madness', this disjunction, so to speak, is actually the fall of the USSR, which plunged America into the sinister illusion of being the 'sole superpower', one that can allow itself to do anything it pleases. The US was unfortunate enough to encounter G. W. Bush, a simple-minded man who has swallowed the 'imperial illusion' whole.

The true ideological creator, or a man who is, at the very least, the 'romantic formulator' of this imperial dream and someone who channelled an old and repressed American discourse, is Richard Haas, the National Security Council member who, on November the 11th 2000, published an article entitled 'Imperial America' (in *The Atlanta Times*). Displaying utter certainty, he wrote: '*America must move from the dimension of a nation to that of a global empire*'. He explained that 'imperial' and 'imperialist' were two different notions, for '*Imperial America must reorganise the world according to what is Good, by adopting the role once attributed to Great Britain and granting it a greater moral dimension*'. Allow me to summarise this bravura piece, which I have in front of me in English: the use of America's new, regenerated power must draw inspiration from the legitimations proposed by John Gallagher and Ronald Robinson, the two famous theoreticians of the British Empire. Haas believes that '*the USA must extend its control over the entire world, even more so than the British Empire*'. In his fusionist and unsophisticated mind, he persuades himself that '*the USA's interests are those of the rest of the world, and vice versa*'. This doctrine is clearly that of a 'Global Coup', a utopian worldview that is just as delirious as universal communism was, an impossible parody of the Roman *imperium*. His is a brilliant, but rather immature mind, which is the case with many American intellectuals (who are as utopian as they are exalted, whereas our intellectuals remain dogmatic and fatigued). Richard Haas thus belongs to those who have influenced the ruling neoconservatives most.

There is a detail that is bound to shock all advocates of OHAA and anti-American Islamophiles, who claim that the neoconservatives are fanatically Islamophobic: Haas is completely unaware of the Islamic threat and the immigrational invasion burdening the EU, and does not take heed of the demographic and ethnic issues that trouble the West. He restricts himself to an immutable, ahistorical vision of the world, one that is generally very faithful to the 19th century understanding of nations. All that he wants is for the US to claim *total hegemony*.

What he has failed to realize is that we are experiencing another Great Migration, a fact that has also evaded the attention of our French intellectuals.

***

In the intellectual and theoretical debate taking place in the US, the principal opponent of neo-imperial theories is political scientist and philosopher Claes G. Ryn, a professor at the Catholic University of America and the author of numerous literary works. Thanks to his solid arguments and his non-polemical attitude, he has imposed himself as the Bush doctrine's most formidable adversary, a doctrine which he demolishes in his latest essay entitled 'America the Virtuous: The Crisis of Democracy and the Quest for Empire' (Transaction editions, 2003). I shall now develop Ryn's main arguments and contrast them with those presented by his primary 'neo-imperialistic' adversaries.

According to Ryn, it is under Reagan's rule that intellectuals first sensed the birth of a New American Imperialism, termed 'imperial ideology' and later reformulated by Haas as 'imperial America'. Strangely enough, shortly before and after his election, G. W. Bush rejected this doctrine and called for the limited use of American power. He stated that America was supposed to display a certain 'humility'. Then, following the 9/11 attacks, he suddenly underwent a remarkable volte-face and proceeded to espouse the imperial policy, which would henceforth be inappropriately referred to as the 'Bush doctrine'.

The latter is characterised by the relinquishment of the notion of American supremacy in favour of the concept of hegemony, or rather that of 'armed world hegemony'. It thus abandoned the idea of surgical and targeted strikes so as to retaliate against anti-American aggressions and conduct grandiose strategic military operations, as implemented in Central Asia and the Middle-East. The pretexts that this ideology resorts to are the four conceptions of 'democracy', 'liberty', 'equality' and 'capitalism'. And it is America that has the privilege of 'supervising the Earth's remodelling in accordance with these 4 principles'. The USA must therefore divide the world into those endowed with *'moral clarity'* and *'virtue'* and the ones that are not.

From Ryn's perspective, there is, in this respect, a striking similitude between American imperial neoconservatives and the Jacobin ideologists of the French Revolution. Both strive to impose commercial freedom, equality, the overthrowing of 'tyrannies' and the toppling of the 'old world', referring to themselves as the 'virtuous'. The only difference lies in the fact that what French revolutionaries attempted to impose upon Europe through forceful means (such was the great ecumenical church back then), American neo-imperialism longs to impose upon the whole world as part of an impracticable and dangerous utopia that threatens collective security. Ryn has baptised the neoconservatives (or neo-imperialists) *'the New Jacobins'*, because they follow the notion of 'liberating' humanity to the letter, a notion proposed by J-J Rousseau in his *Social Contract* (1762) in harmony with the precept that states: *'Man is born free, but is everywhere in chains'*. They apply Rousseau's universalistic principle of *'forcefully liberating those who do not wish to be so'*.

During the Cold War, the legitimation of American supremacist imperialism lay in containing communism and protecting a certain part of the world, meaning the 'free world'. Now that communism has collapsed, the new Jacobins are moving on to hegemonic imperialism and *'taking advantage of the idea that it is necessary to create a better world for mankind, which is America's purpose, thus justifying the continuation and expansion of power'*. Ryn views this tendency as being simultaneously sincere and hypocritical.

As gathered by Allan Bloom in *The Closing of the American Mind* (Simon and Schuster, New York, 1987), this *'American project'* was already discernible during World War II. It is not merely a matter of undoing a dangerous enemy, but also a question of exporting, for universally humanitarian reasons and the sake of Good, the only morally acceptable social model, which allows for the simultaneous prevalence of global American hegemonic will. The American power is thus indistinguishable from all that is good for mankind, and vice versa. As for the NAI, it has taken this principle to an absurd level. In this regard, Bloom first states: '*when we Americans talk earnest politics, what we mean to say is that our principles of freedom and equality, as well as the rights which the latter establish, are rational and applicable everywhere*'. Any and all political particularisms, regardless of location, are thus illegitimate because of their tyrannical dimension. Indeed, Jacobin reasoning was no different. The author adds: '*The second world war was a re-educational project conducted in order to compel those who do not accept these principles to abide by them*'. The successful 'conversion' of both Germany and Japan to 'democracy' has, it seems, rendered such principles globally applicable; but what this attitude truly shows is that these people have bitten off more than they can chew and have come up against an 'impossible' mission instead of actually 'accomplishing' one.

And yet, these neo-Jacobins label 'democratic' all the regimes that they strive to establish to serve their own interests. None but the nations that support the American foreign policy could ever embody a 'democracy' — period. This is what Claes G. Ryn has termed 'democratism'. What is remarkable is that this attitude is strangely reminiscent of Soviet behaviour and its desire to expand its 'people's democracies', which turned out to be fatal in Afghanistan (under Brezhnev). Political scientist James David Barber is the true theoretician behind democratism. This is what he has proclaimed:

> America has both the vocation and the duty to take charge of the international democratic movement and globally impose democracy as we know it here. (*The Washington Post*, 25/01/1990.)

In other words, the purpose is not merely to dominate the world, but also to *Americanise* it, which, in Ryn's view, is but a disastrous notion of an Empire.

What must also be highlighted is the influence that conservatives William Kristol and David Brooks have had on neo-imperialism.

Without flinching, the two stated (in *'What Ails Conservatism'*, *The Wall Street Journal*, 15/09/1997):

> The USA is founded upon universal principles, and its special moral status has bestowed upon it a grand global mission. In order to pursue its universal task, the American government must be strong and energetic, particularly when it comes to military power [...], which presupposes a neo-Reaganian policy of national strength and moral reassurance abroad.

Kristol and Brooks have coined an expression to designate their doctrine: *'national-greatness conservatism'*. G. W. Bush's team has obviously been greatly influenced by these virile words.

Furthermore, renowned foreign policy expert Robert Kagan has also contributed to the neo-imperialistic ideology established by the *neocons*, thus confirming Ryn's claims that they consider themselves the successors of both Jacobinism and Rousseauism:

> As good children of the Enlightenment, Americans believe in human perfectibility. But Americans also believe that global security and liberal order depend on the United States — that 'indispensable nation' — wielding power.

According to Ryn, these intellectual authorities have thus sanctioned *'our country's international adventurism'* through *'ideological and moral passion'*. In his opinion, this represents a *'new nationalism'*, because America no longer takes on real enemies, as was the case during the Cold War; instead, it struggles against virtual foes that are falsely depicted as a menace.

∗∗∗

Nevertheless, Ryn shares Buchanan's belief that this 'new nationalism' is a fake one, since it does not defend America, but is, instead, both harmful and costly to the US, in addition to arousing hatred for it, just like France during the revolutionary and Napoleonian wars:

> Our missionary zeal bears a striking resemblance to that of revolutionary
> France. [...] Like revolutionary France, neo-Jacobin America casts itself as
> a Savior-Nation. Ideological and national zeal become indistinguishable;

which may well shatter the American identity, just as it eventually destroyed the French one. As for Kristol and Brooks, they see things differently, of course. '*Our nationalism*', they write, '*is that of an exceptional nation founded on a universal principle, on what Lincoln called "an abstract truth, applicable to all men and all times"*'. Their position embodies pure homogenising cosmopolitanism.

The American Right that opposes this new imperialism thus believes that both American and French nationalism, inherited not only from Jacobinism, but also from the two sibling-Revolutions, are highly similar. The French-American polemics, therefore, lie at the heart of *the same ideology*. This is not at all the case with US-China rivalry, which is far more serious and fundamental.

The following idea has also been developed: Washington's neo-imperialism and neo-nationalism pay little heed to the American nation, because, just like the French nationalism that we have inherited from our own Revolution, what they actually defend is more of an *ideology* than a nation, which renders them '*anti-patriotic*'. The Bush administration is not interested in the issue of illegal Mexican immigration and cares little for America's profound European roots. The notion of America that Ryn promotes is hardly 'American' at all, since it completely distances itself from Abraham Lincoln's and George Washington's vision of things, which the author castigates for identifying the USA with a '*pure idea*', one that is both theologically moral and commercial:

> American neo-Jacobinism despises patriotism in the ancient sense of the
> word; it is not characterised by devotion to America's concrete historical
> identity with its origins in Greek, Roman, Christian, European and British
> civilization. Neo-Jacobins are attached in the end to ahistorical, supranational principles that ought to replace the traditions of particular societies.
> [...] They equally despise true American traditions and have no respect

for the values and customs of foreign countries which do not share their "democratic" prejudice.

***

This kind of opinion is rather commonplace within the American Right and obviously contradicts America's founding 18th-century principles, allowing us to measure the American contradiction between *specific ethnic belonging* (which, in America's case, is originally rooted in Europe) and *universalist principles*. Neither Ryn nor Buchanan have been able to extricate themselves from this. The very same contradiction is encountered in France: is our country a 'universalist' idea or a 'concrete people' in the ethnic sense? French and American patriotism are both subject to the same tensions.

Ever since the beginning, the USA has longed to become the *Verus Israel*, meaning the land whose duty it is to bestow and impose biblical values upon the entire world, an endeavour that the Bush administration has been implementing on unheard-of levels. Hence the fool's bargain tying America to the Israelis and the Jewish lobby, since Judaism is essentially ethnic in nature and only defends the people of Israel, unlike America, which remains universalistic and utopian.

In actual fact, America's expansionistic ideology merges with Christianity (both with Catholicism, which means 'universality' in Greek, and Protestantism) in a straightforwardly religious form. French universalism, on the other hand, is related to the American kind and thus represents its direct rival, striving to spread a secularised and atheistic form of Christianity (i.e. 'Human Rights'). The difference between the two is both thin and blatant. Let us, however, conclude this topic and return to the description of America's ideological polemic between the anti-NAI camp and those who support it.

Ryn accuses his country's current policy of embodying a 'new universalism' that began under Reagan. In his view, universalism had previously been solely concerned with fostering global cultural exchange or perhaps imposing the American culture through seductive means. America's new universalism, by contrast, has the same ambitions as former Soviet communism, but surpasses the latter in terms of means and skill, attempting to impose, both domestically and internationally, a specific ideological and cultural worldview using straightforward coercion, intimidation and corruption. The author thus thinks that this cultural imperialism goes too far and ends up diverting the world's population away from the 'American model'. By spreading across the planet, authentic American culture peters out. American traditionalists say that it is always preferable to respect others than to spread out, lose one's identity and create a 'neo-universal' culture whose quality is bound to be mediocre.

Their adversaries claim that, on the contrary, the American culture (an anti-pleonasm) must impose itself upon the whole world through virtually forceful means. In its theories, the cultural scope of American neo-imperialism goes far beyond what was once practiced by Hollywood and the producers of television series. The purpose is now to control and Americanise everything, including the Internet, video games, advertisements and information. America's return to the UNESCO is a step in this direction.

In the economic field (which should be understood in the broad sense of the word), the doctrinal initiator of American neo-imperialism is Ben Wattenberg, the famous press and television editorialist who published (in the Washington Times, 01/02/1988) a true manifesto of cultural hegemony evocatively titled A Chance to Champion Freedom, which has since been, of course, a source of inspiration for American governments, especially when callously interfering in the drafting of the European Constitution so as to eliminate any notion of 'cultural exception' from it. Funny how this 'freedom' is always used to generate servitude... 'The time is ripe', says Wattenberg, 'to export American values everywhere. Never before has the culture of a single nation been so capable of conquering all, so omnipotent. There is ultimately only one global language — the American one'. Unfortunately for those who express such wishes, American or even Anglo-Saxon productions have been experiencing a severe global decline since reaching their historical peak in the 1960s-1980s period; this devolution has, for instance, impacted the pop music genre. Let us, however, resume our reading of Wattenberg's manifesto:

> It is absolutely clear that what the international community needs is a glob-
> ally dominant and all-powerful police force. Someone has to take charge of
> this task, and we are the only ones that can.

Merging the concepts of political and cultural imperialism, Wattenberg makes the following specification: *'There is a visionary idea — that of spreading democratic and American values* [AN: which are of course one and the same] *across the whole world'.* He then earnestly adds: *'Our aim in this planetary game is not to conquer the world, but only to influence it so that it ends up embracing our values'.* In another noteworthy article bearing the Americano-biblical title *'Peddling Son of Manifest Destiny'* (in *The Washington Times*, 21/03/1990), ideologist Ben Wattenberg wrote something that has now become a neoconservative creed: *'Remember this American resolution: a unipolar world is an excellent thing, as long as America acts as its pole'.* What must be noted here is that, in truth, the word 'unipolar' surfaced before the actual collapse of the USSR (1990), at a time when the Americans already anticipated it, which confirms the fact that Bush merely jumped onto the NAI's moving train, without having set the latter into motion.

As evidence, I shall quote the words of another neo-imperialistic ideologist, Charles Krauthammer. This statement dates all the way back to 1991, when this political TV and press journalist (the American equivalent of Patrice Duhamel) made the following plea:

> What we urgently need is a powerful interventionist policy, for we are now
> entering a unipolar world that we Americans ought to love and exploit to
> our advantage. Whenever our cause is just and our interests threatened,
> we must act unilaterally, whatever the consequences. ('Bless our *Pax
> Americana'*, *The Washington Post*, 22/03/1991.)

One can hardly be any more cynical and caricatural. As we can see, the neo-imperialist ideology was already in place at the start of the 1990s. Thanks to a bizarre turn of events, the 9/11 terrorist attacks provided it with the necessary implementation tools.

***

American 'democratic imperialism' was also theorised in the 1980s by Michael Novak, whose ideas have equally inspired recent American governments. He argues that the US must implement Christian morals (meaning 'God's intent', basically) on a global scale; this should be done tangibly and politically, and in full compliance with the Protestant doctrine, thus applying a sort of democracy that Christ Himself is said to have wanted and whose sword is allegedly embodied by the USA itself (and yet, nowhere in the New testament can one encounter any praise of 'democracy'). Basing his standpoints on the Augustinian and Aristotelian tradition, Ryn responds by stating that man is not subject to perfectibility and that the Heavens must not be equated with the Earth. Nor must there be any effort to establish Paradise in this world or mix politics with religion. In no way is the USA the hand of God, he says. In Europe, one can only be left in awe in the face of such theological-political debates, which only rage in the US and nowhere else. Let us, however, not forget that America has, since its very beginnings, been marked by the merger of politics and *theology*. Ryn, a Catholic who could be considered Carl Schmitt's American counterpart, has always struggled against the application of Protestant religiousness to the field of politics, because it replaces reason with passion, just as Islam does. This premise has been confirmed by the '*Axis of Evil*', an expression coined by David Frum, who drafts G. W. Bush's speeches.

Ryn also points out that the neoconservatives have taken the idea that the USA is the sole promoter of global freedom to its utmost extreme. Such a notion had already been formulated by American President Woodrow Wilson back in 1919, before being reiterated by general George C. Marshall, but it was not as extreme at the time. Here is what Bush had to say about it:

> Why are some people angry at us? Why do some want to wage war against our country? The answer is: because we love freedom. Exactly. And because they hate it. (West Point, 01/06/2002.)

The neo-Jacobins claim that those who oppose the US are the enemies of 'freedom' and that pre-emptive war is necessary against them. Such was the very precise ideology embraced by French Montagnard[13] revolutionaries in 1793. Confusing the cause of global freedom with American geostrategic interests, Bush did not hesitate to declare in the above-mentioned speech: '*The American flag will not only stand for our power, but for freedom*'. However, many of Bush's American opponents remark that 'freedom' and 'democracy' enjoy less respect in their own country than among other Western nations.

***

The day after the 9/11 attacks, Robert Kagan, one of the chief ideologists behind the NAI, published an article in *the Washington Post* entitled '*We Must Fight this War*', in which he demands a brutal response; not through anti-terrorist actions conducted by American secret services, but through spectacular military strikes. His plea would not fall on deaf ears. Kagan demanded that Congress declare war against every nation involved in terrorism. Here is his grandiloquent proclamation:

> The situation requires that America act with moral clarity and our fathers' courage in the face of the Pearl Harbor aggression. There is no point in wasting time, wondering what we have done to incur the wrath of such inhuman murderers. There is no point for us to seek to understand their motivations, or attempt to reason with and appease those who have spilled our blood.

---

13   TN: Mountaineer.

On the same day, William Bennett, Jack Kemp and Jeane Kirkpatrick, all of whom are also neoconservative ideologists, issued a communiqué that was broadcasted everywhere, in which they called for '*a war against the entire Islamic terrorist network*'.

Ryn highlights the fact that Bush Junior, who began his presidential mandate by promising a greater degree of 'humility' in the American foreign policy, is concluding it with

> ... the greatest thrust of American involvement into global affairs and the American state's historically strongest intrusion into the lives of its citizens.

In his view, the neoconservatives, these 'democratist' neo-Jacobins (who are not 'democratic' at all, in fact), have manipulated Bush the simpleton and, taking advantage of the 9/11 attacks, paved the way for a global policy that aspires to establish an empire. Alongside Charles Krauthammer, these influential ideologists also comprise Midge Decter, who, while advocating 'democracy', of course, and calling for its global establishment, asked Bush to 'cleanse the world' of all that is undemocratic (in *Peace through Democracy*, *The Washington Post*, 28/06/2002).

***

Bush understood the message perfectly. On September the 15th 2002, he sent the American Congress the traditional report on America's foreign strategy known as the '*National Security Strategy*'. This text is of a capital importance because it officially defines the NAI as the 'government's doctrine'. In it, Bush explained that he had relinquished his former vision of a 'humble' American foreign policy and indulged in an exposé centred around the new American imperialistic agenda, which had obviously been dictated by its ideologists. I shall now cover its most remarkable aspects. The struggle against 'terror' was naturally presented as the essential axis of America's new policy, but naively defined as a means to support '*America's extremely ambitious global role*'. Having already set his sights on the Iraqi campaign, he asked for the authorisation to conduct a pre-emptive attack against Iraq. He then engaged in the undisguised advocacy of an '*armed American hegemony over the world*', a longing that had never been previously expressed in such terms by any other American President. This prosody was obviously justified, in harmony with the very essence of the neo-conservative ideology, through the necessity of globally defending and promoting the 4 interconnected principles of democracy, freedom, American security and free trade.

According to the *Washington Post*, this text, presented by the White House itself, was something unheard of, '*bestowing upon the US an almost messianic role*'. It ventured even further than the manifesto that had been published by the *neocons* a few years earlier (and to which Wolfowitz, America's deputy Defence Minister, had greatly contributed) on the topic of an 'American 21st century'. This report-agenda preached an armed form of American activism and specified in a most straightforward manner that

> America's global power and influence are unprecedented and unequalled. [...] Sustained by its faith in the principles of freedom and the values of an open society, the USA has unparalleled responsibilities and obligations, but also opportunities to seize beyond its own borders.

Moralism meets cynicism...

The White House report affirms one of the NAI's foundations:

> [T]o have overwhelming military power in order to discourage any other power from defying us, contesting American hegemony or possessing weapons of mass destruction.

One is left speechless before the naivety of such assertions, proclaimed officially and publicly. As if *pure* military power could ever guarantee domination... It would be a futile endeavour to search the entire history of German and Japanese militarism for such warmongering emphasis, which sounds ridiculously caricatural, just like General Alcazar's rhetoric.[14]

The report also confirms that the new imperialist strategic doctrine has desisted the former concepts of *deterrence* and *containment* once used against America's foes or potential threats, all in favour of direct military intervention. It is in this very text that the latter is defined and legitimised by the White House, taking the shape of *'pre-emptive and unilateral attacks against potentially menacing states or organisation'*, even in the absence of any direct aggression against the US or its allies. Mere suspicion suffices (as witnessed in the case of Iraq), and, as seen in the report, the USA has freed itself from all UN regulations and international laws that only authorise *strictly* defensive wars. One could say that it is 'the Law of Suspects' that prevails, just as it once did during the French Revolution, which, once again, confirms Ryn's view regarding the American 'neo-Jacobins'.

It is absolutely incredible that the famed 'international community' failed to react to this official doctrinal document at the time of its publishing. And yet, a study conducted by *the Washington Post* (21/09/2002) gave a clear explanation of the White House's new strategy: *'Bush Shifts Strategy from Deterrence to Dominance'*. It is obvious that those who oppose the NAI, including William Pfaff (the above-mentioned editorialist at *the International Herald Tribune*), consider this new strategic doctrine to be foolish and liable to spread global insecurity.

The last words of this fundamental report, which allows us to fully comprehend the essence of the NAI, are the following:

> This American strategy can be described as an American internationalism that differs from all others and reflects the unity of our national values and interests.

---

14 TN: General Alcazar is a character in the *Adventures of Tintin*.

There is, however, nothing new about this 'internationalism': Soviet communists could equally have written this exact final sentence.

Although Ryn contests this doctrine, he does think that it has the merit of being clear, unlike the strategic vagueness that characterised previous American Presidents, except for Nixon, who was an anti-imperialist (which, incidentally, cost him his position). The *neocons'* aim is for the US to

> ... establish a global supremacy through which it could impose itself as the world's sole arbitrator of good and evil and reserve itself the right to unilaterally respond and implement its judgements using force.

In short, America would act simultaneously as a procurator, a judge and a police force. Kenneth Alderman, a Defence advisor for the White House, candidly explained in *the Washington Post* (always the same Leftist daily paper, ever open to the neoconservative quill) that the Europeans who advocated 'multilateralism' had failed to understand the facts and *'should thank America for waging the war of civilisation against barbary for them'*. And why not indeed? The only problem is that, considering the manner in which America is fighting this battle, 'barbary' has some great days ahead of it.

***

Here is the final judgement passed by both Richard C. Holbrooke (Clinton's former ambassador to the UN) and Ryn on the conservatives' belligerent biblical messianism. Let us, however, first recall the words spoken by Bush himself during an interview with Bob Woodward (published in *the Washington Post* on September the 19th 2003):

> There exists a value system which we will make no compromise on, and this value system is the one we preach. And if these values are good for our people, they must be good for all others.

As good Americans, Holbrooke and Ryn are not that offended by the messianism pervading this foreign policy, this merger between

America and God's will on Earth. They look upon this propensity with a certain leniency, as the latter mirrors, after all, the 'Christian Right' 's age-old proclivity and traditional American tendency to consider America the world's archangel of morals and goodness. What they severely condemn, on the other hand, is the triumphalism that permeates the New American Imperialism, an imperialism, which, in their eyes, exploits the Christian spirit in favour of sheer warmongering. Ryn thus adopts the Catholic and Christic doctrine of rendering unto Caesar what belongs to Caesar and unto God what belongs to God. He accuses the neoconservatives' fanatically evangelical and Protestant neo-imperialism, which allows itself, for instance, to remodel the Near-East *in order to help the Chosen People of Israel*, of espousing a missionary mentality that is completely out of place, thus behaving in a neo-Jacobin manner.

This position is an interesting one, and was also adopted by the (catholic) archbishop of Boston, who, in May 2003, sent Bush a threatening and very harsh letter in which he denied him the right to label himself a Christian. Furthermore, Ryn highlights the absurd notion of 'global democracy' preached by the neo-Jacobins, whose 'homogeneity and virtuality' do not correspond to the traditions of any single people and which has thus no hope of ever coming to pass.

One could chastise Ryn and all the other Americans who criticise neo-imperialism for remaining, at heart, attached to America's messianic and biblical ideals (even if they do not really acknowledge this) and for not having grasped the fact the G. W. Bush is but the immoderate extension of such standards. Their criticisms are, however, more credible than those used by European intellectuals who have been stricken with OHAA.

***

To round things off, here is a passage taken from Ryn's above-mentioned essay, which embodies one the best critiques targeting the NAI or what the author has baptised 'neo-Jacobinism'. Its tone remains pessimistic throughout.

The neo-Jacobins are attempting to remove any obstacles to the triumph of their ideology and will to power. They exhibit a revolutionary 15 mental disposition that will inexorably lead to disaster. Alongside what President Bush has termed "the anonymous tombs of the lies forgotten by history" [in his speech to the American Congress on September the 20th 2001] expands the historical cemetery of those who have been drugged by their own dogmatic certitudes, those men whose moralism conceals, even from their own eyes, their unavowed hunger for power. As Ronald Reagan once warned, utopian idealists and all ideologies paved with good intentions are responsible for the worst ailments that the world endures. Persuading oneself that one is always the defender of good renders one blind to their own sins. [...] The most generous and most charitable state of mind leads here to inevitable political-religious imperialism. Every observer that is attentive to philosophy and history must remember the terrible and large-scale suffering that sanctions or results from one moral or intellectual Jacobinic concept or another. Communism, one of the most radical and pernicious manifestations of the Jacobin spirit, has disintegrated, at least as a major political force. But there is another global utopia, one that claims universality, which is now taking the latter's place, coming from the USA itself. The neo-Jacobin vision, which claims to know how to redeem humanity, may of course seem less utopian than that of communism. But the essence and spirit of both movements is one and the same and, whether one likes it or not, utopian thinking remains everywhere identical, admittedly almost inoffensive when limited to isolated dreamers and theoreticians, but suddenly dangerous the moment it begins to inspire those who, through politics, act upon the real world. [...] The qualities of prudence, realism, a sense of compromise, and self-restriction, which are all indispensable in politics, have been swept aside, as has the capacity to control the eruptions of collective passion and extremism. The crusaders of the Bush administration are causing the ancient American virtues to disappear. The constantly growing neo-Jacobin power could take on the shape of disaster. By acting under its influence, American leaders may well set fateful consequences

---

15 The term 'revolutionary' has a negative acceptation to it, one that is frequently encountered in the US and relates to an immoderate sort of utopianism which longs to change the world through forceful means.

into motion, tragic sequences which neither they nor their successors will
be able to control.

∗∗∗

The Americans who criticise the NAI often emphasise the idea that
their country's imperial vision is doomed to fail, because it is based on
economic profit above all else.

American historian Hunt Tooley, who teaches at Austin College
and is the author of '*The Hindenburg Program of 1916: A Central
Experiment in Wartime Planning*', has deemed the American neo-
imperialistic military strategy to be completely inappropriate and
out of touch with our world's realities. On September the 18th 2003,
he published an article on the Ludwig von Mises Institute website
(Auburn, Alabama) entitled '*The Bipartisan War Machine*', in which
he predicted the disastrous failure of Iraqi adventurism. In his view,
the '*neoconservative clique*' is taking the '*imperial fantasy*' to ridiculous
extremes, even though it does not have exclusive monopoly over the
latter. Clinton had already implemented '*imperial conquest and domestic repression*', a recurrent combination in American history. All Bush
is now doing is resuming and accentuating the policy adopted during
the first Gulf War and the bombardment of Serbia. Tooley denounces
the hypocrisy of the Democratic opposition to the war in Iraq, an opposition that actually partakes in this imperialism: indeed, they would
have condoned this military operation if it had taken place within the
UN's framework, in addition to not having protested against the first
Gulf War, the 10-year bombardment of Iraq or the intervention in
Serbia. Nowadays, their anti-imperialist posturing is only motivated
by the 'coalition' 's stalemate in the Middle-East, Tooley explains.

He adopts Claes Ryn's analysis regarding American '*neo-Jacobinism*',
which has based its militarism on the legitimacy of expanding democracy and freedom, the demonisation of all opponents and a 'crusade
conducted for the sake of mankind'. In his eyes, the real objective is
to militarily occupy each targeted country by establishing a puppet

government there, so as to 'rebuild' it and appropriate its resources in a manner that profits the corporations that neoconservative leaders are involved in and not the 'American people', which these neoconservatives are entirely indifferent to. Tooley's central assertion is that, unlike European imperialisms (and especially the German one, in which Tooley is a renowned historical expert), American imperialism does not serve the interests of the 'nation' (nor those of some expansive form of nationalism), but rather those of companies and financial institutions whose sales agents are none other than government members and politicians.

In order to mobilise the American public opinion, nationalism and patriotic pride are used as promotional slogans (propaganda) rather than motivations, and moral legitimations are not always sincere.

> The persistence of this mental structure is absolute and is achieved through the alternation between Democrats and Republicans, allowing the latter to move from a belligerent crusader posture to one of rational pacifism, in accordance with electoral needs and the electorate's levels of emotionality and self-blame.

This constant fluctuation between warmongering and pacifism, which enables both Democrats and Republicans to jump from one ideology to another, has not evaded Tooley's attention. He therefore points out that Clinton was castigated by the Republicans for his militarism and interventionism, and yet, in a supremely paradoxical turn of events, G. W. Bush later campaigned in favour of 'refocusing on domestic issues and a humbler foreign policy'! It thus becomes clear that the imperialist choice only depends on the circumstances, as it is essentially driven by economic motivations, or mercantile ones, to be precise. Pacifism and warmongering could each be adopted in turn by the Democrats or the Republicans. America could ally itself to literally anyone, before proceeding to wage war against them (as seen in the case of the Islamists, Iraq, Russia, etc.). This approach is not due to some ideological conviction, but is the result of a purely commercial tactic that changes in harmony with the circumstances. The military operations carried out by the Bush administration in Afghanistan and Iraq do not bear any connection to a genuine imperialistic 'doctrine' of the archeo-European type, but relate to a sort of control strategy whose purpose lies in enabling a certain elite to claim commercial profit.

In this regard, America lacks a real 'foreign policy' to speak of, merely possessing imperialistic strategies that evolve according to the circumstances, are disorderly and fraught with periods of dramatic growth and retreat, somewhat like a company that acts on the spur of the moment in order to claim any potential profit. In no way is the American notion of an 'empire', therefore, 'imperial' in essence; one could say that it is, instead, a mere mockery of 'imperialism'. Tooley believes that it is a 'decorum' founded on imagery and spectacle, one that Bush managed to take advantage of by parading in military disguise, which is as impressive at the beginning as it becomes ridiculous when the bells of defeat finally toll. In a display of great pessimism regarding his country's future, Tooley passes judgement upon those immature American leaders:

> The result will always be the same: a government which, domestically, grows more and more intrusive and authoritarian, and a surrounding world which grows ever more belligerent as a result of American provocations, justified by a desire for perpetual peace.

***

From the Roman empire to the American one: is the USA at risk of becoming a dictatorship? The idea that the American 'empire' will suffer the same fate as the Roman Empire (albeit much more rapidly and with even more tragic consequences) has been theorised by historian and political scientist Chalmers Johnson. The cause, he believes, lies in what he terms 'the scourge of militarism', as stated in his work entitled 'The Sorrows of Empire: Militarism, Secrecy, and the End of the Republic' (Metropolitan books, 2003). He draws a parallel between, on the one hand, the end of the Roman republic and the beginning of the Roman

Empire and, on the other, the end of the American republic and the birth of an autocratic American empire which he considers to be doomed in advance, predicting a much faster and more brutal fall in its case than its illustrious predecessor ever experienced.

On certain levels, his theory converges with André Lama's views on the decline of the Roman empire (in *Of Gods and Emperors* and *Roman Mixtures*). Johnson believes that history *repeats itself*, not as the eternal return of identical events, but as a sequence of identical historical principles. His study is based on the observation that, for a long time, the Roman Empire (which first vanished with Caesar, then with Augustus) continued to invoke the hollowed principle of *Senatus Populusque Romanus*, meaning *In the Name of the Senate and the Roman People*, at a time when its rule was becoming both autocratic and secretive, relying heavily upon the Roman legions and praetorians and placing greater emphasis on the hunger for military conquest than on ensuring the security and prosperity of Roman Italy. The author likens the Roman Empire to today's United States, which is quietly desisting its own republic status to become a venturesome empire, one that is less and less 'democratic' and governed by an opaque autocracy in which the American armed forces are acquiring an ever more decisive role. He states that '*American imperialism shall destroy America as surely as Roman imperialism once destroyed Rome*'.

Just like Rome, America is, according to Johnson, experiencing a transitional period between being a republic and becoming an autocratic and imperialistic empire. The difference, however, is that Rome's imperial phase lasted four whole centuries (of which three were marked by decline), whereas America's imperial stage can only be sustained for a few pathetic decades at most, owing to history's increasing pace.

As Rome gradually exerted enormous military effort to occupy the entire known world, it simultaneously drained itself of all substance and weakened its own ability to protect its own core. Its actions led to the emergence of an ever-greater number of enemies and resulted in an unmanageable financial burden, as is the case today with the

USA itself. What Johnson lacks the courage to clearly formulate (for reasons of political correctness, perhaps?) and André Lama perfectly understood is that the Roman Empire resulted in cosmopolitanism and brought about the end of the 'ancient Roman' ethnic foundation, just as the birth of the almighty American empire coincides with the decline of America's founding European substratum. Whatever the case, the parallel between a Rome that constantly strived to push its *limes* further through relentless military mobilisation (involving the presence of an ever-growing number of foreign mercenaries) and the headlong rush currently experienced by an America that claims to be able to control the world through invasion, occupation and the establishment of permanent military bases is, from Johnson's perspective, a striking one.

Just like the USA, Rome's reasoning was along the lines of a contrast between 'us and the rest of the world', which is the very principle of unilateralism, or rather that of 'unequal bilateralism', as previously defined. Such a geostrategic approach is, however, untenable, because in the long run, the rest of the world will always turn out to be stronger for simple demographic reasons.

***

In short, Johnson's theory is that the USA is attempting to shift from the status of a *'great republican nation'* to that of a *'global, militarist empire'* (just as Rome once did) and that this metamorphosis is bound to be fatal to it. Under the heading *'The Brief and Happy Life of the American Republic'*, he resorts to cruel words and expresses the conviction that his country lacks the ability to enjoy an imperial destiny and is doomed, at best, to become a short-lived caricature of the Roman Empire:

> There are none who would dare claim that the Roman Empire was, after Augustus, an example of enlightened governance, regardless of the enthusiasm borne for it by the neoconservatives, who subscribe to it by supporting the Bush administration, just like Charles Krauthammer of the

Washington Post, Max Boot of the *Wall Street Journal* and William Kristol of the *Weekly Standard*. The reasons for which I invoke Roman history are not aimed at suggesting that Bush, our Boy Emperor, is another Octavius, but rather at guessing what may well happen once he is gone. The history of the Roman republic from Caesar onwards suggests that it was imperialism and militarism which put it to death, a fact that all our conservative politicians refuse to understand. The militarism and professionalisation of a sizeable permanent army establishes new and indomitable sources of power within every political unit. The government is compelled to mobilise the masses so as to eventually utilise them as cannon fodder, leading to an increase in the power of generals that lend an attentive ear to their troops' and veterans' demands.

Following the abolition *of* men's military service in 1973, our armed forces are now a mixed professional corps, whose troops have enlisted for personal reasons, in a general desire to succeed and survive within the American society's "blind economic alley". Overall, they do not expect to face any gunshots and simply hope to benefit from a civil servant's status, with a guaranteed salary, secure lodging, free healthcare, protection against racial discrimination, and the opportunity to travel and enjoy a certain social consideration thanks to their commitment to serving the American nation. They are perfectly aware of the fact that the alternative choice of a civil life in today's America would involve a difficult search for employment, the absence of job security, the regular pilfering of their savings at the hands of the economic-financial leaders and their accountants, "privatised" medical care, low-rate public schools and colleges, and astronomically priced universities. These committed militaries are ripe enough not to abide by the rhetoric of patrician politicians that have graduated from Andover, Yale and the Harvard Business School with the sole ambition of personal fortune and power, but to listen to a new Caesar, Bonaparte or Juan Peron, meaning to populistic military leaders who have little interest in the democratic kowtows of a "republic" and are tempted by imperial proclamation.

Taking into account the calamitous outcome of the Afghan and Iraqi campaigns, Johnson has no means of knowing whether Bush will be re-elected in 2004 or not. However, he does predict the following:

Whoever Bush's successor turns out to be, he will have to negotiate with
the Pentagon, its 725 military bases scattered across the world and the
military-industrial complex. He will have to submit to 55 years of secretive
tradition regarding the true costs of American "Defence" and remain silent
in the face of the devastations that our militaries are capable of inflicting.
Things can only go from bad to worse. Historians have taught us that the
propensity for things to worsen is endless. Roman history suggests that the
American republic's brief happy life is in grave danger and that its metamorphosis into a military empire is a possibility that would definitely not
be the best solution.

* * *

Ever since the publication of his *Empire: How Britain Made the Modern
World*, historian and economist Niall Ferguson, who also happens to
be a professor at the university of New York, has become the idol of
both the anti-Bush American Right and the anti-conservatives. One of
his views is that the American 'empire' has completely failed to learn
the lessons that stem from the expansion and fall of the British Empire
and is thus merely an '*empire in denial*'.

He writes:

> The United States is the empire that dare not speak its name. It is an empire
> in denial, and US denial of this poses a real danger to the world. An empire
> that doesn't recognise its own power is a dangerous one.

With its military bases sprawled across the ¾s of the world and 31 %
of global wealth, the American empire is even more powerful than
the British one was at the time of its zenith in 1920, Ferguson states.
He warns, however, that the American empire '*is taking on the shape
of a military complex all too much*', one that is perhaps even fraught
with militarism and warmongering. It relies too heavily on '*short-term
tactics and interventions*' (Haiti, Lebanon, Serbia, Afghanistan, Iraq,
and so on) and lacks the '*sustained commitment to the dirty work of
rebuilding*' the countries that it intervenes in and disrupts. '*As Iraq
is showing, military commands cannot create law and order. Their
job is to kill people. The British empire learned that the military must*

be subservient to civilian power if you are to build civil administra-
tions'. The very notion of a 'military administration', as applied by
Washington in Iraq, is a plain and simple aberration. From Ferguson's
perspective, the American impotence (in this specific case and many
others, such as Afghanistan) seems to be the result of US ignorance
with regard to the basic political data surrounding imperial hegemony
and the fruit of America's unawareness of its own capacities (through
self-overestimation).

'*When you talk to Americans about empire they say, "but we came*
into existence to fight imperialism"'. And therein lies the American contradiction: the USA has become an 'empire against its own will', going
against its own founding ideology, which accounts for the American
inability to comprehend such a situation and absorb its rules. Ever
since the annexation of the Philippines in 1898, the USA has, whether
the Americans like it or not, entered an imperial cycle. We know that
Donald Rumsfeld, the American Secretary of Defence, once uttered
this unrealistic sentence: '*We are in no way an "empire", nor do we*
act as such'. The hypocritical desire to have America maintain the appearance of a democratic republic, which Chalmers Johnson was well
aware of, is ever present.

> Without admitting to it, military officials have seized the opportunity pre-
> sented by the 11th of September to accelerate the imperial agenda, yet only
> a very small number of neoconservatives have dared to use such a term
> publicly.

Professor Ferguson believes in the existence of good and bad empires.
In his view, the British Empire belongs to the former category, since,
from the mid-19th century onwards, it spread both liberalism and
democracy in the lands it claimed, protected women and reduced
the infanticide rate. It embodied, in short, a civilising factor that tore
entire peoples away from their backward customs, barbaric traditions,
ignorance and famine. He states that '*a liberal empire can do good'.*
He adopts word-for-word the ideology espoused by 19th-century

European colonialism, which was not necessarily foolish, he says, when one compares the current state of those colonised peoples with their situation prior to imperial influence (especially in Africa).

The American empire is, however, an entirely different issue, as it has neither revealed itself to be civilising, nor pacifying, but has, in spite of enjoying a power far greater than that of imperial Great Britain, only been a source of *'troubles and disorder'*. Professor Ferguson is not overall hostile to the concept of an American empire, which is why his ideas have flattered the conservatives that oppose Bush. He merely demands an Empire that draws inspiration from the British notion and no longer embraces militarism. One of his foundational opinions is that *'an American empire must take over from the late British Empire, and still be an anglophone and Anglo-Saxon imperium'*. The American empire must thus, according to him, improve and become more 'gentle'; otherwise, it is doomed to vanish.

It is this kind of doctrine that fascinates Tony Blair and numerous British elites: they are to renounce their 'Britishness', their British identity, and dissolve it within the American imperium, the successor of the British Empire. The problem is that, considering the ethnic modification which North America has been undergoing, this new empire is destined to become less and less Anglo-Saxon. Let us also point out that in the United Sates, those who oppose neo-imperialism and follow the views expressed by Ferguson do not in any way reject the imperial principle of American hegemony. They merely find Bush's methods to be inadequate and counterproductive as a result of their militarism and brutality, but do not reject their basic principle. They also condemn all isolationism. In their eyes, it is always in America's greatest interest to persevere in 'civilising the world'. This goes to show that the NAI is not the opposite of ancient American tradition, but merely its disproportionate expression.

***

The fact remains, however, that the 'anti-imperial' doctrine is gaining strength in America. Following the occupation of Iraq, a group known as the '*Coalition for a Realistic Foreign Policy*' (CRFP) was formed, comprising various American intellectuals and people of influence (university staff, journalists, politicians, and so on). Its objective is to '*persuade Americans that the imperial policy followed by the Bush administration is moving in a very dangerous direction*'. This new thought and pressure group has obviously adopted the arguments often reiterated by Buchanan, according to whom the USA simply lack the necessary military and budgetary means to implement its remodelling policy upon the Middle-East and (a fortiori) the world. The CRFP sees itself as the opposition's metapolitical '*spearhead*' in the face of the neoconservatives.

They state:

> We believe that the headlong rush that aims to transform the USA into an "empire" must immediately be stopped. We stand united in a desire to redirect the American security policy in a realistic direction, by means of serious and applicable measures that protect our vital interests and are compatible with true American values.

The argument that they present is that the fortunes which have been squandered in Iraq in order to pacify and rebuild the country could have been spent on American domestic security and that this fateful occupation procedure has contributed to the Middle-East's instability, given the Islamists a new front to fight along, endangered the global security of all Americans, isolated the USA from its own allies, weakened the US army and its credibility, etc.

Among those who have signed the CRFP manifesto, one encounters Douglas Bandow, Reagan's former advisor, Scott McConnell, an editor at *The American Conservative*, and numerous other Rightist personalities belonging to the business world and the university spectrum. However, one can also find some Leftists such as Charles Kupchan from the Council of Foreign Relations, a man who once acted as Clinton's advisor, which goes to prove the magnitude of the wave rising up against the ruling neoconservative and warmongering ideology. This metapolitical propaganda group has chosen Vice-President Dick Cheney and Defence Secretary Donald Rumsfeld to be its main targets. Christopher Prebble, who is also a CRFP member, believes that the American vision of global strategic and military domination, which is now an openly declared ambition, can only lead to disaster. The CRFP manifesto expounds on that:

> Even if the terms "empire" and "imperialism" are officially rejected, an imperial fever has indeed emerged, overwhelming politicians within the Left and the Right. In order to understand the current state of affairs, all one has to do is to read the following formula expressed by Max Boot, one of the most prominent neoconservative theoreticians: "America's Destiny is to Police the World".

The charter adopted by this new movement, entitled *The Perils of Empire*, emphasises the following argument: the pursuit of the current neo-imperialistic policy will result in a global defeat for America the likes of which the it has never known. It was once the case that the USA became involved in armed conflict so as to defend its allies, even if the pretexts and motivations were not always ideal; today, America resorts to justifications that no one believes in order to attack others and establish an empire:

> We can predict and are already witnessing the emergence of numerous counter-powers against our own. The peoples who experience our domination enter into a state of resistance, considering us to be their enemies. [...] Wanting to build such an empire is problematic, because it subverts public liberties in the US and thwarts the will of foreign peoples. An imperial strategy will only be a threat to America, which will involve itself in unnecessary and unprofitable wars; it will weaken us as a nation, overburden our finances, bleed our economy, and lead our army and federal budget to breaking point.

McConnell adds: '*We are now more isolated from mankind's general perception than we have ever been in our entire history*'. He compares America's current situation to that of the British Empire as assessed by Edmund Burke at the start of the 19th century. According to Burke, Britain's unrivalled power was rooted in a contradiction that was unmanageable in the medium term: the emergence of global opposition to the Empire itself and the ever-increasing costs of various imperial institutions which Albion could no longer bear. The fate of the Ottoman Empire could be also mentioned in this respect.

On his part, Charles Kupchan writes the following words in that manifesto:

> The administration's central mistake is its central assumption, this gamble that has already proven to be crumbling from within, this belief that the stronger America is, the more uncontested its governance, and the more the rest of the world will follow it willingly, with submission. [...] The United States of today is far less secure than it was a few years ago, because we have undermined the international architecture that helped to protect us.

***

This determined yet frantic opposition to imperial temptation could be explained through the following intuition: although it actually lacks the means to do so, the NAI seems to be desperately attempting to conduct a global coup in an effort to exorcise the new planetary landscape emerging from the 21st century, especially when one considers China's irrepressible rise. On its part, the USA appears to be striving (in what would be a very unwise calculation on its part) to take advantage of the historical vacuum that stretches from the collapse of the USSR to the heralded emergence of China and its becoming a superpower, in order to impose itself once and for all and perpetuate its status of the 'world's sole superpower'. Once again, one cannot help noticing the recurrent American mental desire to bring about the 'end of history' and suspend the latter's flow. The NAI's imperial ideology thus becomes a fantastical means of enabling the USA to temporarily prolong its extraordinary monopoly over global power, which it appropriated after the fall of the USSR.

From a Machiavellian perspective, therefore, it is in the interest of China, India, Russia and Islam to have America drown in its imperial *hubris*, a situation that is bound to destabilise it, subject it to hatred and lay it to waste. How upset they all would have been at the sight of a smiling, empathetic and unpresumptuous America, an America that would be 'nationalistic', yet non-imperial, having carefully cultivated its domestic power, stabilised its finances, protected its borders against the Latino-Asian invasion and developed an impenetrably tranquil sort of power, an America that would favour cultural, technological and monetary influence over fatigued brutality and free itself from its poisonous commitment to Israel's unconditional protection. Such a standpoint, espoused by American 'conservatives', would certainly have enabled the great American republic to endure for a long time to come, not in the position of the world's 'sole superpower', which is but a drunkard's dream (right, Mr. Bush?), but as a very strong world power leading a secure existence. There is but one US President, undoubtedly one of the best to have been elected, who could have devised such a policy: Richard Nixon.

✳✳✳

In Patrick Buchanan's eyes, '*the end of the imperial project*' is at hand (WorldNetDaily, 15/10/2003). This project will not have lasted very long: concocted by the neoconservatives right after the collapse of the USSR, it was compromised by the *neocons* themselves and nipped in the bud, so to speak, as soon as the latter seized power and attempted to implement it, mistaking themselves for Roman centurions. There is, however, a level on which American leaders *will* prove to be the most dangerous of all: their obstinacy and refusal to acknowledge obvious defeat. All the better: acting as a creator of disorder, America has proceeded to spin the wheel of History instead of stopping it at the winning number.

***

An even more virulent criticism of the imperial fantasies embraced by the Bush doctrine has been formulated by political scientist Charley Reese and entitled *Road to Darkness* (King Features Syndicate, 29/09/2003). Reese is both an American patriot burdened with disappointment and hurt and a Democrat ideologist. His conviction is that the US government's arrogance is destroying America's global image. He manifests a certain desire for repentance in relation to American imperialism, displaying a very 'anti-Vietnam war' attitude. Reese has close ties to senator Edward Kennedy, whose words he corroborates: '*Bush has involved us in this war through fraud*'. He also mentions the pretext regarding the alleged 'weapons of mass destruction', predicting that the Iraqi (ad)venture will turn out to be worse than that of Vietnam. In contrast with Rumsfeld's theories, he expands on the idea that Washington (or the neoconservative administration, at least) longs to imitate the Europe of yesteryear, and particularly England, in a ridiculous *remake* of ancient British colonialism. Driven half-mad, the neoconservatives mistake themselves for ancient Englishmen, at a time when the English have, in turn, chosen to yield to American order.

Reese writes:

> Bush is only looking to gain a foothold in Iraq for economic reasons, in order to control the country's reconstruction. The myth regarding the reinstatement of a 'democracy' has not fooled anyone. Washington is simply trying to impose a puppet government. Unfortunately, Americans are not able to pay the price for this in spilled blood and spent dollars. [...] Our dream of empire is grotesque. Our President wants a relentless war against the rest of the world. His fantasy of imitating Emperors will turn out to be simultaneously ruinous for America and, paradoxically, fatal to the latter's very power.

In this regard, Reese's analysis highlights the fact that the mechanism that could transform the American republic into a global empire is a passport to the realm of demise. In France, his views were adopted by Emmanuel Todd (as seen in *After the Empire*). He states:

> We Americans are not programmed for the construction of an empire. When those Arab terrorists struck against the WTC twins, the FBI and CIA suddenly discovered that, unfortunately for them, they were part of the category of people who do not understand a single word of Arabic, even though the USA had been involved in Middle-Eastern affairs for more than a century. I even met a general entrusted with selecting the nuclear targets of our American armed forces and, during the conversation, he mentioned Iran, classifying it as an "Arab country", unaware of the fact that it was not.

From Reese's perspective, this utter ignorance of other peoples and civilisations, characterising both the Americans and their leaders, robs them of any and all prospects of building an empire and over-seeing world order. He reproaches his country for its provincialism, a provincialism that is incompatible with any universalistic ambitions. This is because one must first be familiar with others and be able to understand them if one is to aspire to dominate them. Reese adds:

> Our soldiers are scattered across 120 countries around the world. The in-debtedness that stems from our military-industrial complex is above our means. We have a President who advocates a war without end, one that our country will not be able to survive. We are heading towards bankruptcy. If our President aspires to become an emperor, let him re-read Roman history. No emperor, nor even his people, has ever reaped the benefits of his own greed. I pray for the Americans to awaken and re-establish the republic of our Founding Fathers, as well as a military strategy founded on armed neutrality, leaving the quagmires of overseas intervention behind. To choose the path of empire is to sink into darkness.

ANNEXES (PART IV)

Examples of Counterproductive Americanophobia

The Neo-Leftist and Islamophilic Right

The most refined and most caricatural examples of Americanophobic delirium do not come from Leftist or Islamist milieus, whose members are all too cunning to allow it, but from a certain intellectualistic Parisian Right that has become Islamophilic, plagiarising pro-immigration and alter-worldist topics in a vain effort to make the world forget its past. Here are some examples.

Serious analyses and arguments against American imperialism have been replaced with romanticism and low-rate pamphleteering invectives, with exclamation marks and capital letters everywhere, as seen in Alain de Benoist's following text (in *La ligne de mire*[16], published by Le Labyrinthe):

> In France, the wave of Terror left 42,000 fatal casualties in its wake, with the Indian genocide claiming 10 million lives [how did he get such figures, I wonder?] Hail the Algonquin! Hail Little Tortoise, chief of the Miami Indians! Hail Chief Joseph, the one with the pierced nose! [...] Hail Black

---

16   TN: The Firing Line.

Cauldron, the Cheyenne Indian! Hail Mad Horse! Hail Red Cloud! Hail
Sitting Bull! The question is now whether we want to end up like these
Indians.

In other words, we Europeans are at risk of being targeted with genocide and slaughtered by the Americans. We are Indians in the making.
Pursuing his high-standard analysis, de Benoist charges on:

Let them take back their golden boys and yuppies! Their cheerleaders and
pom-pom girls! Their think-tanks and multinationals![17] Their 5 million
obese citizens! Their "moral majority" and junkies! Their cowboys, sheriffs
and saloons!

And so on, and so forth. The counterproductivity of such tantrums is
obvious.

Rightfully deploring Europe's Americanisation and our continent's
subservience to American imperialism, the above-mentioned author
does not call for an Identitarian and 'European' Europe, but for '*a
Europe that is open to all cultures and not the prisoner of a single one*'
(in *La Ligne de Mire*, page 102). In other words, we are to support a
cosmopolitan and Third-World Europe against an American one, but
definitely not an ethnocentric European continent: that would be 'racist', you see.

Those who embrace OHAA have created such a forced portrait of
America that their approach discredits them:

There is undoubtedly no country whose mentality is so profoundly marked
by a hysterical element. America is the land of major collective psychoses.
It is a country where one faints of fear in the cinema while watching horror
films. (Taken from the same source.)

---

17 According to the newsletter published by the OECD in September 2003, only
20 % of all 'multinationals' are actually American. On the contrary, what characterises the American economy is its largest global SME network and a highly
limited externalisation. Some people had better do their homework before
opening their mouths.

And what about the Shiite flagellants? Are they not hysterical too?

Mirroring the symptoms of obsessive and hysterical anti-Americanist Islamophilia, the same author makes the following remark in his personal diary (*Dernière Année*[18], l'Age d'Homme editions, p. 54):

> Two young Muslim girls were expelled from a certain college in Flers for wanting to wear their scarf in the classroom. One symbol for another, then: I personally feel that it would be more adequate to expel the girls who wear jeans.

These words, which no Imam would ever be stupid enough to utter, are the fanatical terms of a future Muslim convert. To prohibit girls from wearing jeans (and mini-skirts as well, perhaps?): this is the level to which our intellectual Parisian anti-Americans and their programme have stooped... This generally common fury against the wearing of *jeans*, this negative attitude towards a pair of trousers that have long since gone out of fashion, relates to a neurosis that has yet to be explained.

The 'New' Right only regards its anti-Americanism as a means of minimising (which basically means glorifying) the Islamisation of Europe, as demonstrated by the following delirious comments made by Robert de Herte (in *Éléments*, April 2003, number 2):

> So as to justify its own actions and legitimise its chokehold, the USA has invented a new scarecrow with the potential to seduce the feeble-minded: the Islamic-Arabian-Muslim-terrorist one. It thus exploits this Islamophobic delirium, which one now encounters everywhere, using it to its own advantage.

Simply put, the Islamisation of Europe is actually a film, a virtual invention by the Great American Satan. As for terrorism, it is but a dream. And the connection between Islamism and terrorism is sheer fantasy, as is, of course, the over-delinquency characterising immigrants. Intellectualism meets cretinism...

---

18   TN: The Final Year.

What we obviously need to draw attention to, within the OHAA camp, are the 'French-Iraqi friendships' and the role played by the movement's inimitable secretary general Gilles Munier, who has declared himself to be both a 'Gaullist' and a 'stout supporter of the Baath party', proclaiming in *Le Journal du Dimanche* (30/03/2003):

> I can understand perfectly well why some Iraqis would choose to wage war against America on its own territory.

His words entail the very same implicit and irresponsible call for terrorism that one encounters among his neo-Leftist friends.

This is because hysterical anti-Americanism goes hand in hand with militant Islamophilia and Arabophilia, both of which feature very prominently in the prevailing ideology's vulgate. In his biography of German philosopher (?) Sigrid Hunke, a pseudo-'pagan' and Islamolatrist who authored a delirious book entitled *Allah's Sun over the Occident* (1960), the inevitable Alain de Benoist reiterates the same old song:

> In this book, Sigrid Hunke has highlighted the things that the European civilisation owes the Arab one, particularly in the fields of science, mathematics, medicine and philosophy. [...] Outweighing the influence of the Antiquity itself, it is essentially Arab science [sic] that enabled a genuine scientific rebirth by liberating the European spirit from the theological Christian mentality during the 12th century. (*Éléments*, November 1999.)

He then goes on to mention a dozen 'scientists' whose names have been Arabized, including the unavoidable Averroes. He somehow forgets to point out, in the process, that none of them were actually Arabian and that every single one of them was condemned by Islam for heresy. Expressing admiration, de Benoist also stresses '*the ancientness of the relations binding the Arab world to the European one*'. The word 'relations', of course, could easily have been replaced with 'wars' or 'sanguinary confrontations'. In short, this great, self-taught scholar and brownnose attempts to make us aware of the fact that we allegedly owe the Arabs more than we do the Greeks.

The denial of the Muslim threat against Europe is an equally recurrent topic:

> Faced with the Muslim "invasion" supposedly taking place in today's France, the catholic Right is most willing to allude to the memory of Charles Martel. (*Éléments*, February 1999, p. 30.)

'Charles Martel', you say? You mean that odious Islamophobe and the first head boasted by the French hydra, right?

***

Another symptom that typifies intellocratic delirium and its disconnection from reality lies in the fact that the 'enemy' of our European civilisation is never specific, nor is he ever visible. The evidence that points to our continent's colonisation at the hands of Islam and the Third World is denied simply because it is all too blinding and excessively simple (and especially too dangerous to mention in the eyes of these slipper-wearing rebels), having been replaced by the following jargonising abstraction:

> It is the global domination system centred around the market-technology-show triptych that remains our principal foe. [...] Michel Marmin highlights the manner in which Hollywood has colonised our imagination [Is the Star Academy a Hollywood product, then?] and, having drafted the astonishing chronology of the European submission to the diktats of American cinematographic industrials, he proceeded to designate the real true current threat: the self-Americanisation of French cinema. (A debriefing of a GRECE colloquium published in *Éléments*, February 1999.)

If it were the case that the principal threat to Europe lay in the 'Americanisation of our cinema' and not in our demographic decline and the ethnic invasion that we are being subjected to, I, for one, would truly be reassured.

***

When reading the '*Manifesto of the New Right*' written by A. de Benoist and C. Champetier, one is quick to realise that this ideological confusion is the result of a desire to be admitted into the neo-Leftist sphere. The manifesto teaches us that '*liberalism is our foremost enemy*'. Such extremism, however, discredits any and every critique of liberalism, which these authors, amateur economists that they are, systematically confuse with *mercantilism*, as well as *materialism*.

The New Right does not perceive immigration to be of any danger and chooses to support the coexistence of various ethnic communities in Europe. Here is an example of the jargon used by these utopians, whose views are tainted by the values of 1968:

> No apartheid, and no melting-pot; the solution can only be found in the acceptance of others in their otherness, from a perspective of mutual dialogical enrichment.

Ignoring all the evidence, these people regard immigration as the 'forced uprooting' of victims who, to use terms that have been borrowed from the Trotskyite-Marxist vulgate, are none other than the unfortunate immigrants themselves, having been '*reduced to the level of relocatable merchandise*' [...] and '*compelled to abandon their native country to live in another, where they are welcomed as the auxiliaries of our economic needs*'. In other words, there is no such thing as illegals and fake refugees that overrun us. In the eyes of the authors, immigrants are all being involuntarily deported...

The authors have thus removed their 'Identitarian' disguise and spoken in favour of Europe's organised Third-Worldisation, chastely labelled '*the communitarian model*':

> The New Right believes that the ethno-cultural identity that characterises the various communities currently inhabiting France must no longer be restricted to the private domain and become, instead, the focus of genuine recognition in the public sphere.

Let us the reassure our beloved authors: this is precisely what is happening with Islam. The System is actually in line with the New Right, and vice versa.

So as to make it perfectly clear that Europe is to become a heterogeneous kaleidoscope, the authors declare themselves to be *'opposed to a "European nation"'* and in favour of a *'federal Europe'*, which they describe, in fact, as a neo-medieval system *'within a plurality of special statuses'*. One can hardly imagine how this headless centipede could ever stand up to American imperialism…

Mimicking the prevailing ideology in a most faithful manner (as well as its Leftist version, if possible), our brilliant theoreticians assert that

> … negotiated reduction and the sharing of working hours must be encouraged […] in relation to all "heteronomous" tasks, meaning that people would work less in order to give a better work performance and gain more time to enjoy life.

They are thus anti-consumerists, anti-materialists and the supporters of a leisure society, all at the same time. Amazing. Then, in a position that surpasses even that of Alain Lipietz and José Bové, our two mental magicians have a go at paleo-Marxist science fiction:

> The impossible return to full-time employment, therefore, implies that we must break with the logic of productivism and henceforth consider a gradual departure from the era when wage-earning served as a central insertion model into social existence.

I see; so, what model are we supposed to adopt, then? The primitive communism of a gathering economy? The African village model? Or perhaps a phalanstery? They never specify which. On the other hand, these shockwave economists present us with the portrait of a novel collectivist paradise:

> It is furthermore imperative [sic] for us to gradually disassociate work from revenue by considering the option of introducing a general living allowance

[Is that so? And who will pay for it, I wonder?] or a "minimal citizen's rev-
enue" that would be given to all citizens free of charge [sic] and last their
entire lives, beginning at birth.

In his above-mentioned private journal, de Benoist also informs us of
the following, making use of his habitual exclamation marks: '*I am in
favour of both work-sharing and the right to be lazy*'! And there we have
it: the remains of Leftism, experienced thirty years later…

In short, we are to earn money without working and take the
welfare state (which has already been criticised), assistantship and
generalised economic irresponsibility to absurd extremes, without
forgetting to strengthen the immigration suction pump through the
granting of allocations: such is their brilliant plan. One can hardly
even imagine how a Europe that has been organised in harmony with
these extremely hackneyed anarcho-unionistic notions could ever resist the American power… Let us not forget, however, the icing on top
of their manifesto's mellow cake: Chirac's own concept of '*cancelling
Third World debts*'.

It is thus very hard to distinguish what sets these 'rebels' apart
from the Greens' nerdiest left-wing members, the Trotskyites of the
Force Ouvrière [19], SUD [20], the French Socialist Party, Attac, or even the
French Communist Party. Unfortunately for them, they could never
join the latter's ranks, as this would definitely cause some clatter…

While denouncing '*American hysteria*', Alain de Benoist has, in
turn, fallen prey to anti-American hysterics. He has replaced every
argument-based demonstration on how American imperialism represents a threat and how one should choose to resist it with demonising
anathemas, formulated using intellectualistic and lyrical political cant
which, having run out of breath, is highly reminiscent of a Maoist style
of expression ('lecherous vipers', for instance) and of the rhetoric used

---

19 TN: The French Workers' Force.
20 TN: A French trade union.

by communist intellectuals during the 1960s. Let us now enjoy his jargon's alluring musical melodies:

> Under the pretext of guaranteeing security, the USA has created a reticular Leviathan founded on technological and military savagery, as well as on the absolute surveillance of our bodies and minds, thus putting an end to human liberties. (*Éléments*, April 2003, p. 2.)

To summarise, this 'reticular Leviathan' (Come again?) is said to be worse in terms of savagery than Stalin, Hitler and Pol Pot combined. Are we truly expected to take this seriously? The Atlanticist milieus must be rubbing their hands with delight at this type of sketchy, demonising and extremist thinking.

To convince those that may yet doubt the 'New Right' 's complete coalescence into the cosmopolitan and multiracial Left and its opposition to European identity, it would suffice to quote the statement made by its leader (de Benoist) in his private journal and read between the lines:

> The Right has risen from Jacobin assimilationism through its nationalistic mystique, which insists on the cultural, judicial, administrative and even ethnic homogeneity of all social members. The Left, by contrast, respects differences and advocates a "multiculturalism" that often mingles with cosmopolitanism. […] It is this very Left that respects human nature and diversity best. (*Dernière Année*, p. 211.)

His diary also contains the following pro-immigrational confession, worthy of the RCL[21]:

> When hearing the expression "too many immigrants", most people tend to remember the word "immigrants". As for me, I spontaneously wonder about the philosophical meaning behind the expression "too many". It is incorrigible. (Op cit., p. 259.)

---

21   TN: The Revolutionary Communist League.

We can thus conclude that, in the eyes of our rebellious thinker, there is an insufficient number of immigrants on our soil….

Stigmatising '*xenophobic propaganda*', our glorious investigator warns: '*The manner in which one speaks of Islamism today so as to denounce its "awakening" is not very convincing at all*' (p. 117). Indeed, it would be a vain endeavour to look for an Islamic mass presence in France or search for any signs of its growth. It must all be a delirious fantasy of ours.

Denouncing the alliance that he believes to perceive between the American Satan and Russia, an alliance which has resulted from the '*colonial war*' that the latter has been waging in Chechnya, the author proceeds, ever faithful to his pro-Islamic bias, to state that

> … capitalism[22] […] is attempting to profit from the Islamophobic wave that it has now triggered on a global scale, in an effort to turn "international terrorism" (or radical Islamism) into a new foil with the potential to legitimise its chokehold. (Taken from an interview with *Le Félin Identitaire*, broadcasted on the Internet in October 2003.)

Such sub-Marxist political cant, which resorts to a snobbish and hollow pseudo-neologism that the author obsessively reiterates (thus betraying his fascination for the term), basically means the following: 'International capitalism is simultaneously exploiting and promulgating the world's hatred towards Islam, in order to justify its domination through a fictitious threat and the fear of alleged Islamic terrorism'.

What is interesting here is that the 'New' Right's foremost thinker has thus taken on the primary role when it comes to formulating the central views of pro-Islamic Trotskyism. What is being implied is that the threat of Islamic terrorism has been exaggerated and is only the desperate result of global, Judeo-American capitalistic greed; that Islam does not actually threaten Europe in any way (unlike what those 'White commoners' claim); that Islamophobia is morally intolerable; and that the principal threat to our civilisation stems exclusively from

---

22 TN: de Benoist uses a French neologism, namely 'Forme-Capital'.

capitalism and the USA. One could apply the Pareto method to this analysis and distinguish the following prejudice and clichés, all of which are fully 'neo-communistic': Americano-centric capitalism represents the devious and oppressive bourgeoisie, the squid, so to speak, with Islam, the Third World, the immigrants and so on embodying the new proletariat and playing the part of sanctified victims and martyrs.

In an attitude that typifies the ideology in which anti-Americanism is but a pretext for people to embrace Islamophilia, Third-Worldism and pro-immigration stances, the 'New Right' leader proceeded to become the zealous spokesman for all Leftist litanies (still in the same interview), explaining that fear of Islam relates to a *'fear culture [...] conducive to all deliria and especially the latter's exploitation'.* He claims that it is all but *'an allegedly menacing threat'* (let us rather not discuss this pleonasm). Turning a completely blind eye to the massive Islamic chokehold smothering Europe (an apparently irrelevant and politically incorrect truth that is unworthy of 'philosophical' analysis,) our second-rate thinker asserts that Washington has invented the Islamist threat *'in order to legitimate its own domination'.* He thus remains blatantly oblivious to the fact that the roots of Islamism reach deep into the latter's core and that, even if America and Israel did not actually exist, Islamism would still remain equally menacing, as history has repeatedly confirmed since the 8th century.

The author then goes on to explain that

> ... our greatest foe is not necessarily the one for whom we feel the greatest hate, nor the one for whom we have the least amount of sympathy. Our main enemy is simply the one endowed with the greatest strength. As long as one fails to comprehend the fact that we are now living in the world of international capitalism [always the same hollow words] and the realm of mercantile imagination [...], one has not, in my view, understood anything at all.

Let us now reformulate things more explicitly:

> Our main enemy, my dear prejudiced and stupid people, is not the one that
> targets us specifically with harm, nor the one who imposes his customs and
> presence and who you have no sympathy for. Our main enemy, in fact, is
> Uncle Sam, along with his bombs and international finances.

The French Communist Party's own discourse has basically been
adopted by a bunch of bohemians, who are attempting to negotiate
(quite unsuccessfully) their repenting conversion from the extreme-
Right to the extreme-Left.

A grave confusion regarding the very notion of 'power' is to be
noted here. Europe's chief enemy is thus said to be the one possessing
the greatest material power from an international perspective. This
conception is utterly materialistic and superficial. Does the power
that characterises the immigration wave, its demographic fertility,
the Islamic mentality, the devastation of European societies, and the
feeling of dereliction and abandonment burdening European natives,
who watch as their lands and ethnic identities are betrayed, not matter
ultimately at all? All of this is allegedly harmless in comparison with
the Yankee hydra and the terrifying sword of Damocles that hangs
above our heads, embodied by

> … the world of international capitalism [again!] and the realm of mercan-
> tile imagination […], which generates global conditions of self-deprivation.

What we are facing here is a textbook case of the intellectual delirium
that ails our French mentality. By copying the Leftist jargon and
adopting the (misunderstood and unreferenced) formulas of Debord,
Lefevbre, Bourdieu and Baudrillard, plagiarist de Benoist presents us
with the perfect example of pure *bourgeois thinking*.

The latter is characterised by a complete denial of reality as specifically perceived by our people, meaning by society as a whole. It is a
mixture of pretentious contempt and sententious intellectual laziness.

What you see is not real, my dear folks; your suffering and apparent foes are nothing but an illusion. It is we intellectuals who, as the sole keepers of science and veracity, can explain to you all that your main enemy is not at all the one that you perceive as such, for you are all foolish and uneducated, belonging to the category of people who "ascertain things in a purely reactive fashion, instead of granting analysis and reflection due priority". (As stated by the same author in the very same text.)

What threatens you most, therefore, are the scholarly conceptions and abstractions which we have specified. Instead of wallowing in racism, learn how to recognise your foe in international capitalism and 'the axiomatic system' impelled by the American military-industrial complex.

This priggish reasoning was both normal and usual within the dogmatised, Leftist intellectual bourgeoisie, whose members have always preached that whatever people experienced in their everyday lives was nothing but an illusion and that those who 'spoke the truth' were demagogues. In the above-mentioned text, de Benoist has adopted this very same illusionism:

Apart from a ceaseless pedagogical effort, I fail to see the potential of any other daily strategy to lead people's minds towards maintaining a greater critical distance from both the state of things and themselves.

In other words, it is through propaganda ('pedagogy') that one must persuade common people, who are all simpletons and readily fanaticised, that the things they experience are false and what they feel is of little importance when compared to the metaphysical and moral truth which we, as enlightened intellectuals, are alone to possess. We must convince them of the fact that immigration, Islam, insecurity, foreign preference, and decadence are all mere delusions.

The above-mentioned enlightened intellectual bourgeoisie is obviously completely unfamiliar with the issues of insecurity or precariousness experienced by our native people. It can thus allow itself to 'maintain' a 'critical distance' and advise others to follow suit. What

could ever be more normal and logical than for this contemptu-
ous — and contemptible — attitude to prevail within the 'New' cosmopolitan Left? There is, however, something quite tragicomic about
seeing these Parisian intellectuals, who once made much hay out of
our 'European identity' and still continue (albeit with ever-increasing
difficulty) to live off the Identitarian public, repeat word-for-word
the ideas advocated by the bohemian Left. This desperate about-face,
conducted in the hope of being forgiven by the System for one's capital
sins and being accepted as 'righteous rebels' under the sublime pretext
of embracing philosophy and freedom of thought, is but a priggishness
that cannot deceive anyone (as A. de Benoist himself has stated, 'when
View from the Right *was reedited a year ago, it might as well have been
entitled* View from the Left'.

The Anti-Americanism of Those Ignorant about America

I shall now allow myself to refute the anti-American vulgate that
usually characterises Identitarian milieus, a vulgate that only serves
to reinforce American positions through its fallacious arguments,
especially those which attempt to demonstrate that the USA is actually
the main, or even the sole, enemy that threatens European survival.

The Polémia website (www.polemia.com) usually comprises
excellent analyses which always defend Europe's power and identity.
It sometimes happens, however, that one comes across some biased
arguments there, arguments in which ideology has replaced practical
reasoning and neglected facts that are mostly too blatant to ignore.

For a certain time now, I have been defending the notion that it is
mass immigration, paired with Islam's tightening grip and supported
by all the collaborators who exacerbate the situation, that actually represents our *principal foe* (a fact that I have made particularly clear in
this book). I have also been stressing the idea that the American policy
has, for a long time (since the 1892 war against Spain, in fact), been the
main *adversary* that Europe has had to contend with as a power, which

applies to the economic, geostrategic and cultural level. An enemy is not an adversary. The former seeks to erase your presence, even physically, and longs to settle into your home. The danger he embodies is an urgent one to tackle and may turn out to be fatal in the medium term. An adversary, on the other hand, only strives to weaken you and subjugate you, but never to eliminate you completely, for he requires you to be his vassal.

Such a distinction and hierarchisation of threats, however, often remains unacknowledged, as it conflicts with ideological *passion*, which, in this case, happens to me an emotion-based Americanophobia that uses clichés and untruths as its main arguments. The analysis published by this Polémia editor does not, of course, drown in extremism, nor has it been rendered blind by OHAA; its logic does not, therefore, crumble, nor does it pretend that the US is our *sole* enemy and that the twofold threat of Islam and immigration does *not* actually exist.

In no way does Polémia's openly declared doctrine neglect the immigrational and Islamic menace, but merely subordinates the latter to the American threat, considering the latter to be its very source. I will attempt to prove that this viewpoint is not only political in essence, but also counterproductive and especially flawed, since its understanding of things is virtual and does not reflect the reality of our society and world.

***

Let us now analyse and refute Polémia's arguments one at a time, all of which have the merit of being both concise and precise.

> Nowadays, our principal enemy is embodied by the United States. The "Yankees" represent a powerful danger that the "Arabs" could hardly ever incarnate, except of course on our own soil.

First of all, the fact of generalising the 'United States' is an effort to regard it as a bloc and fully identify it with Washington's policy, as if the latter were never going to change in future. The USA is thus perceived

as an immutable civilisation, akin to the Islamic one, which constitutes a first error in judgement. Next, the 'Yankee' appellation denotes
a polemical and emotional tendency to substantialise the Americans,
whose ties to the Northern camp of the American civil war are,
however, growing ever thinner. Last but not least, one detects a grave
confusion when the author asserts that the 'Arabs' (in a likely reference
to the Muslim-Arab world) represent a lesser power compared to that
of the USA. This may be obvious on a geostrategic and economic level,
but this is hardly the issue here, since what we are focusing on are
direct, first-hand threats that have been burdening Europe. The author
is, in fact, guilty of a surprising antilogical periphrasis and reduces
his previous argument to naught when stating: 'except of course on
our own soil'. For it is obviously 'our soil' that matters most. A gram-
matical analysis of the author's words shows that he acknowledges the
fact that, on a global scale, the 'Yankees' represent a more dangerous
power than the "Arabs", even with regard to our own interests, but
it is in fact the opposite that applies 'on our own soil'. Either that, or
my interpretation of the preposition 'except' differs from the author's.
Through his syntactic lapse, the latter pre-demolishes the very idea
that he plans to defend and expresses his genuine, secret opinion,
while implicitly acknowledging that he abides by ideological thoughts
rather than common sense.

∗∗∗

The text then continues in a manner that confirms our suspicion
thanks to the farfetched arguments that the author resorts to:

> He [the 'Arab'] is only accepted in France because of our adoption of the
> American multiracial model (which is publicised on a daily basis through
> American films, television series, videos, games and records). It is because
> we have been Americanised that we are mentally prone to being invaded;
> territorial occupation will only cease when our mental colonisation does.

We are drowning in delirium at this stage. The author has truncated
the sociological reality, history and very nature of American society

and culture, which he is clearly unfamiliar with. According to him, it is allegedly our mental Americanisation that has triggered our acceptance of uncontrolled immigration flows, our 'multiracial society', our loss of ethnic identity and our tolerance towards the massive and ever-increasing Islamic presence…

To believe this is to forget that this cosmopolitan, egalitarian and multi-ethnic ideology is definitely of French origin and that those horrible 'Yankees' cannot be blamed for any of it. The roots of the above-mentioned ideology reach deep into the Encyclopaedist world and the Enlightenment period (the secularisation of Catholic charitableness), with its initial manifestation dating back to the start of our colonial adventure and World War I. The 'family reunification' introduced by Giscard and Chirac was neither inspired by the Pentagon, nor by American TV series. Claiming otherwise is synonymous with bestowing a fictitious and oneiric sort of importance upon 'cultural Americanisation'; to seek a cause-and-effect connection between mental Americanisation and the acceptance of our 'invasion' relates to a bazar-like type of sociology, if you do not mind my saying so.

Incidentally, if the author were truly familiar with American mass culture, especially in the cinematographic and audio-visual sphere, he would have noticed that the topics of miscegenation, immigration, the social melting-pot and even behavioural decadence are very rarely encountered there, while remaining prevalent in all of our French productions. Generally speaking, anyone that has ever lived in the USA (which is obviously not the author's case) can testify to the fact that the general mental and cultural atmosphere can hardly be described as favourable to ethnic intermixing. Provided that he has cable TV access, the author could have a closer look at American and French advertisements and compare the two. His findings would definitely come as a surprise to him.

The criticism of American culture is only credible when the focus is actually on the latter and not on our impression of it based on some ideological grid. Allow me to add something that I have repeatedly tried to explain to those emotion-driven Americanophobes (but all in vain): the most apologetic productions regarding our European culture and its profound ethnic roots have (unfortunately, one might say) come from this ever-abhorred 'planet Hollywood', whose sense of epics is far more developed than that of our subsidised national cinematographers. There is simply no denying this. For no theory could ever be proven correct through imaginary 'facts'.

It is of course certain that, on an audio-visual level, American mass culture is mostly far from being brilliant and that its ambition is to homogenise people's minds. However, it must not be subjected to any caricaturing; instead, one must acknowledge the fact that such criticism is hardly applicable to *all* American productions. Furthermore, the frenzied desire to praise the sociological 'model' of ethnic chaos (often encountered in Europe) is absent from even the most pathetic American productions.

Moreover, in order to invalidate the absurd suggestion that the Americanisation of European minds has led to our mental acceptance of the invasion (according to the author's claims), it is the example of Japan that serves as an *argumentum a contrario*. How is it possible that this country, which has been subjected to forced Americanisation for almost sixty years now and is an island of great wealth and a magnet, so to speak, has always rejected immigration and remained mono-ethnic? The reasoning according to which 'mental Americanisation implies colonisation at the hands of foreign migrants' is thus precisely what rhetoricians would term 'a sophism'.

***

The Polémia author then engages in a sociological attempt at analysing 'suburban youths'. He accumulates numerous clichés that one, unfortunately, often hears in Identitarian milieus:

> Our second enemy is not Islam, but immigration. Those "suburban youths" are only Muslims on the surface, whenever indulging in temporary acts of provocation; they are, however, profoundly Americanised, as confirmed by

their caps, tracksuits, trainers, ghetto-blasters, rap music, tagging, drugs, attacks against teaching staff, and their use of gangrape as a gang cohesion rite, none of which bears any connection to the Islamic culture. Such behaviour, in fact, has but one source: North American gang culture. Islam only plays a certain role through Americanisation itself, meaning through young people's imitation of the Black Panthers, Cassius Clay, Farrakhan, and so on. Immigration is not, above all, an Islamisation factor, but one of Americanisation: from the second generation onwards, immigrants find themselves unable to live in accordance with their original culture, with a far lesser capacity to integrate into the French one. They are rootless parasites, only able to assimilate into the sole civilisation that has turned rootlessness into its very foundation: North America.

The first thing to notice here is the author's strange concern with treating Islam with utmost care, attempting, at the very least, to minimise the latter's role. His ignorance regarding those 'housing estate youths' is, however, complete: unlike what has been falsely claimed, Islamisation is progressing at a brisk pace (even if it is not mystical in nature and only serves as a 'banner of ethnic assertion'), at a time when American clothing and alimentary trends are experiencing a general decline in favour of ostentatious 'neo-Islamic' behaviour. The re-learning of the Arabic language is currently soaring, while all references to Americanism and the 'black' American syndrome have actually been dropping, especially since the occupation of Iraq, with the majority of North African 'Brown-Blacks' now considering the USA to be the Great Satan. In such areas, the first names given to newborn babies are neither American, nor French, but in 95 % of all cases Muslim-Arab; and let me tell you, 'Usama' is far from being at the bottom of the list.

The new generations of immigrant descent have, unlike what the author blindly claims, been massively reembracing their original culture, reinventing it and even readapting it at times, all in accordance with an aggressive kind of ingeniousness. They are all far more 'rooted in this original culture' than their parents ever were (even if their ways are new and different). Any attempt to turn them into miserable and rootless individuals is a grave mistake, a cliché spread by the extreme

Left. For it is in fact the 'little Whiteys' that find themselves in this situation today. Those immigrants are perfectly content with living in a society that they can sponge off of and which they have the impression of invading. They have no desire to be 'frenchified' at all, as they have created a new identity for themselves, one that is, unfortunately, much stronger than that of our native French people. To present them as being the destitute victims of a 'rootlessness' imposed upon them by the USA is an absolutely ridiculous claim and a potential source of laughter for the subjects themselves. Let us not linger on this matter, though.

A small side-comment: regarding 'rap' (a popular music genre characterised by a 'rapping' rhythm that initially surfaced in the black parts of Brooklyn during the 1970s), the similarity between the American and French kind is becoming less and less evident, as the latter is now openly racist and anti-European. Also, since American pop music has been accused of perverting young people's minds, *rock'n'roll*, *country music* and the *crooners' melodies* should equally be mentioned at this stage, for their message is in no way degenerative, nor is it spiteful towards Whites, and all three are broadcasted a hundred times more often in the US than 'rap', which remains highly marginal in radio programmes and record shops. Johnny Hallyday, Eddy Mitchell and many others who have drawn inspiration from them and have thus objectively 'Americanised' French songs never engage in spreading pro-immigration, multiracial, Islamophilic or even politicised messages! Apart from the 'Black-White-Brown' rap genre heavily broadcasted on all private and public radio channels, it is, in fact, the famous 'politically committed' French music genre (including, for instance, murderer Bertrand Cantat's band known as 'Noir Désir' and subsidised by Jack Lang) that served as a tool for the immigrationist, 'tolerant', multiracial and Trotskyite ideology to exploit under a veneer of feigned rebellion and romanticism. This 'politically committed' French music, usually involving Americanophobic composers and singers, has remained prevalent since the 1960s — just think of Moustaki, Ferrat, Ferrer, Nougaro, Perret, Reggiani, Renaud,

Balavoine and, further back, impostor and pseudo-poet Boris Vian, along with an entire horde of musicians who are all very French indeed. The messages spread by this music (considered 'artistic' and therefore listened to much more often by our elites than neutral rock music or insignificant and artificial American dance music) are clearly more dangerous to our profound identity and values than all those popular and industrial American music genres, which, incidentally, are not all necessarily rubbish.

And don't even get me started on the pro-immigration and cosmopolitan plugging that our National Education, Radio France, France 2, France 3 TV series, Arte shows and many others indulge in. What I detect in them is much more of a Trotskyite, progressive Christian, champagne socialist and bohemian-bourgeois influence than a Yankee one.

✳✳✳

The author continues his argumentation in the same vein:

> In its Islamist form, however, Islam is definitely our enemy, occupying third position in this hierarchy. And yet, it is only our foe because the United States has enabled its rebirth by supporting global decolonisation efforts that target European states, including France (the fact that America supported the FLN is by no means a secret), by financing the armed Islamist re-emergence during the war in Afghanistan', and last but not least, by supporting the expansion of Islamic republics across Europe, all of which tend to undermine the development of European power from within [...], or exerting immense pressure upon European member-states to allow a re-Islamised Turkey to enter the European Union.

Why did the author choose to begin with the words 'in its Islamist form'? Would a non-Islamist version of Islam be acceptable in France? Why, that sounds just like what Sarkozy would say! A very ambiguous statement on his part...

He then sinks, once again, into sophistry and flawed analysis. It is perfectly clear that Washington has exploited both Islam and Islamism by encouraging fundamentalism, subsidising the *mujahideen* and arming them first against Russia and now against our own continent. The author, however, displays astounding naivety in his belief that, without Washington's involvement, Islamism and the global Islamic outbreak would not exist! In actual fact, nothing would be different at all. I would also like to respond to those who claim that Ariel Sharon's policy, and that of his Israeli administration, is among the main causes of global Islamic terrorism: even if the Israeli state did not exist, even if Palestine had never experienced the Jewish chokehold, the Islamic conquering wave (with Islamism acting as its spearhead and not as its dissident aspect) would remain unchanged, making use of other pretexts instead. This is because the Koranic tactic requires Muslims to always depict themselves as the victims of an attack or aggression in order to justify their own offensive. They always manage to designate someone else as being an oppressor, thus turning themselves into martyrs.

Islam's historic global surge, experienced as a kind of rebirth, and the simultaneous rise of fundamentalism embody a groundswell that has strictly nothing to do with Washington's policy. Muslim immigration into Europe (totalling 90 % of the overall influx) is neither caused by the USA, nor is it the result of disastrous liberal management; it is, in fact, triggered by the suction pump of financial aid, subvention, protection against deportation, and all the other guarantees offered by socio-democratic states that have been gangrened by humanitarianism and cosmopolitanism, whose moral roots are actually found right here, in Europe. It is likewise perfectly possible for Europeans to oppose any prospect of Turkish EU membership; The USA is obviously pushing for this to happen, as it is all fair game; but it is essentially European leaders (as heard in Chirac's and Schröder's declarations) that are choosing to yield to Turkish demands, going as far as to *desire* Turkish membership. As already stated, it would be unwholesome for me to systematically justify our ailments through the actions of the Great American Satan, as this Polémia author has clearly chosen to. Doing so would exempt us from taking any responsibility.

***

Let us now focus on the next part of the argumentation, whose author is confident enough not to fear derision. What does he claim is the main purpose of American imperialism?

> The ambition is to create a homogeneous market with endless opportunities for American products, one that would be omnipotently governed by Washington.

On the contrary, however, it is widely known that the American problem lies in its commercial deficit and delocalisation; that America is being flooded by foreign imports, especially Asian and European ones; and that the USA has not been attempting to 'submerge the world with its products' for more than 30 years. The reason behind American neo-imperialism and the latter's economic foundations are entirely different:

1) To gain control of raw material sources.

2) To continue attracting 75 % of all global investment savings.

3) To acquire a monopoly over high technology.

Here is yet another passage taken from the very same text: it is a text-book case of truly ill-argued anti-Americanism, one that is emotional and must at all costs be avoided, since it clearly plays into the hands of Atlanticist milieus through its accumulation of indefensible clichés.

> We are facing the rapidly materialising nightmare of witnessing the global expansion of what life in the urban agglomerations of the American Northeast is like: an absence of history, an absence of popular tradition, the absence of any aristocratic substratum, an absence of art, and an absence of mystique, paired with omnipresent multiracial delirium, generalised rootlessness, blatantly selfish individualism, and energic wastefulness, in addition to the prevalence of a showbiz society pervaded by a culture of immediacy, degenerate pop art, primal Protestant puritanism and a corresponding worship of money.

Europe is thus said to be polluted by this model, for we have

> ... racial chaos, and particularly Africanisation, urban anomy, an ugly and stench-infested tube, omnipresent advertising, fast-food establishments, tagged walls, and the sound of rap music being played on all radio channels […], not to forget jeans, the uniform that the forces of occupation have managed to impose where others have failed. And, above all that, what we have in our offices is an arrogant international lobby fashioned according to the trends of Wall Street, Manhattan and Hollywood.

Such a text is both distressing and unworthy of Polémia. Everything in this adolescent and impassionate condemnation is either false or excessive (perhaps even hateful). The vocabulary itself is childish ('nightmare'?). The tragedy of such analyses lies in the fact that they draw those European patriots who are at least somewhat familiar with the US away from anti-Americanism, giving up on the latter. Standard-wise, it is akin to the clumsily anti-American Stalinist propaganda of the 1950s, thus discrediting all that motivates the resistance to American imperialism.

Here are some examples of plain and simple untruths: those 'urban agglomerations of the American North-East' are far more European in nature than the French, Belgian, Dutch and German conurbations are. It pains me to say this, but it is true. Is this 'absence of history, popular tradition, aristocratic substratum, art and mystique' (what on earth is 'mystique' anyway?) supposedly characteristic of the USA? How can anyone write such rubbish (pardon my choice of words, but there is no other way for me to express this)? Is the USA the land of 'racial delirium', then? This is undoubtedly the reason why at Palm Springs, where I was tasteless enough to live, an interiorised social practice of ethnic separation is rigorously implemented, just as it is in thousands of other American counties. Furthermore, the USA is allegedly the model of 'generalised rootlessness'. I am certain that this is what accounts for the fact that uniforms are imposed upon children at school and that the school programmes in 20 American states comprise the learning of folk songs. A country of 'blatantly selfish individualism'? When one considers the entire West, it is in the USA that one finds the highest number of associations that focus on social support and familial solidarity. 'Rap' is played on all radio channels, you say? A hundred times less than in France! In the US, one can actually only listen to it on a small number of Black radio channels. 'Racial chaos and Africanisation'? Our Polémia author is clearly unaware of the fact that there are dozens of TV and radio channels in the US that are characterised by a very high cultural level, do not include any advertisements at all and are financed by private foundations. He is, likewise, oblivious to the fact that American universities fund various courses centred around the teaching of our French culture and our country's history (thus replacing the 'Alliance Française' without receiving any credits) and that these courses offer a quality that is superior to that of our French universities.

To depict the USA as a cultural desert is not to understand this land, and to restrict this country to the presence of couch potatoes, popcorn-munchers who watch baseball games, and dumb TV series is demagogically easy. This, however, does not explain why the world's best European classical musical orchestras and dance groups (among many others) are to be found in the US.

One cannot help noticing, furthermore, the condemnations that pervade the author's text, forming an ambiguous mixture that combines jeans, a uniform that is allegedly imposed all around the US and is somehow considered worse than the chador itself, with an 'arrogant international lobby' (Which one? Why does the author not pluck up the courage to specify which, just as I have in this book?). Jeans are decidedly a receptacle for people's fantasies to pour into. We are supposedly being colonised by them, which is why they represent a grave danger. I will not waste any time refuting these endless clichés. All I wanted to do is to use them as an example of the kinds of ideas that one should avoid in order not to make one's arguments seem ridiculous. Fighting a specific adversary presupposes sufficient familiarity with the latter. In this regard, the central issue that plagues French anti-Americanism is that it targets an adversary whose true nature is completely unknown to it.

OHAA thus succumbs to the very same flaw that the NAI has fallen prey to: virtualising, meaning the fact of expanding upon (and acting on) a state of affairs that does not actually exist, but that one still imagines to be real. The tragedy that pervades both intellectualism and fanaticism lies in the fact of thinking before observing, as the plough simply precedes the oxen.

The Prevailing Ideology's New Anti-Americanistic Position

During the 1960s, in the wake of the Vietnam war, anti-Americanism was part of the prevailing ideology's arsenal. Orchestrated by the Soviets and relayed by all Leftists, the struggle against 'American imperialism' was an imperative for all courtyard intellectuals. Things were, however, to begin changing during the 1980s, as we witnessed an intense acceleration that started with the collapse of the USSR: anti-Americanism was becoming obsolete among the European intelligentsia and it was pro-Americanism that now had a binding value in terms of fashion.

The USA embodied a cosmopolitan model in the face of European enrooting, considered tasteless and reactionary. An irrepressible sort of Americanomania spread throughout the entire 1990s; in people's minds, any comments regarding 'American imperialism' were always linked to Fascism, antisemitism and 'our history's darkest hours'. The only ones to have been anti-American since the first war in Iraq were the French National Front and the supporters of French sovereignty, which automatically meant that this position was to be condemned by our self-righteous elites.

And then, quite recently, came the emergence of the NAI, trudging through the world like a bull in a china shop and triggering a new situational reversal, as well as a return to the cartography of the 1960s: anti-Americanism was once again part of the dominant ideology's vulgate. Although this turning point began in the aftermath of the war in

Kosovo (1999), it was actually the military campaigns in Afghanistan (2002) and especially Iraq (2003) that defined the new landscape once and for all.

As a result of the ridiculous war waged against a small, harmless Arabian country, the USA came across (quite mistakenly, in fact) as an anti-Islamic and anti-Arab power. Due to the fact that our intelligentsia has espoused the obligation to advocate antiracism and xenophilia, the prevailing ideology has now chosen to integrate anti-Americanism and Islamophilia as its main paradigms, with Third-Worldism acting as an added bonus, of course. And it is at the highest levels of government that the tone is now set, which is an unprecedented development. Incidentally, it is the first time that a consensus has been observed between the position adopted by the governmental apparatus and the one embraced by the majority of our intellectuals. This ideological reconfiguration is highly damaging to all those who, like myself, intend to desist such a binary and Manichean mentality and *simultaneously* reject both Americanophilia and Islamophilia.

***

Pierre-André Taguieff provides us with a very subtle analysis of this phenomenon (in *'The Grip of Neo-Progressivism'*, Le Figaro, 02/07/2003). Pointing out the fact that neo-progressivism *'has fervently adopted the legacy of its communist and leftist ancestors, namely Third-Worldism, anti-capitalism and anti-imperialism'*, he outlines the ideological panorama upheld by the new vulgate, whose 'new' ideologemes are but recycled old ones, speaking of

> … an absolute hatred of America (a land that is viewed as a repulsive and mythical entity which is both hyper-powerful and hyper-declining), an unconditional siding with the (ever idealised and blameless) "Palestinian resistance", and a pronounced complacency towards Islamist terrorism.

He also tackles the denunciation of *'Western capitalistic greed'* and offers the following analysis, aimed simultaneously at a whimsical extreme Left and a capricious extreme Right that always shadows the former: *'The new "single mindset" is both (openly) Islamophilic and (more or less secretly) Judeophobic, with these two aspects always remaining inseparable. Is "Zionism" not "a form of racism"? Is Islam not the "religion of the poor"'*? In P-A Taguieff's eyes, this *'subversive miserabilism'* lies *'at the heart of the new dominant ideology'*, which is divided into 4 parts or prejudicial stances: *'the demonization of America and Israel'*, which have joined forces as part of the *'American-Zionist conspiracy'*; the *'negation or minimalization of the Islamist threat'*; *'the litanic denunciation of Islamophobia (which is overestimated whenever witnessed and invented wherever absent)*; and last but not least, *'the negation and minimalization of Judeophobia'*.

***

In this respect, Pierre-André Tanguieff suggests that this ideology, which, despite using *Le Monde*'s news columns as a means of expression, longs to be the embodiment of 'resistance' and 'rebellion', is the exact replica of the old Marxist schematic: the USA (ever associated with the 'Zionist entity') is equated to the conductor of the orchestra in an aggressive, imperialistic, over-exploiting and satanic neo-liberal conspiracy; by contrast, Islam and the Third World (along with the ever-present Palestinians) play the role of the exploited, virtuous and martyred proletariat.

In the extreme-Rightist version of this vulgate, Third-Worldism, anti-Americanism and Islamophilia are accompanied by an ethno-pluralist rhetoric in favour of 'the cause of peoples' (an expression borrowed from the late Jean-Edern Hallier), whose purpose is not so much to act in defence of European identities as it is to protect those of Third World peoples, who are all necessarily threatened by the Great Satan. It is all an amusing standpoint when one considers the fact that these very same neo-Leftists look upon Islam with enamoured eyes, even though 'the cause of peoples', their diversity and their cultural liberties do not rank high on the Islamic concerns list, to say the least…

Final Warning

It is not because one denounces hysterical anti-Americanism that one is immediately pro-American or 'Uncle Sam's servant'; if one neither supports the 'Palestinian cause', nor militant anti-Zionism, this does not imply that one is automatically pro-Zionist; and just because one does not succumb to obsessional anti-Judaism, this does not mean that one necessarily acts at Israel's behest.

Being a free-spirited person is becoming increasingly difficult these days, as one simply shocks everyone with their views. It is truly complicated for anyone to promote a genuine European Identitarian position in the fanaticised world that we inhabit.

In its darkest imaginable shape, binary and Manichean reasoning reigns supreme. Advocating a *terzia posizione*, meaning a third path, is a highly strenuous endeavour, even among those who dream of this notion and have deified it.

It is crucial, furthermore, not to misidentify our enemy. The political theatre is not one of passion, but one of reflexion; it entails an arduous effort that precedes all actions. And as for reflection itself, it must always be rooted in observations, meaning in the analysis of facts. Any ideology that is founded upon the exaltation of verbal expression and the cult of fashion, or one that submits to power pressure, has no hope of making an impact. The only valuable approach lies in the *experimental method* that asks: what exactly is happening? And what conclusions are to be drawn? This attitude presupposes an unperturbed sort of lucidity, in which everything that is 'intellectual' must be banned.

The second requirement in the face of adversity is that of responsibility, meaning the fact of wondering whether the historical ailments that have befallen us have truly been caused by others. I, for one, have both an answer and a solution. Unfortunately, this recipe is an American one and is bound to shock people: *be yourself* and deal with things accordingly. And for goodness' sake, stop complaining.

It is not 'American imperialism' that lies at the source of Europe's horrendous decadence, nor can the Jews, extra-terrestrials and commodification be blamed. All of these are easy targets for lazy publicists to accuse. What accounts for this decadence is, in fact, a mental disease, the crumbling of our self-defensive reflexes and self-confidence, our fatigue and inner cancer; it is the latter that simultaneously generates our demographic collapse, the deliquescence of our traditions, our devirilisation, the loss of our collective memory, and the relinquishment of our ethnic consciousness. The underlying cause behind our decadence is not exogenous in nature, but *endogenous*. Spengler may well have been right: civilisations do run out of breath and expire, just like the light of an oil lamp does once the oil that fuels it is depleted.

It is, incidentally, bizarre to notice that those claiming to be 'anti-economists' actually identify economic factors (capitalism, liberalism, etc.) as the culprits behind all these ailments. Unlike what would-be intellectuals believe, it is not 'globalisation', 'commodification' nor 'international capitalism' that have hastened Europe's decline, nor even Islam and immigrational pressure themselves that can be held responsible for this development, even if it is necessary for us to resist them, of course. I say this all the more gladly as I have always condemned mercantile globalisation (in favour of a model centred around the 'autarchy of great spaces'), in addition to denouncing Islam and colonising immigration.

These factors and symptoms are mere consequences. The cause itself is, above all else, a spiritual and cultural one. Uncle Sam and his influence have no bearing upon the European decline. The fact is that both China and India, which are subjected to the same international environment as Europe, and particularly to worldwide mercantilism, are not experiencing any waning at all; they are, instead, growing. A people that maintains its inner strength can face the worst tempests, akin to a well-constructed and well-secured ship.

***

In my view, European decadence stems from a highly specific inner viral disease, one that took centuries to make its presence felt and develop its symptoms. There are three ailments that have been weakening European peoples and undermining their immune system's responses: individualism, universalism, and abstract charitableness (otherwise known as xenophilia). This results in the destruction of our *ethnic consciousness* and *collective subjectivity*.

The origin of this affliction can, from my point of view, be found in *Christianity*, namely Paul's understanding of Christendom. The latter bears strictly no connection to Judaism, which is an ethnic religion (hence the absolute falseness of the notion of Judeo-Christianity). I have, in this regard, drawn inspiration from the views of Louis Rougier, who was both a historian and philosopher. It is not traditional Catholicism that we are talking about here, of course; the latter was a mere syncretism comprising numerous ancient pagan religions. What we are focusing on is the accelerating secularisation and 'mundanisation' (in the aftermath of Vatican II) that have afflicted the Christian principles of universal charity, generalised equality, individual salvation, and the oneness of the human race. To be simultaneously selfish (i.e. a frenzied consumer that lacks both ethics and progeny) and express solidarity with the rest of mankind: such is the 'religion of human rights' through which Europeans are committing mass suicide, in a display of utter indifference. I, personally, am of the opinion that the above-mentioned virus originates from a *specific* ideological drift to which Christian morality has yielded.

Incidentally, the US has begun its own descent upon this very same slope... On the other hand, Asian civilisations and Islamised peoples are not burdened with such a handicap at all. It seems to me that this fact clarifies contemporary events better than any economic essays ever could; History's infrastructure has an ethno-cultural, alchemical aspect to it — it is an 'unstable mixture', as chemists like to say.

***

One must remain optimistic, just like historian and writer Dominique Venner, in whose eyes historical determinism is a sign of myopia, even in relation to demographic decline. He states:

> Periods of decadence are saturated with toxic emanations. Through reversals or reactions, however, the latter have the paradoxical power to bring about salvational awakenings. [...] And just because we are said to be wallowing in mud, this does not mean that history itself is motionless. Nowadays, for instance, everything points to the fact that it is indeed in motion, moving in a manner that entirely transcends the general consensus.

The European civilisation is *metamorphic*, capable of overcoming its terrible crises and of pursuing its own history by transforming its outer forms. Its principle is one of *rebirth*, and it is the Phoenix that acts as its model. Unlike the USA, it has its own *destiny*. The disease could thus still give birth to a healing elixir, and it is from the embers of a seemingly dying fire that a new conflagration may arise. *Sol Invictus*: the sun is waning and setting in the midst of a hopeless twilight; but soon enough, dawn shall break, casting the light of a new day. The simple truth is that such a metamorphosis, impacting one age after another and brought forth by Clio, the goddess of History, always presupposes a tragedy lined with hecatombs. Once Europeans have globally banished Christian charity from their souls, *Septentrion* shall be born in a river of blood and pain. Under the weight of the facts, the most inconceivable of outcomes is rendered possible. *Fiat spes ac imperium.*

Index

OTHER BOOKS PUBLISHED BY ARKTOS

OTHER BOOKS PUBLISHED BY ARKTOS

OTHER BOOKS PUBLISHED BY ARKTOS

RAIDO	*A Handbook of Traditional Living*
STEVEN J. ROSEN	*The Agni and the Ecstasy*
	The Jedi in the Lotus
RICHARD RUDGLEY	*Barbarians*
	Essential Substances
	Wildest Dreams
ERNST VON SALOMON	*It Cannot Be Stormed*
	The Outlaws
SRI SRI RAVI SHANKAR	*Celebrating Silence*
	Know Your Child
	Management Mantras
	Patanjali Yoga Sutras
	Secrets of Relationships
TROY SOUTHGATE	*Tradition & Revolution*
OSWALD SPENGLER	*Man and Technics*
TOMISLAV SUNIC	*Against Democracy and Equality*
ABIR TAHA	*Defining Terrorism: The End of Double Standards*
	The Epic of Arya (2nd ed.)
	Nietzsche's Coming God, or the Redemption of the Divine
	Verses of Light
BAL GANGADHAR TILAK	*The Arctic Home in the Vedas*
DOMINIQUE VENNER	*The Shock of History*
MARKUS WILLINGER	*A Europe of Nations*
	Generation Identity
DAVID J. WINGFIELD (ED.)	*The Initiate: Journal of Traditional Studies*

Lightning Source UK Ltd.
Milton Keynes UK
UKOW04f2107241017
311595UK00002B/371/P